A Guide to Prayer for

All Who Walk with God

A Guide to Prayer

for

All Who Walk with God

Rueben P. Job

Norman Shawchuck

John S. Mogabgab

*Sunday Scripture Readings from
The Revised Common Lectionary*

UPPER
ROOM BOOKS®
NASHVILLE

A Guide to Prayer for All Who Walk with God
© 2013 by Upper Room Books
All rights reserved.

Unless noted otherwise, scripture quotations are from the Common English Bible. Copyright © 2011 Common English Bible. Used by permission. Scripture quotations identified in the text are used by permission: ASV, the American Standard Version. AT, author's translation. JB, The Jerusalem Bible, copyright © 1966 by Darton, Longman & Todd, Ltd. and Doubleday, a division of Bantam Doubleday Dell Publishing Group, Inc. Reprinted by permission. KJV, The King James Version of the Bible. NEB, the New English Bible, copyright © Cambridge University Press and Oxford University Press 1961, 1970. All rights reserved. NIV, the Holy Bible, New International Version®, NIV®. Copyright © 1973, 1978, 1984, 2011 by Biblica, Inc.™ Used by permission of Zondervan. All rights reserved worldwide. www.zondervan.com. NJB, The New Jerusalem Bible, copyright © 1985 by Darton, Longman & Todd, Ltd. and Doubleday, a division of Random House, Inc. Reprinted by permission. NRSV, the New Revised Standard Version Bible, copyright 1989, Division of Christian Education of the National Council of the Churches of Christ in the United States of America. Used by permission. All rights reserved. RSV, the Revised Standard Version of the Bible, copyright 1952 (2nd edition, 1971) by the Division of Christian Education of the National Council of the Churches of Christ in the United States of America. Used by permission. TEV, the Good News Translation in Today's English Version-Second Edition Copyright © 1992 by American Bible Society. Used by permission

Lectionary tables from The Revised Common Lectionary. Copyright © 1992 Consultation on Common Texts. Used by permission.

At the time of publication all websites referenced in this book were valid. However, due to the fluid nature of the internet some addresses may have changed, or the content may no longer be relevant.

Excerpts from *Weavings: A Journal of the Christian Spiritual Life* are used by permission. While every effort has been made to secure permissions, we may have failed in a few cases to trace or contact the copyright holder. We apologize for any inadvertent oversight or error. All scripture within the articles from *Weavings* are taken from NRSV, unless otherwise noted.

Book cover and design: Bruce Gore/gore@gorestudio.com

Typesetting: PerfecType, Nashville, TN

Printed in the United States of America

LIBRARY OF CONGRESS CATALOGING-IN-PUBLICATION DATA

Job, Rueben P.
  A guide to prayer for all who walk with God / Rueben P. Job, Norman Shawchuck, John S. Mogabgab.
      pages cm
  Includes bibliographical references and index.
  ISBN 978-0-8358-1226-0 (print)
  1. Devotional exercises. 2. Meditations. 3. Church year. I. Title.
  BV4832.3.J63 2013
  242'.3—dc23

                                                                      2013003752

NOTE ON LANGUAGE: While effort has been made to select and edit material to be inclusive, some texts retain original language that uses male nouns and pronouns in reference to humanity and to God.

For Norman Shawchuck
a soul friend

Contents

Preface

This *Guide to Prayer*, like the previous three, was prompted and formed by our own need for help as we seek to walk with Jesus every day of our lives. Like the previous *Guides*, this one grew out of the need for direction along the way of Jesus. However, it differs from the other three in that John Mogabgab is the primary editor and author, while Norman Shawchuck and I have had a more limited role in the development and writing. We are each and all pleased to lend our efforts to the goal as we share together the experience of learning to walk with God.

John brings an incredible list of accomplishments to the task as well as the experience of a remarkable spiritual journey. He was teaching, research, and editorial assistant to Henri J. M. Nouwen from 1975 to 1980, founding editor of *Weavings: A Journal of the Christian Spiritual Life*, and is special projects editor for Upper Room Books. John is currently working on the Henri J. M. Nouwen Spirituality Series on behalf of the Henri Nouwen Society.

A Guide to Prayer for All Who Walk with God attempts to provide an easily accessible resource for all who desire God and need a simple daily pattern of spiritual discipline to assist them in their quest. The pattern offered here draws on ancient and contemporary wisdom to assist us on the journey that will lead to transformed and abundant living.

The scriptures and wisdom of spiritual leaders across the generations are more relevant today than ever before. As the world struggles to find an equitable and balanced way of life that is fulfilling and rewarding, the daily practice of spiritual disciplines can help us all find the pathway that leads to a closer relationship with God and all God's children.

We have discovered that the practice of these daily spiritual disciplines brings new depth to our spiritual lives. We have found greater peace, comfort, joy, and hope as well as a deeper awareness of and commitment to healing the social injustices of our communities and our world. We invite you to join us in this journey, confident that God not only desires but also is able to lead us all to new levels of faithfulness. May it be so!

Rueben P. Job
Norman Shawchuck

Acknowledgments

The first *Guide to Prayer*, published in 1983 by The Upper Room, was born in the hearts and minds of the authors fifteen years before the publication date. Norman Shawchuck and I first met in the late 1960s and developed an immediate and lifetime friendship. The first *Guide* was the result of our own hunger for God and for a resource that could be our constant companion on the journey toward a deeper and more consistent walk with God. At the time, we did not realize the widespread nature of this deep yearning. In the years following, with sustained encouragement and editorial guidance from Upper Room staff, we published *A Guide to Prayer for All God's People* (1990) and *A Guide to Prayer for All Who Seek God* (2003).

A Guide to Prayer for All Who Walk with God began with a request from The Upper Room and a meeting with John Mogabgab to discuss the possibility of publishing a fourth *Guide*. This time it was clear that Norm and I would need help in accomplishing such a large project. In the ensuing months, with time for prayer, reflection, and continued adjustments, the current *Guide* took shape.

To research, design, assemble, and integrate a resource as complex and inclusive as this one takes the gifts and skills of more than one person. This project could not have been completed by the publisher's deadline without the unstinting help of Vanderbilt Divinity School intern Andrew Garland Breeden and part-time Upper Room Books staff member Craig Dustin Katzenmiller. With energy, creativity, and deep commitment to the shared vision of what a new *Guide to Prayer* might offer seekers, Andrew and Dusty made substantive contributions to every stage of this volume's development. They have earned my profound gratitude.

Because of Norm's declining health, it became apparent that his wife of fifty-six years, Verna Shawchuck, would need to help John and me in finding and selecting a significant gathering of Norm's work for inclusion in the *Guide*. She has been untiring in her efforts to find significant passages from Norm's published and unpublished writings as well as his personal daily journal.

Norm's death came after a long and valiant struggle with Alzheimer's disease. The title of the homily at Norman's memorial service was "Journey of a Soul Friend: Strong Mind—Tender Heart—Adventurous Soul" and is a mirror reflection of his life. Roger Heuser, longtime colleague and soul brother, preached the homily and gave the commendation that appears on the following page. It is introduced by the greeting and welcome that appeared on the worship bulletin for Norm's service.

In the opening paragraph of his homily, Roger said, "Norm's passion in his vocational calling and private existence was spirituality. He often used the metaphor 'journey' to describe this reality. The French Jesuit theologian and scientist Pierre Teilhard de Chardin once said, 'We are spiritual beings on a human journey.' I think Norm saw it this way—we are spiritual beings on a human journey. And thus he became a soul friend to many."

Norm's theology was first and foremost practical. I believe you will see this expressed in the selections from Norm's work included in this *Guide to Prayer*.

—*Rueben P. Job*

On this day the Shawchuck family welcomes you to this memorial service. May you witness the love of God the Father, the grace of the Lord Jesus Christ, and the comfort of the Holy Spirit.

COMMENDATION

God of faith, hope, and love!
Creator of heavens and earth,
> sea and sky, river and prairie.

"Our first glimpse of reality this day—everyday—is
> your fidelity.
We are dazzled by the ways you remain constant
among us,
> in season, out of season,
> for better, for worse,
> in sickness and in health.
You are there in watchfulness as we fall asleep.
You are there in alertness when we awaken . . ."*

This day we trust, O God, that all you have given us
is yours.
You first gave Norman to us—husband, father, grand-
father, brother, soul friend—and our lives have
been so blessed!
Now we give him back to you.
Receive Norman into the arms of your mercy.
Raise him with all your people.
Receive us also, and raise us into new life.

We pray for one another in our need
> and for all who mourn with us this day.

* Walter Brueggemann, *Awed to Heaven, Rooted in Earth: Prayers of Water Brueggemann* (Minneapolis, MN: Fortress Press, 2003).

We pray for all who sorrow . . . your peace and comfort,
for those who doubt . . . your light,
for those who are weak . . . your strength.
Bind us in together in your love with which we hold
one another.

We pray especially for Verna, that in the days and
months to come she would find a deep reservoir of
love that "bears all things, believes all things, hopes
all things, endures all things."

God of faith, hope, and love!
Creator of heavens and earth,
sea and sky, river and prairie,
You are also Redeemer and Friend,
who remains our true home forever. Amen.*

* Prayer of Commendation offered by Dr. Roger Heuser at
the Memorial Service for Dr. Norman Shawchuck on June
1, 2012, at Zion Evangelical Lutheran Church, Elgin, North
Dakota.

How to Use This Guide to Prayer

Welcome to your personal copy of *A Guide to Prayer for All Who Walk with God*, the fourth in the series of *Guides* to prayer. This book contains materials for daily prayer and monthly retreats. While the patterns of the daily and monthly practices are similar to past volumes, there are also some marked differences.

The Revised Common Lectionary will continue to provide the scripture readings for Sunday. However, the daily scripture readings for the rest of the week are different. The pattern of prayer has also been modified and is more centered on scripture and ancient forms of prayer than the previous *Guides*.

If you do not already have a daily pattern of prayer, we urge you to begin using the one suggested here. We do not mean it to be followed slavishly or without modification. Rather, we have designed it to serve as a guide for your spiritual journey. The pattern is simple to understand and easy to follow. We trust you will find that it provides an abundance of material to nurture your life of prayer and your walk with God.

While we believe the materials in this book are of great value in developing your life of prayer and your life with God, we also believe that God is your guide and spiritual director. We encourage you to permit each of the scriptures of the day and the anthology of readings for the week to be a time and place of listening for the voice of God. Our prayer is that this resource will increase your joy, confidence, trust, and hope as you continue your faithful walk with God.

Weekly
Guidance

The Season of Advent

Advent is not just about Christmas! Rather, it is about the beginning of the Christian year. The focus is on the future of all things as seen through the eyes of those who follow Jesus. At the same time, the season of Advent takes history seriously and encourages us to remember and reflect upon God's mighty acts and how they affect us today.

Long before Jesus' birth, liturgical practices were in regular use. Jews observed times of daily prayer (Pss. 55:17 and 119:164) and honored a Sabbath day of rest and prayer (Deut. 5:12-15). Christians observed Sunday as a holy day and by the fourth century were beginning to formalize regular times of prayer, worship, and fasting. The Christian year we observe today has ancient roots in these early Jewish and Christian practices of prayer, worship, and faithful living. This kind of daily, weekly, and yearly rhythm has a varied history that ranges from full embrace and practice to condemnation and avoidance. Most Christians today practice some elements of the Christian year.

The contemporary liturgical year observed by Christians contains at least Christmas and Easter. The more liturgical denominations begin with the season of Advent, include Christmas and Epiphany, and end with Reign of Christ Sunday, concluding the period usually called the season after Pentecost.

The season of Advent offers a time of expectancy and hope as we prepare to celebrate the birth of Jesus. It includes the four Sundays before Christmas and often begins with hymns like Charles Wesley's "Come, Thou Long-Expected Jesus." The yearning of all who wait for God finds expression in hymns such as "O Come, O Come, Emmanuel," "Savior of the Nations Come," and scripture texts like the Canticles of Mary and Zechariah.

The message of Advent is about God's astounding intervention in human history—an intervention that makes the world's attempt to market Christmas seem hollow and empty. Advent is the announcement that God is offering a new revelation of reality that will turn the world's way of thinking about life and its meaning upside down. The birth of Jesus marks the beginning of a new dawning of light and truth about who God is and who we are as God's children. Be alert, look, listen, reflect; and be ready to experience "God-with-us" as never before.

First Sunday in Advent
Sunday between November 27 and December 3

1. Active Waiting

Affirmation
My whole being thirsts for God, for the living God.
When will I come and see God's face? (Ps. 42:2).

Psalm: 27

Psalm Prayer
You offer us a refuge amidst the trials of life. May our
waiting prepare us to see glimpses of your face, even
as we long for the full appearance of your goodness
throughout all the earth. Amen.

Daily Scripture Readings

Sunday	A.	Isaiah 2:1-5; Romans; 13:11-14; Psalm 122; Matthew 24:36-44
	B.	Isaiah 64:1-9; 1 Corinthians 1:3-9; Psalm 80:1-7, 17-19; Mark 13:24-37
	C.	Jeremiah 33:14-16; 1 Thessalonians 3:9-13; Psalm 25:1-10; Luke 21:25-36
Monday		Matthew 25:1-13
Tuesday		Psalm 130
Wednesday		Isaiah 26:7-10
Thursday		Lamentations 3:19-26
Friday		Luke 2:25-32
Saturday		2 Peter 3:8-13

Silence

Daily Readings for Reflection

Reflection: Silent or Written

Prayers: For the World, for Others, for Myself

Offering of Self to God
Holy God, we will wait with patience for what we do not yet see. Amen.

Blessing
May the goodness and loving-kindness of our God sustain us in our longing, and transform the desert of our waiting into a garden of fertile expectation. Amen.

Readings for Reflection

❧ "If it sounds too good to be true, it is." We have all heard this with the warning about scam artists that are waiting to take our money and our property. And it is true that there are those who prey on the naïve, the trusting, and the innocent. Most of us can remember hearing about that seductive bargain that turned out to be a disaster. We have seen it happen and have promised ourselves it will never happen to us.

Because we see such deception in our world, it is not unusual that we guard ourselves against the truth of the gospel story. We are afraid that it is indeed too good to be true. What if we believed and then found out it was only myth and hype? Better to keep our distance. We listen to the gospel story, let it creep into the edges of our lives but never can bring ourselves to embrace it fully. What if it is just another cheap commercial trick that has nothing to do with our need or destiny and everything to do with the storyteller's need and fortune? Since it is better to be wise than to be a fool, we stand near the edge of the Advent story and keep all our options open.

So often I stand on the edge of the light, afraid to believe, afraid to act, afraid that this story is too good to be true. But then in my better moments, when I listen closely to the story, move closer to the light, my fears seem to evaporate like an early morning mist; and I can believe again. I can believe that God who made all that is became clothed in our human flesh so that we might become clothed in God. I can believe that God claims me as a beloved child. I can believe that all my days are in God's strong and tender hands. I can believe that life is good, beautiful, and eternal. I can believe that not only my days but all days are in God's good and able hands. I can believe, rejoice, and wait trustingly and expectantly for the unfolding of God's promise given so many ways and most clearly in the Advent story. Thanks be to God!

We are not unlike Zechariah in the presence of God's messengers. Our questions are like his. How can this be? The angel speaks to us as to him, "Do not be afraid . . . for your prayer has been heard" (Luke 1:13). God gives the promise, and God keeps the promise. So even though it does sound too good to be true, it is true! Thanks be to God, it is true! Two thousand years of Christian experience and testimony declare that the preposterous promise is true. Today, believe that your prayer is heard, and the light and presence of God will lead you through all your days.

—Rueben P. Job

❧ The basic foundation for all spiritual growth is God's loving gift of Jesus. Through God's promises and initiatives, God assures us that we are already loved just as we are. We don't have to go anywhere or do anything to gain God's love. This love is unconditional and unmerited. To fall into the hands of God is to fall into the arms of unfailing love (Mic. 7:18-19).

There is a divine initiative in our every encounter with God. Even before we knew our Creator, God loved us. Even before we turned to look toward God, God was moving toward us.

Our faintest yearning for God is assurance that God is already longing for us. Our first feeble step toward God is possible only because God has already been moving toward us, drawing us nearer by the divine magnet-heart of love.

—Norman Shawchuck, Rueben P. Job, and Robert G. Doherty, *How to Conduct a Spiritual Life Retreat*

ᴥ We live in an age of instant answers; we want the Lord to reveal God's plan for us immediately in response to our prayers. The psalmist suggests just the opposite. The psalmist speaks of waiting on God: "I waited patiently for the LORD." The psalmist, like many of us, was probably not very good at waiting. The psalm's last words indicate a desire for immediate relief: "O my God, do not delay" (Ps. 40:17, NIV).

God's purpose for our lives unfolds gradually as a tree grows into fullness. It cannot be forced or achieved overnight. Jesus himself pointed out that the beauty of lilies does not result from their own efforts, for "they neither toil nor spin." Their growth comes about by their yielding to the friendship of the sun and the rain in purposeful waiting.

—Costa Stathakis, "God's Purpose for Our Lives," *The Upper Room Disciplines 1999*

ᴥ In many ways, Advent is a "not yet" season. Mary and Joseph have *not yet* traveled to Bethlehem, the infant Jesus has *not yet* been born, the angels have *not yet* appeared to the shepherds, and the star has *not yet* come to rest over the manger. Still, with all these "not yets" embedded in the Advent story, we spend these days and weeks living in faith that God will provide what has been promised—a long-awaited Messiah, a living hope.

—Pamela C. Hawkins, *Behold!*

ᴥ The right time for seeking God is always *now*. "Now is the acceptable time, now is the day of salvation," and He promises, "Before they call upon me, I will say, Lo, I am here." And if it is by good works that we seek God, while we have time, let us do good unto men; and that

all the more because the Lord Himself warns us that the "night cometh, wherein no man can work." Do you expect to find some future time in which to seek God and do good other than this present day of mercy?
—Bernard of Clairvaux, *Selections from the Writings of Bernard of Clairvaux*

❧ Advent is a season of good news. In this season we prepare, by faith, to celebrate the birth of God-With-Us, Immanuel. According to the prophet Isaiah, this good news comes not just for us whose lives have been attuned to listen for, celebrate, and receive it; it comes also for the many others who wait day and night for us to act upon it—the oppressed; the brokenhearted; the captives and prisoners; the mourning, ruined, and devastated.
—Pamela C. Hawkins, *Behold!*

❧ Advent is a time of the unexpected gift, both in our remembering and in our hoping. It is a season when we recognize that God became flesh in a place emptied of comfort and privilege, a presence that took form in a forlorn crib as the start of a journey that would carry all the way to an ignominious cross. It remains a season haunted by such memories . . . , longing as we do for some trace of the One who was among us for a season and whose coming again we await in life's long winter.
—Mark S. Burrows, "The Hardest Love We Carry," *Weavings*

❧ People who wait have received a promise that allows them to wait. They have received something that is at work in them, like a seed that has started to grow. This is very important. We can only really wait if what we are waiting for has already begun for us.
—Henri J. M. Nouwen, "A Spirituality of Waiting," *Weavings*

Second Sunday in Advent
Sunday between December 4 and December 10

2. Hope in God

Affirmation
Hope in the LORD! Be strong! Let your heart take courage! Hope in the LORD! (Ps. 27:14).

Psalm: 33

Psalm Prayer
You brought all things into being and know the secrets of the furthest galaxies as well as those within the hidden universe of the human heart. May we always hope in your faithful love, which surrounds us all our days. Amen.

Daily Scripture Readings

Sunday	A.	Isaiah 11:1-10; Romans 15:4-13; Psalm 72:1-7, 18-19; Matthew 3:1-12
	B.	Isaiah 40:1-11; 2 Peter 3:8-15*a*; Psalm 85:1-2, 8-13; Mark 1:1-8
	C.	Malachi 3:1-4; Philippians 1:3-11; Luke 1:68-79; Luke 3:1-6
Monday		Genesis 17:1-8
Tuesday		Psalm 119:159-170
Wednesday		Zechariah 9:9-12
Thursday		Matthew 12:1-23
Friday		Romans 8:19-29
Saturday		1 Corinthians 15:12-22

Silence

Daily Readings for Reflection

Reflection: Silent or Written

Prayers: For the World, for Others, for Myself

Offering of Self to God
Lord of all hopeful horizons, in your word of promise to our father, Abraham, and in the promise of your Word incarnate, Jesus Christ, you have given us solid ground on which to build our lives. We offer you the toils and struggles of our days in faith that by your grace they will become sources of hope for others who seek to walk in your ways. Amen.

Blessing
May the God of hope fill [us] with all joy and peace in faith so that [we] overflow with hope by the power of the Holy Spirit. Amen.

Readings for Reflection

⮞ Zechariah was a deeply religious man, a man full of years and full of experience. He was a leader in the religious life of his community, and he was filled with a question that would not go away. Even an angelic visit did not calm his fears or answer his questions. "How can I know that God's promise is true for me?"

Zechariah is not the only one who hears the nagging questions. We hear them too. How will I know God is guiding me? How will I know God will provide for me? How will I know God will forgive me? How will I know God loves me as an individual? How will I know? How will I know God? These are the nagging questions that lurk close in many of our lives, and to deny them is to give them power they do not have. To face the questions honestly and directly is to see them for what they are—a response of fear to our lack of faith. So what shall we do? Continue our life as Zechariah did—praying, serving, listening. And as we continue our disciplined listening for the voice of God, we will be called to remember that God does care for us and provide for us in wonderful ways, even when we are unaware of that provision.

After living with the questions, the apostle Paul said, "I am convinced that neither death, nor life, nor angels . . . , nor anything else in all creation, will be able to separate us from the love of God in Christ Jesus our Lord" (Rom. 8:38-39). The assurance that we are enfolded in the loving arms of God can still the nagging questions and grant us the grace, peace, and serenity to live all of life fully and faithfully every day. Grant us this blessed assurance today and always.

—Rueben P. Job

&. From firsthand knowledge Jesus understands our inevitable times of being enclosed in imprisoning narrowness, with no way out. Christ not only understands these moments because he has had his own, he also comes to share ours with us: to lighten our darkness, to love us beside us, from inside our walls of stone.

This is the inestimable gift that we approach in this season of Advent: the saving gift of the love of God in the Incarnation, the unfailing presence of God-with-us in all our darkness. This Presence is so powerful and all-encompassing that absolutely nothing can divide us from it. As Saint Paul reminds us, neither life nor things present nor things to come nor anything else in all creation can separate us from the love of God in Christ Jesus (Rom. 8:38-39).

—Deborah Smith Douglas, "Enclosed in Darkness,"
Weavings

&. Everything that is done in the world is done by hope. No husbandman would sow one grain of corn, if he hoped not it would grow up and become seed; no bachelor would marry a wife, if he hoped not to have children; no merchant or tradesman would set himself to work, if he did not hope to reap benefit thereby, &c. How much more, then, does hope urge us on to everlasting life and salvation?

—Martin Luther, *Table-Talk*

❧ What I have come to see is that there is nothing more important to human beings than hope. Certainly in our own day, many people live without explicitly religious faith. And evidence of loveless lives is tragically abundant. But people usually do not survive long without hope. They cannot, because hope is the very heart of a human being. . . .

We live in a profoundly disruptive and disorienting age. On every street, behind every door, lives someone who is deeply disheartened, if not actually despairing. This may be brought on by the awareness of massive and meaningless death, the randomness of violence, the onset of early illness, the loss of a loved one or job or sense of meaning and value. Or by the loss of cherished and heretofore reliable ways of thinking and speaking of God. Indeed, even by the loss of faith in God. But this loss too can beckon us to deeper levels of openness to hope, the kind of hope that is absolutely and altogether gift. . . . Hope is not the same thing as optimism that things will go our way, or turn out well. It is rather the certainty that something makes sense, is worth the cost, regardless of how it might turn out. Hope is a sense of what might yet be. It strains ahead, seeking a way behind and beyond every obstacle.

—Michael Downey, "Gift's Constant Coming," *Weavings*

❧ Hope is a constant force working to enliven us, and its energy is immediate. Although we are neither its creator nor master, hope comes to us and dwells in our bodies. Our bodies are sacred creations of God that are a home for hope. We embody hope. . . .

Jesus taught that our salvation (being in right relationship with God) depends on loving. Care for the body exemplifies his focus on love. He spoke of the hungry body being fed, the thirsty body being given drink, the strange body being welcomed, the naked body being clothed, the sick body receiving care, and the imprisoned body being visited (Matthew 25:31-46). Body conditions are holy matters. To deny loving care

to persons and their body conditions is to deny love to God. The body, as a recipient and giver of loving care, is of holy and ultimate significance to the work of hope.
—Luther E. Smith, "The Work of Hope," *Weavings*

༝ The reason for the hope of the Christian is that in the Incarnation, Eden has been restored. The gifts of life, fullness, and future, once refused, are offered yet again. We are "fore-given," given before we would even think to ask. The most appropriate response to this gift is not to grab or to hide but to receive and then to live freely from this gift, a gift that can never be repaid. The great call to the spiritual life amounts to little more than learning how to receive what first and finally can only come as gift and then to live freely in and from that gift. Every inch and ounce, every moment of our life is to be lived in the presence of God. In Christ, all has been embraced. All of human life is a precinct of epiphany. But the gift half understood, the hint half guessed, is that it is ours to receive amidst the most mundane of human realities—the daily round of life's ordinary experiences—and here. Yes, especially here, if we only could see.
—Michael Downey, "Gift's Constant Coming," *Weavings*

༝ *Hope is a force of God that enlivens us to life.* We can easily miss the radical significance of this definition to our lives. Hope is often described as the expectation that desires will be fulfilled or as a feeling of assurance about current and future circumstances. When someone thinks positively or believes deeply about desired outcomes, so this line of reasoning goes, then hope happens.

However, hope is more than a positive attitude or elevated feeling of assurance. Like faith and love in 1 Corinthians 13, hope is *a force*. Yes, it functions within individuals to transform their lives. But hope also resides and functions outside an individual's attitudes and feelings. The very character of hope as *energy that comes to us from God* means we encounter hope as a transforming force that we do not control.

Hope's mission is to save us from a false sense of aliveness. Rather than fulfill whatever fantasies claim our hearts, hope rescues us from a diminished life. Its mission to us is congruent with its mission to the world: to enliven *all* to life and to save the world from a false sense of aliveness.

The opportunities to experience hope are as close to us as we are to our neighbors and our bodies. God has given us the capacity to pay attention, imagine, and enter into the wonder of life together. This capacity is also our God-given assignment. God created us to be a home for hope, to discern its work, and to be a people of hope.

—Luther E. Smith, "The Work of Hope," *Weavings*

3. *Prepare the Way of the Lord*

Affirmation

Look, I am sending my messenger who will clear the path before me; suddenly the LORD whom you are seeking will come to his temple (Mal. 3:1).

Psalm: 96

Psalm Prayer

You have inspired a new song of justice and peace to carry our hopes and dreams. May we find joy in singing it not only with our lips but also with our lives as we prepare a place for you in our hearts, our communities, and our world. Amen.

Daily Scripture Readings

Sunday	A.	Isaiah 35:1-10; James 5:7-10; Psalm 146:5-10; Matthew 11:2-11
	B.	Isaiah 61:1-4, 8-11; Luke 1:47-55; 1 Thessalonians 5:16-24; John 1:6-8, 19-28
	C.	Zephaniah 3:14-20; Isaiah 12:2-6; Philippians 4:4-7; Luke 3:7-18
Monday		Exodus 19:1-11
Tuesday		Luke 12:35-40
Wednesday		Psalm 98
Thursday		Romans 13:11-14
Friday		Mark 13:28-37
Saturday		1 Peter 1:13-16

Silence

Daily Readings for Reflection

Reflection: Silent or Written

Prayers: For the World, for Others, for Myself

Offering of Self to God
Faithful God, our hearts are unwavering. Help us to
stand firm in our faith so that all we do may be done
in love. Amen.

Blessing
May the Spirit of the Lord be with us, giving us strength
to resist conformity to the patterns of this world and
grace to receive God's transforming renewal of our
minds. Amen.

Readings for Reflection

❧ Mary's song of praise must have been a shock—
even to Elizabeth and surely to everyone else who
heard it. It bordered on treason and blasphemy and
must have left every adult who heard it angry, confused, embarrassed, surprised, curious, or frightened.
And it could be that all these feelings were swirling
around in the hearts and minds of those who heard
this message of radical revolution.

First of all, here was Mary, a simple peasant girl,
announcing that God had chosen her for great responsibility, honor, and blessing. Only Elizabeth could hear
this song without a knowing smile, attributing all this
nonsense to teenage idealism. As a matter of fact,
Mary's declaration would likely have been dismissed
as teenage daydreams if it had not all come true!

And what about this prophecy that God would
bring down the rich and powerful and lift up the weak
and powerless? Where did Mary get this nonsense?
We might say it was youthful idealism out of touch
with reality and an absolute absurdity in our world. We
could say that—if we didn't know about Jesus and his
proclamation and practice of the same truth.

The final straw was the youthful confidence that
God can be trusted to keep promises. Where did a mere

child get the wisdom and the faith to bear witness to God's trustworthiness so boldly? Perhaps from the same God who dwelt within and spoke through the voice and actions of Jesus. Jesus trusted God as loving Abba and taught and lived his faith in a God who was absolutely trustworthy. He not only taught people to receive God's love, but he also taught them how to trust, love, and obey this trustworthy God.

God's promise seems no less preposterous today. Turn the values of this world upside down? Rich become weak; poor become strong? Each of us chosen to be God's special witness to God's promise of love and justice? It does seem like a preposterous promise, until we listen carefully to the Advent story, observe the life of Jesus, and listen to the Spirit's voice today. But then we see that the promise is for us. The responsibility to tell the story is ours. And yes, the blessing and honor come to all whose lives point to Jesus Christ and God's revolutionary purpose in the world.
—Rueben P. Job

❧ *In those days John the Baptist appeared in the desert of Judea announcing, "Change your hearts and lives! Here comes the kingdom of heaven!" He was the one of whom Isaiah the prophet spoke when he said: The voice of one shouting in the wilderness, "Prepare the way of the Lord; make his paths straight"* (Matt. 3:1-3).

A rough and wild John the Baptist seems to interrupt Advent's gentler story. But the way of the Lord, the path of Jesus, had to be prepared so that people did not miss what God was doing right before their eyes. John's life was full of sacrifice. He lived and died so that Jesus could bring hope into the world. John lived and died so that God's word could be fulfilled.
—Pamela C. Hawkins, *Simply Wait*

❧ From the wilderness comes a voice crying out: "Prepare the way of the Lord, make his paths straight" (Luke 3:4). On the road ahead someone is coming toward us, someone for whom we must prepare by undertaking massive new construction. Valleys of loss and despair are to be filled with new hope. Mountains of self-assigned virtue are to be replaced by humility. Crooked minds are to be straightened through compassion and misshapen ideologies graded by truth. Yet even before we have begun this great work, the visitor is among us, knowing full well the meager measure of our capacities. Here is One who will freely labor with us and for us along the wilderness road so that, eventually, "all flesh shall see the salvation of God" (Luke 3:6).

But before this expansive vision can come to pass, the road must narrow drastically. It shrinks to the width of a virgin's womb; it conforms to the proportions of a worn manger; it follows the line of a jaw set toward Jerusalem. This road shares the dimensions of a rough beam thrust on abused shoulders. It fits within the space of a grave separating old and new creations; it tapers to the time between a decision to follow or not to follow; it narrows to the distance between the One who bids us come and the One who is the end of all our seeking.

The One who sets the course of this road and whose entry into it defines the way forward is the same who walks beside us, flesh of our flesh, God with us. Therefore, we can trust without reservation a journey whose future turns we cannot see.

—John S. Mogabgab, "Editor's Introduction," *Weavings* (November/December 2001)

༠ "That same night he rose, and taking his two wives and his two slave-girls and his eleven children he crossed the ford of the Jabbok. He took them and sent them across the stream and sent all his possessions over too. And Jacob was left alone. And there was one that wrestled with him until daybreak" (Gen. 32: 23-26, JB). It was Philo of Alexandria (d. 50 AD) who first saw Jacob as the archetype of the ascetic. Jacob wrestled with God and emerged from the contest with a blessing. His struggle with the Holy One bore Jacob a new name, a new identity, a new future.

If the deepest meaning of asceticism is to wrestle with God, what is the place of spiritual disciplines in the encounter? The story of Jacob offers a clue. It tells us that before he met God, Jacob sent his wives and servants and all his possessions to the other side of the river Jabbok. Jacob cleared an arena in which God could meet him "face-to-face," a place apart from the supportive relationships and material resources that sometimes mask our true self. Spiritual disciplines are like ground-clearing exercises aimed at providing room for God to confront us unmasked. The initiative for such a meeting always rests with God. Yet like Jacob, we can set aside our usual commitments and relationships for the sake of transforming encounters with God. The practice of such spiritual discipline truly prepares a way for the Lord.

—John S. Mogabgab, "Editor's Introduction," *Weavings* (November/December 1988)

❧ Life brings numerous opportunities to move from illusion to reality. Some illusions are inherited from culture, nation, or family. We see ourselves as better, more generous, or more intelligent than others. It is also possible to cling to the illusion that we are not worth anything or that we are incapable of good actions. Other illusions are created as defense mechanisms. We have illusions about ourselves, about our children, about our situation in life, about friends, about God. In some situations the illusion is more positive than the truth. In others, less so. In either case, they are false and therefore incapable of serving as a foundation for building a loving and authentic life.

In general, we like our illusions. They are familiar and comfortable, and we cling to them even though they lead to a dead end. We close our eyes when the truth intrudes on our picture, and we rarely seek outside perspectives from persons who might see more clearly than we do. Responses from other people that make us especially upset or angry can point to some part of the truth about ourselves that we are not willing to face.

An asceticism of everyday life points to an alternative in which we grow in the desire for the truth of our situation. We undergo the necessary stripping as the layers of illusion are peeled away. We engage in the discipline of seeking the truth, of being on the watch for clues to the false dimensions of our lives. We become willing to die to the old, self-centered self so that a new creation may emerge. Such an asceticism may involve the time and energy required to get at the truth of some political situation, local or global, and the action one must take as a result of knowing the truth. For others, it may mean facing up to the growing chasm between true inner feelings and dispositions and the self that is presented to others. It may mean watching attentively for the signals that others send us about the blocks to truth we have set up in our work and relationships. Such a process entails pain and suffering but can lead to new life.

—Elizabeth Ann Dreyer, "Asceticism Reconsidered," *Weavings*

❧   Holy preparation,
counterweight of surprise,
plumb line of hospitality;
you are fresh hay quickly strewn,
soft linen bands newly torn,
to hold the One who is to come.
O Preparation, catcher of the off guard,
leveler of all things high and low;
you are the smoother of rough edges
and bearer of good news.
Come, reveal our webs of apathy
with holy, sweeping light.
Amen.
—Pamela C. Hawkins, *Behold!*

❧ God had a lot to say in the various stories surrounding Jesus' birth, and many other individuals engaged in the practice of listening. Zechariah and Elizabeth listened to God telling them that Elizabeth would have a child in her old age—and that he should be named John (Luke 1:5-25, 57-80). Mary listened to the angel's news of her impending pregnancy and the future promise of the son she would birth. Joseph listened to the proclamation of the angel that he should not be afraid to take Mary as his wife because the son she would bear was from the Holy Spirit (Matt. 1:18-25). All this listening was critical to the outcome of the story. What if Joseph had not listened to the angel and had refused to take Mary as his wife?

God also calls us to listen. We may not receive visits from winged angels proclaiming that God has a message for us, but God still speaks to us. Our task as those who would hear is to do all in our power to listen to God's voice speaking to us.

—Beth A. Richardson, *Child of the Light*

❧ O Expectancy,
born of fertile wonder,
belabored by narrowed hope;
craning curious lives forward,
drawing in the lonely and longing.
You are imagination's sister
and the brother of holy surprise.
Come, startle awake
our dozing apathy, our complacent dreams,
that we may behold your borning Advent cry.
Amen.

—Pamela C. Hawkins, *Behold!*

4. Welcome the Stranger

Affirmation
He was despised and avoided by others; a man who suffered, who knew sickness well. . . . He bore the punishment that made us whole; by his wounds we are healed (Isa. 53:3, 5).

Psalm: 81

Psalm Prayer
Holy God, your ways are strange to us, and the language of radical love you speak is unfamiliar to our ears. Help us to welcome your presence among us and to receive your word as the finest food for nourishing a generous spirit within us. Amen.

Daily Scripture Readings

Sunday	A.	Isaiah 7:10-16; Psalm 80:1-7, 17-19; Romans 1:1-7; Matthew 1:18-25
	B.	2 Samuel 7:1-11, 16; Psalm 89:1-4, 19-26; Romans 16:25-27; Luke 1:26-38
	C.	Micah 5:2-5a; Psalm 80:1-7; Hebrews 10:5-10; Luke 1:39-45
Monday		Exodus 23:1-9
Tuesday		Genesis 19:1-13
Wednesday		Psalm 121
Thursday		Jeremiah 7:1-7
Friday		Luke 9:51-58
Saturday		Matthew 25:31-46

Silence

Daily Readings for Reflection

Reflection: Silent or Written

Prayers: For the World, for Others, for Myself

Offering of Self to God
Lord of all who wander far from home, we place ourselves in your good care, trusting you to teach us the arts of welcoming those who are different from us. Amen.

Blessing
May the God who became a stranger so that we could become friends with God and one another transform our wary hearts into welcoming ones. Amen.

Readings for Reflection

꙳ So many of the entries in my journal end, "I am yours." It appears so often because that is the way I want to live my life every day. It is also there because I know how easily I am distracted to "belong" to something or someone else. I genuinely want to belong to God fully and without qualification. But living in our culture, we easily tend to brush aside that desire.

Mary made this incredible leap of faith and offered herself without qualification to God for whatever God chose to bring into her life. At the moment of this confession, recorded in Luke 1:38, she could not have known the magnitude of her decision. Yes, the angel messenger clearly reported God's desire for her, but it was still a huge step to say a willing and faithful yes to whatever God would choose. The risk to her reputation, the commitment of faith to an unknown path, the simple trust that God would provide today and tomorrow were not unlike the ingredients of our decision to offer ourselves to God without qualification.

In our better moments we know that it makes little difference what others may think of us. We know deep within our hearts that pleasing God is far more important than pleasing those around us. And yet risking our reputation for God is difficult for us. It is easy to remain silent and hidden when my colleagues make decisions based on the cultural norms rather than in the way of Christ. I don't like being called "too spiritual" or "unrealistic," and so I'm tempted to remain silent when I should speak a clear and simple word of faith. Yes, "I am yours." Help me to live that way.

We like to think that we can know the future, and so we make plans, make investments, and seek to determine what the future will be. Planning, investing, and preparing are wonderful practices that we should incorporate in our lives. However, these practices should not dull our readiness to say yes to that call. "I am yours." Lead me always in your path.

We know we are entirely dependent upon God, yet we forget and try to make our own provision for tomorrow or waste our energy in anxiety and fear that we will be forsaken when tomorrow comes. Mary was able to entrust her life fully to the everlasting arms, sure that she would be upheld no matter what the future brought. "I am yours." Help me to remember you provided for me as a helpless baby; you provide for me now and will provide for me through eternal ages. Help me to live as one life totally given to you.
—Rueben P. Job

❧ "Foxes have holes, and birds of the air have nests; but the Son of Man has nowhere to lay his head" (Matt. 8:20). In Jesus, the strange God and the strange neighbor dwell together in the extraordinary intimacy of one flesh. In him, the full measure of our alienation is revealed. He dwells among us as a foreigner in a tent (John 1:14). He is rejected in his hometown (Matt. 13:54-58) and depends on the hospitality of others (Luke 10:38-42).

Jesus' teaching provokes misunderstanding (John 3:1-7) and hostility (Mark 14:1-2). He dies outside the walls of the city (Mark 15:22-24) and is buried in someone else's tomb (Matt. 27:57-61). Yet throughout the harsh litany of his sufferings, one insistent question wells up from Jesus' heart, in which the heart of God and the heart of humanity are once again united: "Do you love me?" (John 21:15-17).

Jesus asks this question still, no less present today than he was in the dust and heat of Galilee. And so, says Dorothy Day, we have the same opportunity as his first friends to welcome him into our lives.

—John S. Mogabgab, "Editor's Introduction," *Weavings* (September/October 2003)

᠕ Our Wednesday night Bible study group has become a rather odd community of sorts. We gather about 5:15 p.m. and share whatever food people have been able to bring. While we eat, we share joys and sorrows, celebrations and concerns, and all the stuff that falls in between. There are usually six to ten of us—two or three people who are struggling with mental health problems, three men who are homeless, several dealing with time in prison, and others wrestling with emotional and physical scars. Folks come with a hunger for healing, wanting food for the body and soul and a place to be at home. . . .

John, one of the men who is currently homeless and staying, as the others who are homeless do, at the downtown mission, started out one night: . . .

"Stayed down at the mission again last night—house of pain for real. Woke up this morning and my shoes were gone. Somebody stole my shoes. I didn't even have to think about what to do—I pulled out my knife and I went looking. I was walking all up and down the dining hall, table by table, and I meant to get my shoes back. Kept thinking: in the old days wouldn't anybody tried to touch my shoes—'cause they'd know I'd get 'em 'fore they could ever put 'em on. Oh, yeah. I was mean and folks knew it. Didn't care. And that's how it was this morning. It's one thing to give up drinking and drugging. It's another thing when they steal your shoes.

"And I'm hollering, threatening, and walking up and down with my knife out where everyone can see. I'm going to get my shoes. Then old Jim here (points to another homeless man in the group) starts hollering from the other side of the room: 'Bible says if they take one cloak give them your other one; if they took your shoes, give 'em your socks. Put that knife away and give 'em your socks.'

"And I'm swearing and getting madder. Ain't givin' nobody nothin'! I want my shoes! And old Jim, he just keeps hollering: 'Give 'em your socks, John!'

"Folded up my knife. Took a long time doing it, too. Walked barefoot to the service center this morning—and got me some more shoes—but ain't it hard to live this stuff out!"

—Janet Wolf, in *A Guide to Spiritual Discernment*

❧ The pain that distances us from ourselves reflects a larger wound in the connective tissue of life with God and others. To welcome our lives because God has already done so in Jesus establishes the healing peace that allows us to recognize God's face in the gaze of the stranger and live.

—John S. Mogabgab, "Editor's Introduction," *Weavings* (September/October 2003)

❧ More urgently than ever before, the biblical mandate to "show hospitality to strangers" (Heb. 13:2) summons us to create a world where strangeness breeds not estrangement but engagement. We seem to be faced with strangers at every turn. Different cultures, religions, ethnicities, and values now confront one another in ways unanticipated one or two generations ago. Isaiah's vision of every valley being "lifted up, and every mountain and hill . . . made low" (40:4) is coming true, sometimes with a vengeance. Ancient, isolated, mountain-separated valleys of tribe, tongue, religion, and clan are being connected by rapid transportation, high-speed communication, and vast international migration. Even with nations, the conflict of majority groups with minorities and the emergence of "identity tribes"—movements based on ethnicity or race, sexual orientation or gender, theological or moral fervor—can create a heightened sense of estrangement from the other and an increased chance of xenophobia.

—Robert Corin Morris, "Fear or Fascination?" *Weavings*

❧ Each of us is a mystery. Today we are encouraged to psychoanalyze, understand, and fix the problems that have contributed to our sense of alienation or disease. We forget that we will never plumb the marvelous depths of our own being. What we see and know is like the tip of an iceberg. Below the surface is God's handiwork in all its richness and depth. We are strangers to ourselves, and the most appropriate posture we can adopt is awe and a willingness to allow the Spirit to reveal more of what is hidden below the surface. This is pilgrimage, a journey of discovery and surprise, and the welcomed stranger within enables us to honor the mystery of others who travel with us. On pilgrimage we learn to travel light, discarding the heavy load of judgment and appreciating the gifts of those we meet along the way. Sharing resources, stories, and needs creates hope. In an inequitable world dominated by fear, those who follow the Christ-path will embody pilgrim hope—the hope that on this journey together God has not "forgotten the recipe for manna." There is enough for us all and together we are invited to sit at God's table in an ever-widening circle of belonging.

—Elizabeth J. Canham, "Strangers and Pilgrims," *Weavings*

❧ The biblical mandate to welcome the stranger comes with the promise that we may be blessed by unexpected grace. This belief was common to both ancient pagan and biblical societies. Hospitality to strangers may lead not only to "entertaining angels without knowing it" (Heb. 13:2) but also to encountering the Divine itself in disguise (Matt. 25:35).

Welcome goes beyond people to ideas. There's general consensus among scholars that the biblical text is filled with many borrowings from surrounding cultures. The creation story in Genesis 1 uses imagery borrowed from Babylonian mythology. The covenant language in Exodus is in the common style of Middle Eastern overlord-and-vassal covenants. Psalm 104 seems to echo Pharaoh Ahkenaten's famous "Hymn to the Sun," and Psalm 29 may have originally been addressed to Ba'al, the Canaanite rain god. The Song of Solomon probably finds its roots in Canaanite hymns about the marriage of the sky god and earth goddess, and the whole of Wisdom literature is influenced by the Egyptian and Babylonian wisdom traditions.

Nor is the New Testament without its links to wisdom from beyond the borders of Jesus' fellowship. The prologue to John's Gospel, while deeply Jewish, seems also to refer to the Stoic idea of the *Logos*, and Stoicism may well have influenced Paul's idea of the virtues. All this material has been "baptized" into Israel and the church, reshaped and revised by central biblical values, but it is the gift of strangers nonetheless. Nor should this surprise us, since the biblical God "has left himself nowhere without witness" (Acts 14:17).

Thus, biblically rooted people have more reason than many to show hospitality to the stranger. The God who created "of one blood all nations of men for to dwell on the face of the earth" (Acts 17:26, KJV) is working toward a kingdom in which the true riches of every culture are brought as offerings (Rev. 21:24). We can never tell when the strange person, idea, or custom is grace presenting itself to us as one small part of God's project of weaving the world together in love.
—Robert Corin Morris, "Fear or Fascination?" *Weavings*

The Season of Christmas

Christians believe that the birth of Jesus marked human history's most revealing moment about the nature of God. The author of the letter to the Hebrews puts it this way: "In the past, God spoke through the prophets to our ancestors in many times and many ways. In these final days, though, he spoke to us through a Son. God made his Son the heir of everything and created the world through him. The Son is the light of God's glory and the imprint of God's being" (Heb. 1:1-3*a*). The author of Colossians declares the same message: "The Son is the image of the invisible God, the one who is first over all creation" (Col. 1:15*a*).

As we view pictures taken of our universe and examine closely the earth that provides an abundance of all we need to sustain life, we are constantly overwhelmed by the extravagance of the creation we can, to some degree, see and understand. Yet, we know that what we see and what we understand is but a tiny speck of that creation. Our minds cannot grasp the immensity of a creation measured in billions of light years, and they understandably fall helpless trying to define the One who created and sustains it all.

While creation reveals much about both ourselves and the God who authored it, creation is also limited by our inability to unlock its mysteries and its inability to speak our language and understand our condition. The birth of Jesus changes all of this. His life reveals the character and person of God in remarkably clear and understandable ways.

Because of Jesus we know and understand more fully not only who God is but also who we are. Through Jesus we know that God is transcendent and ever beyond us but also near, loving, compassionate, the initiator of love, justice, and goodness in the world. Through Jesus we know that we are made to be God's beloved children, fashioned in God's image and created for good works as our way of life (Eph. 2:10).

This loving and gracious creator God is always with us. We will never be outside the reach of God's presence and love in this life or the next. This is the good news we celebrate during the season of Christmas—and all year long.

Christmas Day or First Sunday after Christmas

5. The Word Became Flesh

Affirmation

What are human beings, LORD, that you know them at all (Psalm 144:3)? And yet each of us is precious in your sight and carried lovingly in your all-embracing heart. Indeed, you have made our heart your heart in the life and ministry of Jesus, our brother and Lord.

Psalm: 67

Psalm Prayer

In your unbounded love you have shown us your face and made your way known among all the nations. May we recognize in your decision to become one flesh with us an invitation to live gratefully with others as one family, gathered and held together in your holy name. Amen.

Daily Scripture Readings

Sunday	A.	Isaiah 9:2-7; Psalm 96;
		Titus 2:11-14; Luke 2:1-14
	B.	Isaiah 62:6-12; Psalm 97;
		Titus 3:4-7; Luke 2:8-20
	C.	Isaiah 52:7-10; Psalm 98;
		Hebrews 1:1-12; John 1:1-14
Monday		Matthew 10:16-31
Tuesday		Luke 13:31-35
Wednesday		Mark 6:31-44
Thursday		Philippians 2:12-15
Friday		John 3:1-3, 7-12
Saturday		Hebrews 5:7-10

Silence

Daily Readings for Reflection

Reflection: Silent or Written

Prayers: For the World, for Others, for Myself

Offering of Self to God
Gracious God, you are bone of my bone and flesh of my flesh. Let nothing in this world separate me from you, for you are my life and my hope in every trial and every joy. Amen.

Blessing
May the God of untrodden ways, who has chosen to live as one of us, guide us and keep us on the road to fullness of life. Amen.

Readings for Reflection

❧ New discoveries about our universe seem to emerge every day. Telescopes in space enable us to see into the created order farther and more clearly than ever before. But even with all of this marvelous technology we have not been able to chart the boundaries of creation. And even if we could, the idea of a created order many billions of light years in depth is too much for us to comprehend. So how can we comprehend the One whom we call Creator? Clearly, an infinite God has a communication problem with finite humankind. Christians find the answer to that problem in Jesus Christ. The mystery of this magnificent universe finds resolution in the mystery of the birth in Bethlehem. Jesus Christ came and was clothed in human flesh to let us know who God is and what God is really like. In Jesus Christ we see that God is approachable and, to a degree, knowable by creatures like us. God can understand our condition because God has made us. We can know God because God has been revealed in Jesus Christ.

Colossians 1:15-16 says it so well. "He is the image of the invisible God, the firstborn of all creation; for in him all things in heaven and on earth were created, things visible and things invisible, whether thrones or dominions or rulers or powers—all things have been created through him and for him." In Jesus we have the perfect reflection of God. While the Creator of this vast universe may seem distant and unknowable, we can see, understand, and know Jesus of Nazareth. While it may seem too much to ask the Maker of the complex creation to hear us as we pray, we remember Jesus listened to everyone. So we, you and I, can know the One who knows us and we can communicate with the One who is author of all.

Our earthly existence takes on fresh, new meaning when we remember that God chose to put on our humanity and chose to wear that humanity as an ordinary working man. Our ordinary existence is not so ordinary when we remember that God chose this existence to give us a true picture of the divine. Therefore there are no unimportant moments in any lifetime. All are precious gifts of opportunity to know and serve the One who made us and chose to stand with us and be like us in the gift of life.

—Rueben P. Job

❧ [O]ur high God, the sovereign wisdom of all, bedecked himself willingly in our poor flesh in this low place so that he himself could perform the service and office of motherhood for all things.

—Julian of Norwich, *Encounter with God's Love*

❧ In unimaginable love, God has taken on our humanity—including all our mortal terror, sorrow, and pain—and invited us, in exchange, to participate in the mystery of eternal life that is God's own nature. God offers us, in that exchange, a partaking of divinity so deep that it amounts to union, what the Lady Julian called "one-ing" ourselves to God. God in Christ is so profoundly with us that that "with-ness" is who he is: Emmanuel.

—Deborah Smith Douglas, "Enclosed in Darkness," *Weavings*

❧ The Word of God is indeed a living and effective arrow, sharper than any two-edged sword to pierce the hearts of men. There is another, chosen dart: the love of Christ.

This love of His is tender, wise and strong. Tender in that He took on Him our flesh; careful and wise in that He guarded against sin; and strong in that He suffered death. It is a thing beyond all measure sweet to look upon man's Maker as a Man . . . a loving Friend, a prudent Counsellor, a mighty Helper He! I trust myself entirely to Him who willed to save me, knew the way to do it, and had the power to carry out the work. He has sought me out and called me by His grace.

—Bernard of Clairvaux, *Selections from the Writings of Bernard of Clairvaux*

❧ What an admirable foundation for thus associating the ideas of time and eternity, of the visible and invisible world is laid in the nature of religion! For, what is religion,—I mean scriptural religion? For all other is the vainest of all dreams. What is the very root of this religion? It is Immanuel, God with us! God in man! Heaven connected with earth! The unspeakable union of mortal with immortal. For "truly our fellowship" (may all Christians say) "is with the Father, and with his Son Jesus Christ. God hath given unto us eternal life; and this life is in his Son." What follows? "He that hath the Son hath life: and he that hath not the Son of God hath not life."

Soon you will awake into real life. You will stand a naked spirit, in the world of spirits, before the face of the great God! See that you now hold fast that "eternal life which he hath given you in his Son."

—John Wesley, *Journal of John Wesley*

❧ For many people, the body continues to be a problem outright. Restless under the extreme stress imposed by the avid lifestyles of affluent Western cultures, the body may either be ignored or subdued with tranquilizers available in bewildering variety. For others, the body is not so much a problem as a project. In a world where fresh frontiers of heroic endeavor have dwindled and feelings of powerlessness have grown, the body has become the new focal point of personal achievement. In fitness centers across the United States, tuned and tanned bodies have replaced big cars and suburban homes as symbols of success and well-being.

Is it possible to acknowledge the limits our bodies impose on us without despising them? Can we seek the health our bodies desire without exalting them? Might we perceive the body neither as inconvenience nor idol but as icon disclosing our origin and destiny as God's beloved creations? Could we receive the body neither as problem nor project but as promise of renewed intimacy with God, other human beings, and the creatures of the earth? . . .

The foundation for responding to these questions is evident through scripture. Both Old and New Testaments affirm a positive view of the body as part of a good creation. Soul and body together, like two facets of a finely cut crystal, give us glimpses into the mystery of our psychophysical unity as persons. When Jesus points to the relation between faith and wholeness or forgiveness and healing, he confirms the irreducible unity of the human being as body and soul. Paul employs the metaphor of the body to refer to the equally irreducible unity of Christ and those joined to Christ through baptism (1 Cor. 12:12-13). For Paul, our indwelling in Christ is a bodily reality consummated in sharing the resurrection body with the Lord (1 Cor. 15:35-44).

—John S. Mogabgab, "Editor's Introduction," *Weavings* (November/December 1987)

❧ For the Christian, the body is far from being the less important, the less "noble" or "divine" aspect of the human person. If I accept as fact the Incarnation—that the Infinite Spirit broke into time and space as Jesus

Christ; taking on our human body-spirit nature; linking in a new creation the matter of our bodies and of all the universe to his divinity; nourishing us, body and spirit, with his body and blood; uniting us with himself by incorporation or assimilation into his body; promising us eternal joy in a resurrected body like his own—then the implications are staggering for the objective preciousness of these bodies of ours, which we take so much for granted. They are our most obvious underlying connection with the whole of the created universe and, through the body of the incarnate Word, with the divinity of our Creator. And every impulse toward liberation from human weakness and sinfulness, toward growth in union with the living God, comes through God's Holy Spirit working in our body-selves, so that, as St. Paul asserts, our bodies (ourselves) are in truth living temples of the Holy Spirit (1 Cor. 6:19-20).

—Theodore Tracy, sj, "The Body: Pivot-Point of Salvation," *Weavings*

❧ Any form of Christianity which is not incarnational, which does not celebrate "the Word made flesh," which tries to separate us from our own bodies, the bodies of our communities, the body of this earth, is not the Christianity of our Lord Jesus Christ. In Christ the walls of hostility, the walls of division and fragmentation within us and among us are encountered, touched, healed. The Christ moves lovingly and with power through our closed doors and confronts our frightened selves, just as the risen Christ moved through the closed doors of the house where the disciples hid. And the loving hands were stretched out, showing the wounds that were not wasted or swallowed up in glory but that had become sources of redemptive love.

If we take those hands stretched out to us, our own wounds of body and spirit become to us no longer signs of hopeless pain but also sources of new springing love!

—Flora Slosson Wuellner, *Prayer and Our Bodies*

New Year's Day or Second Sunday after Christmas
(If this is the first Sunday after Epiphany, use Week 7.)

6. The Poverty of God

Affirmation
[Jesus] emptied himself by taking the form of a slave
and by becoming like human beings (Phil. 2:7).

Psalm: 14

Psalm Prayer
You created us in love and desire only that we love
you in return. How can we measure the depth of the
poverty you endure because we foolishly love you
poorly? Infuse us with the wisdom that will help us
turn our faces to you with loving regard and joyful
celebration. Amen.

Daily Scripture Readings

Sunday	A.	Jeremiah 31:7-14; Psalm 147:12-20; Ephesians 1:3-14; John 1:10-18
	B.	Jeremiah 31:7-14; Psalm 147:12-20; Ephesians 1:3-14; John 1:10-18
	C.	Jeremiah 31:7-14; Psalm 147:12-20; Ephesians 1:3-14; John 1:10-18
Monday		Exodus 32:1-8
Tuesday		Psalm 74:1-10
Wednesday		Isaiah 3:1-5
Thursday		Mark 6:1-6
Friday		Luke 2:1-7
Saturday		1 Corinthians 1:18-31

Silence

Daily Readings for Reflection

Reflection: Silent or Written

Prayers: For the World, for Others, for Myself

Offering of Self to God
Extravagant God, in your love you have assumed our human impoverishment. May we become empty enough to receive the riches of life you offer us in the community of those who call you Lord. Amen.

Blessing
May the Lord who has blessed our poverty by embracing it empower us to embrace the poverty of our brothers and sisters in their sorrow, sickness, or any other hardship. Amen.

Readings for Reflection

❧ Today I read Acts 17:1-32, and I was deeply impressed by Paul's ability to put his thoughts and ideas into the beliefs and faith-stance of his dubious listeners. The account of this event says, Paul "argued with them." Certainly this sermon was not a one-way communication—and it brought results.

When Paul "argued" in Thessalonica, some believed and joined sides with him. Others cast the city into an uproar and set out to do harm to Jason (Paul's host) when they could not find Paul.

Wherever Paul and the others went, people were divided—some accepted, some opposed Paul's preaching. Is this not better than what we see today? Virtually no preacher or teacher can cause a riot by reason of his or her preaching or teaching today; our words and our certainties are too banal and too bland.

When I consider my own teaching, I know I am safe. No one comes into my classroom without already being convinced. My students are "on my side" from the beginning. My only problem is to keep them awake and motivated to learn.

There are no stonings or riots in my classroom. What a pity!
—Norman Shawchuck

❧ The nothingness from which we are created permeates human existence like rain forest mist. It is an impoverishment so profound, so persistent, that no self-improvement efforts can diminish it, and every illusion of self-sufficiency will compound it. This poverty God fully assumed in the manger birth. That this choice might be visible, the One who was flesh of our flesh shared without reserve the afflictions of the poor. Like them, his wisdom was despised, he was unjustly treated, left without friends, mocked and humiliated, "crushed and abandoned." These and many other sufferings have been gathered into the very heart of God. The destitution of human life is now eternally and inseparably part of the poverty of God.

God's poverty, however, is greater than the human poverty God has willingly embraced. God is forever poor because the gates of God's heart, opened to receive the full burden of our poverty, are also opened for the outpouring of God's love in the freedom that only love creates. Who can measure the poverty of divine love as it seeks a hearing in a hostile, self-absorbed world? Love bade God take a place with the poor, who are waiting—waiting for someone to stop, acknowledge their dignity, listen to their voice: "O Israel, if you would but listen to me!" (Ps. 81:8). Love cast God into the dependency of the poor, who must look for the response of the other: "And he could do no deed of power there. . . . And he was amazed at their unbelief" (Matt. 13:58). It is to what Clare of Assisi calls a "life of the highest poverty" that God invites us with the words: "Come to me, all you that are weary and are carrying heavy burdens, and I will give you rest" (Matt. 11:28). This is the deep soul rest, the holy poverty, of learning to love in freedom.

—John S. Mogabgab, "Editor's Introduction," *Weavings* (November/December 2003)

❧ By desiring wealth for the power and distinction it gives and gathering it on this motive, people may become rich. But since their minds are drawn in a way distinguishable from the drawings of the Father, they cannot be united to the heavenly society where God is the strength of life. "It is easier," says our Savior, "for a camel to go through the eye of a needle than for someone who is rich to enter the kingdom of God." Here our Lord uses an instructive similitude. As a camel while in that form cannot pass through the eye of a needle, so someone who trusts in riches and holds them for the sake of the power and distinction attending them cannot in that spirit enter the kingdom. Now every part of a camel may be so reduced as to pass through a hole as small as the eye of a needle. Yet such is the bulk of the creature and the hardness of its bones and teeth that it could not be so reduced without much labor. People must cease from the spirit that craves riches and be brought into another disposition before they inherit the kingdom, as thoroughly as a camel must be changed from the form of a camel in passing through the eye of a needle.

When our Savior said to the rich youth, "Go, sell what you own, and give the money to the poor," though undoubtedly it was his duty to have done so, yet to enjoin the selling of all as a duty on every true Christian would be to limit the Holy One. Obedient children who are entrusted with great outward wealth wait for wisdom to dispose of it agreeably to God's will, in whom the orphan finds mercy. It may not be the duty of all to commit at once their substance to other hands but from time to time to look around among the numerous branches of the great family as the stewards of God, who provides for the widows and fatherless. But as disciples of Christ, although entrusted with many goods, they may not conform to sumptuous or luxurious living. For as he lived in perfect plainness and simplicity, the greatest in his family cannot by virtue of their station claim a right to live in worldly grandeur without contradicting him who said, "It is enough for the disciple to be like the teacher."
—John Woolman, *Walking Humbly with God*

❧ Without paying any fee we have all been admitted into a wonderful world; and if, in addition, we come into touch with the love of Jesus, how can we remain unmoved? After all, we entered the world naked, and therefore we ought to leave it in the same condition. I cannot admire a man who, while calling himself a disciple of Jesus, yet says he must have a cultured life and wants to live in luxury in a big house. For his whole life Jesus wandered from village to village, spending his life on foot, and having no place to rest. Do we not need once more to return to Jesus?

—Toyohiko Kagawa, *Living Out Christ's Love*

❧ Saint Francis was known to his contemporaries as the *poverello*, the poor one. It was a name that explained him utterly. Not only was Francis a great champion of the poor and marginalized (one of the earliest stories about him tells of his giving his cloak to a beggar), he also preached of the blessedness of poverty. His early followers were literally to imitate the gospel by carrying no money with them. They were to own no property, covet no titles, and claim no goods as their own. But Francis's love of poverty went deeper than concern for the material goods to which the involuntary poor are entitled and which can keep the rich, like the young man of the Gospels, from following Christ. Francis thought of himself as married to lovely Lady Poverty. And he knew that the marriage was not one of convenience but a matter of two becoming one.

Even more profound than his romance with voluntary material poverty was Francis's passion for spiritual poverty. In this the saint from Assisi understood himself to be an imitator of Jesus, the poor one, who was born naked and vulnerable in a stable, and who died naked, vulnerable, and abandoned on a cross. He wanted his brothers in Christ, the Friars Minor, to do likewise, to be the little ones, the lowly ones. He wanted them to share in the powerful, kenotic reality of the Christ-life, that life of unexpected reversals, of paradox, of the world and its assumptions turned upside down. He wanted them to preach the redemptive poverty of God with their lives.

From the beginning, the mysterious poverty of the Incarnation was the focus of Francis's spirituality, and he took its implications very seriously. The naked, cross-hung man proclaimed in the Gospels became the template for his transformation. A youthful dream led him to question his desire to become the vassal of a local prince. "Who do you want to follow, Francis," the dream challenged, "the great lord or the lesser one?" Awaking, he understood that the poor one, Jesus, was the greater lord. Once his heart was captured, Francis quite literally began his imitation of—or better, his participation in—the poor Christ. He followed the dictates of a divine locution: "Repair my church." Taking bolts of cloth from his wealthy merchant father's warehouse, he sold the goods for building materials to restore a shabby local chapel. Then, in the town square, before his irate father, the bishop, and the assembled townsfolk, he stripped himself naked and declared that he no longer called any man father except his father in heaven. He, like the Lord he loved, abandoned everything to follow. He carried no money, went barefoot, and owned no more than his rough tunic.

—Wendy M. Wright, "The Freedom of the Children of God," *Weavings*

&. It is an awesome thing to see the good gentle Jesus, the one who rules and feeds the whole universe, in such great want and need that no one else has ever been as poor as he. He is so poor that Mary hasn't a blanket to wrap him in. In the end he dies naked on the cross so that he might reclothe us and cover our nakedness. Our sin had left us naked; we had lost the garment of grace. So Jesus gave up his own life and with it clothed us. I tell you, then, the soul who has discovered love in the love of Christ crucified will be ashamed to pursue it in any other way than that of

Christ crucified. She will not want pleasure, status, or pomp but will prefer to be like a pilgrim or traveler in this life, with her attention focused wholly on reaching her journey's goal. And if she is a good pilgrim, neither any prosperity she may encounter along the way nor any difficulty will slow her down. No, she will go forward bravely in love and in eagerness for the goal she hopes to reach.

—Catherine of Siena, *A Life of Total Prayer*

Saint Paul rejoiced in the "unsearchable riches of Christ" (Eph. 3:8) and counted the loss of everything else as gain "because of the surpassing worth of knowing Christ Jesus my Lord" (Phil. 3:8). These riches are eternally ours if we want them, but we cannot have both the unfailing treasure and the failing kind: we cannot, Jesus declares bluntly, serve both God and mammon (Luke 16:13). "Do not lay up for yourselves treasures on earth, where moth and rust consume and where thieves break in and steal, but lay up for yourselves treasures in heaven. . . . For where your treasure is," Jesus observes, "there will your heart be also" (Matt. 6:19-21).

We must choose which riches matter; we must decide where our hearts belong.

—Deborah Smith Douglas, "Unfailing Treasure," *Weavings*

The Season after Epiphany

A friend once patiently explained a depiction of the Lord's Supper crafted in wire and steel. I tried to see the message in this piece of abstract art, but it was invisible to my eyes. Was I too distracted? Was my mind too full of other renderings of this familiar scene that blinded me to this simple and profound image? I am not sure, but I do know that as my friend traced the outlines with her finger I was able to see the dramatic figure of Jesus gathered at table with the disciples for the Last Supper.

Epiphany is the day and the season of the church year when we patiently watch and listen as God is quietly revealed before us once again. Sometimes, even when we try hard to do so, we just don't see God in our everyday lives or in the events of our troubled world. Epiphany gives us the time and the resources to watch, wait, listen, look, anticipate, and discern the light, life, and truth of the Lord's presence in our midst.

Contemporary observances of Epiphany include the coming of the wise men with gifts for the Christ child and the baptism of Jesus. The season concludes with Transfiguration Sunday, when the church remembers the radiant vision of the disciples who saw Jesus' garments turn bright and they heard a voice from a cloud that overshadowed them saying, "This is my Son, whom I dearly love. Listen to him!" (Mark 9:7).

Epiphany is the time when the church gathers to remember and reflect on the mighty acts of God in the birth of Jesus Christ. As we watch and wait for the light of Christ to overcome the darkness, we see the Christ child who will become prophet, healer, teacher, and savior. Much of the story remains to be told, but the biblical readings for Epiphany remind us of the direction in which this one sacred life is moving. Here was life at its purest and best. Life lived as it should be lived. Life that came from God, walked with God in the world, and would one day be fully with God in the world to come (John 13:3). The life of Jesus is our light and model for how we too may live. As we recognize the image of our true humanity in the life of Jesus Christ, we also begin to understand that we have come from God, are invited to walk in faithfulness with God in this world, and one day will be welcomed to our eternal home. There we will still be with the God who loves us beyond our capacity to fully understand.

7. You Stand on Holy Ground

Affirmation
The LORD is definitely in this place, but I didn't know it. . . . This sacred place is awesome (Gen. 28:16, 17).

Psalm: 114

Psalm Prayer
In your awesome presence, faithful Lord, even the sea and the mountain stand back, and the rock pours forth pure water to refresh the weary and heavy-laden. May we join all creatures great and small in acknowledging the life-giving strength of your love in all things and treat your creation as the holy ground you intend it to be. Amen.

Daily Scripture Readings

Sunday	A.	Isaiah 42:1-9; Psalm 29; Acts 10:34-43; Matthew 3:13-17
	B.	Genesis 1:1-5; Psalm 29; Acts 19:1-7; Mark 1:4-11
	C.	Isaiah 43:1-7; Psalm 29; Acts 8:14-17; Luke 3:15-17, 21-22
Monday		Genesis 1:24-31
Tuesday		Exodus 3:1-6
Wednesday		Psalm 77:11-20
Thursday		1 Samuel 3:1-10
Friday		Matthew 2:1-12
Saturday		Colossians 1:15-23

Silence

Daily Readings for Reflection

Reflection: Silent or Written

Prayers: For the World, for Others, for Myself

Offering of Self to God
We desire to be your faithful companions, incarnate God, as you hallow the ground under our feet by your presence with us. Amen.

Blessing
May the Lord of heaven and earth strengthen our knowledge that in Jesus Christ heaven has come to earth and earth has become the holy ground of God's saving work. Amen.

Readings for Reflection

ๆ "Why do you spend your money for that which is not bread, and your labor for that which does not satisfy?" (Isa. 55:2). How often in my seventy plus years have I disregarded Isaiah's admonition and sought, sometimes desperately, that which is not bread and does not satisfy. Seeking God first is not just good advice; it is the only way to a joyful and faithful life in companionship with the One who made us and loves us without limit.

When I saw my first airplane as a child, I knew at once that I wanted to fly. I became a farmer, student, pastor, husband, father and still wanted to fly. Throwing caution and common sense to the wind, I joined a flying club and soon was ready for my first solo flight. I will never forget the thrill of breaking the bonds of gravity. When the aircraft broke free from the ground and slowly climbed, I was bursting with the joy of realizing a dream I had nurtured for a lifetime.

Flying still holds a thrill for me, although I have not had the controls of an aircraft for over thirty-five years. When flying club members asked why I quit flying, I responded then, "I would rather fly than eat, but my children would rather eat." It is costly to fly! Several decades later, I realize something else was

going on: a growing love and desire for God and a growing awareness of stewardship. I still look up when a light plane passes overhead and for a moment feel the sensations of flight, but then I rejoice in the companionship of the One with whom we can all break bonds that hold us down and rise to heights greater than we imagine.
—Rueben P. Job

❧ *Christ reveals to us as much of his own kingdom vision as we are able to bear.* Whenever we take a step toward Christ, he responds in a way that tells us the step did not go unnoticed. His response is always designed to give us further insight into the nature of the kingdom of God and our place in it. It is as though Jesus were saying, "Now that you have turned my way, I want to share with you something of my vision of how good life can be for you and for all creation, as you journey farther into the kingdom of God."

Our letting go of former attitudes and behaviors has made it possible for Christ to create within us a new consciousness of the kingdom of God and its rightful claim upon our lives. Jesus does this by setting up a situation in which we must again decide our response to him. The situation may seem almost trivial, but the consequences of our response will prove to have life-altering effects.
—Norman Shawchuck, Rueben P. Job, and Robert G. Doherty, *How to Conduct a Spiritual Life Retreat*

❧ Holy ground is the stable place of clarity and confidence in a turbulent human landscape of shifting values, crumbling hopes, frayed trusts, uncertain commitments. Holy ground is the place of life-giving rootedness in something larger than our own lives, something deep enough and enduring enough to keep us anchored and oriented in the storm. Holy ground is the place at once attractive and fearsome, where God speaks and we listen; the place of empowerment, transformation, and sending forth to live victoriously in a world too often disfigured by the defeat of justice, peace, and human dignity; the place where the gracious rule of God is known and the new creation becomes visible; the place where faith can move mountains (Matt. 17:20).

—John S. Mogabgab, "Editor's Introduction," *Weavings* (September/October 1992)

❧ I feel like I'm swimming in the dark.
> On a moonless night, my frail arms and legs thrash about in black despair.
> I can't see where I'm going or where I've been.
> I can't see the danger lurking beneath the surface, but I know it's there.
> I am terrified of losing what little independence I have left.
> I grope for a glimmer of purpose to keep me afloat, but I cannot find it.
> Floundering. Gasping for air.
> In thick water I can feel but cannot see.
> Then I sense your voice speaking to me stirring my soul:
> "Look up, child.
> Put your feet on the rock bottom.
> It is solid ground. Holy ground.
> Stand up and live."

—Missy Buchanan, *Talking with God in Old Age*

❧ An altar, a pew, a seat on the bus, a kitchen table: all become holy places when we confess before God. Today, in this holy place, God meets us, hears us and forgives us. In this holy place, God empowers us with genuine love to share with a hurting world. Be for God, a holy, loving people.

—Kwasi Kena, *The Africana Worship Book*

❧ Make us like the wind—ever-moving and ever moving others. And with joy we will dance with the

leaves. In submission we will linger in the shade, cooling the skin of those scorched by the sun's heat. In awe we will pause and be still enough to hover over creation, admiring your world and waiting for your command. And when you move us, we will fly with more strength, reminding people that you are present even in times you may seem invisible. Breathe into our souls, Lord, and make us like the wind, like your Holy Spirit—in the name of Jesus Christ. Amen.
—Ciona D. Rouse, *The Africana Worship Book*

• Going barefoot is not always easy; it is a profound act of intimacy, freedom, reverence, responsibility, and vulnerability. Yet only when our feet are bare can we truly relish the earth, wiggle our toes freely in the fertile soil of life, and root ourselves firmly in the Holy Ground.
—Jean M. Blomquist, "Barefoot Basics," *Weavings*

• I believe Scriptures tell us that the whole creation is holy ground. "O Lord, how manifold are your works! In wisdom you have made them all; the earth is full of your creatures," says the psalmist (104:24), who goes on to describe a Creator active not only in the design of the universe but also in maintaining and sustaining each creature in its relationship to the environment. This Creator provides not only food and drink for all the variety of creatures but also thoughtfully makes high mountains for the goats and rocks to be refuge for the badgers. This was not my understanding of God as Creator. I grew up a functional deist, I think; I believed that God created only "in the beginning." I remember the day a door opened onto a new perception. I was sitting on the lawn with a group of college students studying the story of the healing of the paralytic in John's Gospel. When I came to the words "My Father is working still, and I am working" (John 5:17, RSV), I pointed to a blade of grass and said, with utter conviction, "Here is incontrovertible evidence." It was overwhelmingly clear to me that in that moment God was at work creating this blade of grass. A blade of grass was transfigured before my eyes. God's creating continues now; God is present and actively shaping creation everywhere around us, in our midst, with us. That sense alone, could we recover it, would ensure that we regard *all* ground as holy ground where God is present.

—Elaine M. Prevallet, SL, "Grounded in the Holy," *Weavings*

8. The Kingdom of God Is among You

Affirmation

Your kingdom is a kingship that lasts forever; your rule
endures for all generations (Ps. 145:13).

Psalm: 24

Psalm Prayer

O Lord, the world and all that is in it belongs to you.
Let us give praise to your glory and give thanks each
day for the kingdom you have established among your
people, a kingdom unlike the ones of this earth that
fade and fall but a heavenly and everlasting kingdom
that endures throughout all ages. Amen.

Daily Scripture Readings

Sunday	A.	Isaiah 49:1-7; Psalm 40:1-11; 1 Corinthians 1:1-9; John 1:29-42
	B.	1 Samuel 3:1-10; Psalm 139:1-6, 13-18; 1 Corinthians 6:12-20; John 1:43-51
	C.	Isaiah 62:1-5; Psalm 36:5-10; 1 Corinthians 12:1-11; John 2:1-11
Monday		Luke 17:20-21
Tuesday		Mark 12:41-44
Wednesday		Psalm 145
Thursday		Matthew 5:1-12
Friday		Deuteronomy 30:11-14
Saturday		Hebrews 12:18-29

Silence

Daily Readings for Reflection

Reflection: Silent or Written

Prayers: For the World, for Others, for Myself

Offering of Self to God
Don't be afraid little flock, because your Father delights in giving you the kingdom. Sell your possessions and give to those in need. Make for yourselves wallets that don't wear out—a treasure in heaven that never runs out. No thief comes near there, and no moth destroys. Where your treasure is, there your heart will be too (Luke 12:32-34). Amen.

Blessing
Now is the time! Here comes God's kingdom! Change your hearts and lives, and trust this good news! (Mark 1:15). May the knowledge of God's kingdom established among us bring us joy and comfort this day and always. Amen.

Readings for Reflection

᪥ There was a light drizzle in the air as I walked along a darkening road, hands in my pockets, head down, thinking of a task I was to do and quite oblivious to the world around me. Suddenly a voice called my name. My head came up, I looked around, and there spotted a friend who was driving by and had stopped his car to greet me. We were several thousand miles from my home and a hundred miles from his. I suspect much of my life has been like that, preoccupied with personal issues and oblivious to the voice of God calling to me every day and in every circumstance.

The Bible and saints who have gone before us give ample evidence of God's consistent call to each of us. The Bible and the saints who have traveled this road before us also make clear the universal nature of God's call to all humankind. No one is left out, exempted, or overlooked. All are of equal worth and all are called. While we may think of certain vocations as callings,

God appears to consider all of life as our calling, and that includes every honorable vocation.

Regularly practicing disciplines of the holy life puts us in position to hear God's call clearly. Those disciplines include prayer, fasting, community and personal worship, acts of mercy and compassion, and faithful living.

Hearing is an important step in saying yes to God's call. But once we hear, we must still decide whether we will go where invited or sent. In other words, hearing may be the easy part of saying yes to God's call. Once we have heard and counted the cost, the most difficult task remains. However, with deep faith in the living God who calls us, the only reasonable response is to say yes. For in our best moments, we know God will ask us, only us, to say yes to an invitation that is right and good for us. Listen closely, think deeply, pray fervently, and you will be led to the right answer to God's invitational call. In my experience the right answer is always yes. The good news is that even when I was unable to give the right answer, God was patient and gave me opportunity to grow in faith until I was able to say yes and to claim another part of my inheritance as a child of God.
—Rueben P. Job

ﺈ The kingdom of God is near, but how near? It is not easy to perceive this realm of light and life in a world so tortured by suffering. John's Prologue offers a clue: The kingdom becomes flesh in the life of Jesus and in the lives of his followers. The story is told of a seeker who met a wise woman on the road. The seeker asked, "How do I find my way into the Kingdom?" The wise woman responded, "It's just up the hill." "What hill?" questioned the seeker. "The hill of your longing," said the wise woman. "But how far is this hill?" pressed the seeker. Her reply: "How far is your heart?"
—John S. Mogabgab, "Editor's Introduction," *Weavings* (January/February 1995)

▪ The word *epiphany* comes from the Greek word meaning "appearance." The church proclaims that God revealed God's self to the world in Jesus. God appeared in the life, death, and resurrection of Jesus.

The church's celebration of Epiphany recalls three events of Jesus' life. First, the coming of the magi from the East signifies the universality of God's self-revelation. The magi symbolize the whole world that God has come to save. Jesus' baptism is the second event. Matthew tells us that God speaks from the heavens, and the Holy Spirit descends like a dove. The third story from the Epiphany tradition tells of Jesus' first miracle at a wedding in Cana (John 2:1-11).

The church is to be a continuing "appearance" of God's presence in the world. The gifts the magi bring us are the practical gifts for ministry.

Rulers appeared upon their palace balcony to reveal their presence to the people. The ruler "made an epiphany" before the people: "This is who I am. This is what I offer you. This is what I ask of you." Using the palace balcony as a metaphor, God in Jesus made an appearance (epiphany) on the world's balcony. We are to stand on the balcony of our own time and reveal the presence of God through our lives.

—Joseph P. Russell, "Baptized for Ministry," *The Upper Room Disciplines 1999*

▪ When our souls are utterly swept through and overturned by God's invading love, we suddenly find ourselves enmeshed with some people in amazing bonds of love and nearness and togetherness of soul such as we never knew before. In glad amazement we ask ourselves: What is this startling new bondedness in love which I feel with those who are down in the same center of life? Can this amazing experience of togetherness in love be what people have called fellowship? Can this be the love which bound together the early church and made their meals together into a sacrament of love? Is this internal impulse which I feel, to share life with those who are down in the same center of love, the reason that the Early Church members shared their outward goods as a symbol of the experienced internal sharing of the life and the love of Christ? Can this new bondedness in love be the meaning of being in the kingdom of God?

—Thomas Kelly, *The Sanctuary of the Soul*

⁑ Each of us has a unique combination of personality traits and gifts. When we are able to put into practice the design that God has put within us, we find high levels of energy, fulfillment, and purpose. Ideally, what we are to do as Christians is to live in loving service to God in the world, according to the way we were created. We share in the ministry of Jesus who gave himself completely for us.

—Gerrit Scott Dawson, *Companions in Christ*

⁑ The church—in theory—is here to help us make our home in the silence of adoration and the holy; to give us courage to carry it into ordinary life, into the kingdom of noise—that is, what ancient writers have called "the world"—so that it too may be transfigured. "The world" in this context does not mean the creation, which is good, but rather the arena of illusion, of power struggles and conspicuous consumption, imagined in the mind but acted out in the suffering of the material creation and the body. It is this shadowy and contentious world of avidity, not the body, which Paul refers to as "the flesh." This phantasmagorical world cannot bear silence, for silence reveals it for the delusion it is. It adores only what it can consume and lives for the adrenaline rush of power over people and things. It is this noisy world of delusion and lies that the humble Christ defeats by self-emptying silence.

—Maggie Ross, "Practical Adoration," *Weavings*

❧ In the upper room, Jesus gently and imaginatively equipped his disciples to set aside their old dreams of who he was and what kind of world to hope for. He gave them new images of himself and his kingdom: the washing of feet, the sharing of bread, praying, dying, rejoicing amid suffering. He gave them a new image of God's face just by calling them by name and getting them to look him in the eye. By faith we believe that God's reign is more than just a dream. It is reality. Yet, we only seem to catch it in glimpses. Most of our lives, we live in between visits to the kingdom. If we practice spiritual discipline, our prayers and Bible readings and songs and silences keep us watchful for the kingdom, but we do not hear its music just yet. We hear all of creation groaning in anticipation of it, and our prayers only seem to blend in with the collective moan that rises into the cold darkness of outer space. If we do not practice a regular life of prayer or meditation, God's face occasionally arrests us, but in between those epiphanies we live in the desert of our routines.
—J. Marshall Jenkins, *A Wakeful Faith*

❧ The pressure in our culture to secure our own future and to control our lives as much as possible does not find support in the Bible. Jesus knows our need for security. Because it is such a deep human need, he is concerned that we not place our trust in things or people that cannot offer us real security. "Do not store up treasures for yourselves on earth, where moth and woodworm destroy them and thieves can break in and steal. But store up treasures for yourselves in heaven, where neither moth nor woodworm destroys them and thieves cannot break in and steal. For wherever your treasure is, there will your heart be too" (Matt. 6:19-21, NJB). We cannot find security if our heart is divided. So Jesus says something very radical: "No servant can be the slave of two masters: he will either hate the first and love the second, or be attached to the first and despise the second. You cannot be the slave both of God and of money" (Luke 16:13, NJB). What is our security base? God or mammon? That is what Jesus would ask. He says that we cannot put our security in God and also in money. We have to make a choice. Jesus counsels: "Put your security in God." We have to make a choice whether we want to belong to the world or to God. Our trust, our basic trust, Jesus teaches, has to be in God. As long as our real trust is in money, we cannot be true members of the kingdom.

—Henri J. M. Nouwen, *A Spirituality of Fundraising*

❧ Righteousness and justice characterize the kingdom of God, and Jesus came to announce, embody, and inaugurate the kingdom of God. The kingdom was the unifying vision in all of Jesus' preaching and teaching and the primary motif of his parables. In fact, Jesus called the reality and availability of the kingdom of God the good news.

What is the kingdom of God? It's the divine order of reality that results when and where God's sovereignty and lordship is fully realized. Jesus himself incarnated that divine order. The nature and character of his life perfectly illustrates what it looks like. If you want to know what the kingdom of God is and what are its results, simply observe the life of Jesus as he lived on this earth. The qualities of life that he admonishes in us are the qualities he exhibited fully and perfectly during his brief time here.

The kingdom Jesus incarnated and exhibited is the divine order that has come, is coming, and will come in its future fullness. This order has already dawned within human history; we can glimpse it among us, though imperfectly, in churches, cells, and congregations. But it awaits consummation. When the kingdom comes in its fullness, there will be justice for all the oppressed. There will be no disparity between rich and poor, no divide between people because of race or social class. There will be no violence and aggression, and there will be peace.

As individuals in whom the presence of Christ dwells, we are to seek this kingdom above all else. We are to order our lives according to its ethic and pattern our behavior after the one who incarnated it. We are to serve this kingdom, pray for its coming, and live expectantly for its full realization.

—Daniel Vestal, *Being the Presence of Christ*

&. I have been watching as a friend's mother dies, participating, as I could, in the dying. I watch her body work to keep breathing, lungs pumping, taking in oxygen from the air around us. I imagine her, each of us, as an experiment of the universe, each an irreplaceable part of a vast whole. Death is in some ways an example of God's kingship, God's power over us. One has to yield. But ever since I saw the icon of earth viewed from outer space, I've had a different sense of life and death. Sometimes I imagine myself out there in space looking at myself here on earth: this tiny little speck in this one particular tiny spot on the globe, relating to this particular environment. I begin to sense that death is somehow *for* life, for its continuance. I feel my way into a sense of kinship or communion throbbing through it all.

God's life, as Christians describe it in the symbol of the Trinity, is a continuous joyful exchange; and creation is shot through with that same life, giving and receiving, living and dying. I keep waiting to separate the life from the death, but life and death are so intricately joined at every moment in the process that for practical purposes they are nearly inseparable. The truth is that I am always and inevitably both—living and dying at the same time. Our little lives are caught up in a much larger process. Our dyings, large and small, are in fact always an exchange, always *for* something or someone else, enabling life in some other form—we just don't see how it's working. That is at least one application of the central symbol of Christ's death: "always carrying in the body the death of Jesus, so that the life of Jesus may also be made visible in our bodies. . . . So death is at work in us, but life in you," says Paul (2 Cor. 4:10, 12). And, since "one has died for all; therefore all have died. . . . if anyone is in Christ, there is a new creation" (2 Cor. 5:14, 17). The new creation is coming to be every moment if we have eyes that can see, if we have hearts willing to play our part, to participate in the process. Some persons, at least momentarily, *experience* the truth of that ongoing creation. For most of us, most of the time, willingness to participate is the most—and perhaps also the least—we can offer.

—Elaine M. Prevallet, SL, "Dancing around the Kingdom," *Weavings*

The Season after Epiphany
Sunday between January 21 and January 27

9. The Extraordinary in the Ordinary

Affirmation
Heaven is declaring God's glory; the sky is proclaiming his handiwork. Let the words of my mouth and the meditations of my heart be pleasing to you, LORD, my rock and my redeemer (Ps. 19:1, 14).

Psalm: 104

Psalm Prayer
Gracious and loving God, the earth and all that is in it speaks of your glory, from the animals and hills of the earth to the clouds and stars of the heavens. It was through your infinite and eternal love that creation was spoken into existence and it is through you that we are sustained and have our being. Give us eyes to see you not only in the big things but in the small things also, for nothing exists apart from you. All glory and honor is yours, O Lord. Amen.

Daily Scripture Readings

Sunday	A.	Isaiah 9:1-4; Psalm 27:1, 4-9; 1 Corinthians 1:10-18; Matthew 4:12-23
	B.	Jonah 3:1-5, 10; Psalm 62:5-12; 1 Corinthians 7:29-31; Mark 1:14-20
	C.	Nehemiah 8:1-3, 5-6, 8-10; Psalm 19; 1 Corinthians 12:12-31*a*; Luke 4:14-21
Monday		Colossians 2:1-6
Tuesday		Matthew 17:1-13
Wednesday		Genesis 21:1-7
Thursday		2 Corinthians 4:1-15
Friday		Isaiah 51:1-16
Saturday		Hebrews 4:14-16

Silence

Daily Readings for Reflection

Reflection: Silent or Written

Prayers: For the World, for Others, for Myself

Offering of Self to God
We are constantly reminded of your presence, O Lord, in all that surrounds us. May we always be mindful that you are found not only in the extraordinary places and moments of life, but also in the routine and ordinary. Amen.

Blessing
The Lord laid the foundations of the earth with wisdom, establishing the heavens with understanding. With his knowledge, the watery depths burst open, and the skies drop dew . . . don't let them slip from your eyes; hold on to sound judgment and discretion. They will be life for your whole being, and an ornament for your neck. Then you will walk safely on your path, and your foot won't stumble (Prov. 3:19-23). May the peace of our Lord Jesus Christ be with us this day and always. Amen.

Readings for Reflection

❧ History presents examples of humankind and the church horribly missing the mark of God's will. Times when God's will was not followed, and wars, schism, hatred, and racism infected the world. There are also some examples of wonderful times when individuals *and* the church listened for, heard, and obeyed the voice of God in beautiful and healing ways. Perhaps the church and individuals usually have fallen somewhere between unqualified hearing and obedience to the voice of God and ignoring the voice of God as a result of being overpowered by voices of the world.

Finding God's voice in the midst of this noisy world is not easy. So many voices clamor for our attention, and so much noise tends to shield us from the voice of the One who, as Evelyn Underhill said, "has everything to tell us and nothing to learn from us." However, millions of people have learned how to "read the signs," that is, to observe how God has acted and is acting now, to listen attentively, and to receive knowledge and direction from a source greater than they are.

The foundation for reading the signs is the desire to know God's will and the confidence that God desires that we know, understand, and obey God's will. For some, such a desire has become a way of life. That is, there are persons who habitually ask, "Lord, what is your will in this matter? In my life, in my church?" For such persons, discernment is a way of life and an unconscious process. They do not look for special times to listen to God's voice; they simply listen, trust, and obey. These persons see all experiences, ordinary and extraordinary, as conveying God's presence and message. When such persons read the Bible or the daily paper, they are aware of another Presence speaking and guiding. These individuals experience the ordinary events of life as filled with meaning and direction from God. For them, all of life is a conversation, a dialogue with the One who made them. For them, discernment is a way of life.

—Rueben P. Job

❧ To view reality from a slightly different perspective often yields a view of things totally unlike what they appeared to be. If we take just a couple of steps in another direction, what we view as reality is often profoundly changed.

—Rueben P. Job

❧ When we seek to be like Christ we come to realize that we are facing an eternal paradox—the more we become like him the greater is our realization that we are not yet fully like him. This growing similarity makes us more conscious of the vast dissimilarity. But there is increased faith that he will never stop drawing us until we are fully formed in the image and likeness of God. He is ever moving toward us with transformation as the goal (Rom. 12:1-2).

The realization of transformation brings with it two crisis-laden insights. The first regards our resistance to enter into full personhood. Jesus is much more than savior. He is Lord. Many persons are willing to have Christ as savior. Far fewer are willing to surrender everything they possess and desire to his lordship. But union with Christ makes this possible: all that we have is already his—and all that he has is already ours. It is a small, albeit momentarily painful, sacrifice to surrender what we fleetingly possess in order to make room for all he is desiring to share with us forever.

The second insight regards the fullness of Christ's mission. Union with Christ means we will share not only his glory but also his passion and suffering. He invites us not only to live with him but also to die with him (Mark 8:34-38). The mystery here reminds us that Christ yet suffers for the redemption of God's creation, and we can share his suffering. Because of us he need no longer be alone in the garden of suffering. We can shed his tears and bear his stripes.

—Norman Shawchuck, Rueben P. Job, and Robert G. Doherty, *How to Conduct a Spiritual Life Retreat*

❧ The prayer of adoration, in which we behold the beauty of the Lord with awe and reverence, savoring the sweetness of God's presence and the majesty of God's way, places us in the atmosphere of divine goodness—an atmosphere of silent communion unclouded by anxious preoccupation with our own desires. Just as the weaned child on its mother's breast seeks no physical nourishment but enjoys the riches of unspoken love given and received (Ps. 131), so the soul in quiet adoration lays its head against the heart of Love and absorbs all that Love yearns to bestow. This Love draws out what is truest and best in all it touches, shapes all things toward the wholeness proper to them, is quietly victorious amid the strident self-importance of the world.

—John S. Mogabgab, "Editor's Introduction," *Weavings* (March/April 2008)

❧ We can never forecast the path God's energy of rescue will take. It is never any use saying to God, "I am getting desperate! Please answer my prayer by the next mail and please send a blank check." God *will* answer but not necessarily like that; more probably God will transform and use the unlikely looking material already in hand—the loaves and the tiny fishes—looking up to Heaven and blessing it and making it do after all.

—Evelyn Underhill, *The Soul's Delight*

❧ The Christian is proud to be a fool for Christ. Such a fool is obedient, yet free; under law, yet walking by grace; sinful, yet forgiven; unlovable, yet unconditionally loved; a believer, but with a healthy skepticism; certain, but only by making the ultimate gamble. The Christian claims that God is definitely revealed in Christ, yet is still the Hidden One; knows deeply, but in a cloud of unknowing; believes, but only by faith; and acknowledges that while all things have been made new, everything remains much the same.

Above all, the Christian is a citizen of the church universal. While we delight in the uniqueness of each individual, our deepest joy is to be part of the community that Christ embraces as his own body. Invited to his marriage feast yet to be, we partake of his body and blood. And at these sacred moments, it is enough just to stand around, passing the peace for which the world yearns, being the church adorned as a bride awaiting her divine Lover.

—W. Paul Jones, *The Art of Spiritual Direction*

ᔄ God is active in the world and in our lives in many ways. We may feel the mystery of God as we view storm clouds brewing over an azure ocean. We may experience the love of God when we are comforted by a friend. We may be filled with the compassion of God as we attend a conference on the plight of the homeless. We may be blessed by the peace of God during prayer or troubled by the challenges of God as we study the Bible. God comes to us in our conscious and unconscious experiences, for God is in all of life.

There are times when God's activity seems clear: a specifically answered prayer, the saving of a seemingly unredeemable situation, strength which is wondrously given at just the right moment. Other times, we recognize God's interaction with us only in hindsight when we take time to reflect on our lives.

—Anne Broyles, "One More Door into God's Presence," *Weavings*

ᔄ God prescribes our duty; and it were wrong not to believe that if we undertake God's real work, God will attract us into a nicer observation of wisdom in our humble duties and concerns. We shall more admire the healthiness of that which grows up in God's natural springtimes, and ripens in the air of his common days. The ordinary will thus grow dignified and sacred in our sight; and without discarding all invention in respect to means and opportunities, we shall yet especially love the daily bread of a common grace, in our common works and cares. And all the more that it was the taste of our blessed God to make the ordinary glow with mercy and goodness. Him we are to follow. We are to work after no set fashion of high endeavor, but to walk with him, performing, as it were, a ministry on foot, that we may stop at the humblest matters and prove our fidelity there.

—Horace Bushnell, "Living to God in Small Things," *Weavings*

10. Behold the Beauty of the Lord

Affirmation
I have asked one thing from the LORD—it's all I seek—
to live in the LORD's house all the days of my life, seeing the LORD's beauty and constantly adoring his
temple (Ps. 27:4).

Psalm: 97

Psalm Prayer
Lord of the whole earth, the heavens proclaim your
beauty. May we behold your splendor, glory, and majesty, O Lord, in all the forms they assume, seen and
unseen, obvious and hidden. We rejoice in you and
give thanks and praise to your holy name. Amen.

Daily Scripture Readings

Sunday	A.	Micah 6:1-8; Psalm 15; 1 Corinthians 1:18-31; Matthew 5:1-12
	B.	Deuteronomy 18:15-20; Psalm 111; 1 Corinthians 8:1-13; Mark 1:21-28
	C.	Jeremiah 1:4-10; Psalm 71:1-6; 1 Corinthians 13:1-13; Luke 4:21-30
Monday		Deuteronomy 4:31-39
Tuesday		Psalm 93
Wednesday		Isaiah 40:10-31
Thursday		Matthew 27:27-31
Friday		Romans 15:7-13
Saturday		Hebrews 1:1-9

Silence

Daily Readings for Reflection

Reflection: Silent and Written

Prayers: For the World, for Others, for Myself

Offering of Self to God
LORD my God, how fantastic you are! You are clothed in glory and grandeur! (Ps. 104:1). Let us praise the Lord. Amen.

Blessing
May God's beauty surround, strengthen, and direct us all our lives. In the name of the Lord, whose glory and grandeur is ours to behold. Amen.

Readings for Reflection

❧ Through the Holy Spirit at Pentecost, God in Christ became available to every believer. Christians now had firsthand experience with God in Christ. From Pentecost on, the good news was not held only by a select few who had been with Jesus, felt his hand upon their lives, and sought to follow him throughout his earthly days. Now everyone could experience that touch of the Savior's hand; all could know the healing and saving presence of Jesus Christ. No Christian need ever walk alone, for now God was present with every believer who chose to accept this holy presence.
—Norman Shawchuck and Rueben P. Job

❧ "In him we live and move and have our being" (Acts 17:28). Paul's words to the Athenians, which echo a saying of Epimenides of Knosses (6th century BC), anticipate the majestic vision developed by theologians such as Gregory of Nyssa, Athanasius, and Augustine that the spiritual life is nothing less than participation in the life of the holy Trinity. Through union with the risen Christ, we are drawn into the intimacy of love and freedom enjoyed by the three Persons of the Trinity. In this mysterious communion of mind and heart our lives are being transformed, and from this same communion we go forth into the world as emblems of the hidden truth that God is making all things new.

—John S. Mogabgab, "Editor's Introduction," *Weavings* (January/February 1993)

❧ Christian community, like beauty, often presents itself in the intimate, the common, the close at hand. It comes to bud and flower in the simplest of places. Race by, and we miss it. Wait to see it in some idealized state, and we pass without knowing it is there.

"Where two or three are gathered in my name, I am there among them" (Matt. 18:20). As Jesus' followers, if we are to find true community with one another and with him, then we should look not just to the massive throng or the dramatic moment. We should look as well to the simplest instance of one life brushing up against another. We should open ourselves to the small and intimate moments when persons draw together in their joys and in their needs.

If love flows among us, even briefly, God is there— in traffic jams, in places of staggering beauty, in the realms of darkest communal pain. If we find ourselves bound together even momentarily, God is present. We taste with our spirits the community God longs to build.

To honor these occasions of community is to acknowledge how widely and all inclusively God works to fashion bonds among us. It is to open ourselves in wonder to the One who beckons toward wholeness at every turn.

And yet by honoring these experiences, we do not hold them up as substitutes for formal religious communities that gather in Christ's name. Only in the long-term bonds of such community will we learn where all these matters point. The formal community itself stands as a sign of what our passing experiences of closeness suggest. And rather than distracting us, these experiences of wider beckoning may ultimately be a means by which the living God calls us to fuller immersion in the community of faith that is both our home and our place of ongoing growth.

—Stephen V. Doughty, "Simple Places," *Weavings*

❧ Lord, when was it that we saw you . . . ? (Matt. 25:37). The bafflement of the righteous and unrighteous alike is understandable. They are standing before Jesus, who is resplendent in unearthly glory and surrounded by a vast multitude of shimmering angels. The beauty of the Lord is stunning, attracting the rapt gaze of the throng. He is, as Augustine said, the "beauty in all things beautiful." And so it is perplexing indeed when Jesus tells the crowd that they had encountered him in all things destitute, despised, downtrodden. He was the one in desperate want, the one who lacked even basic human comeliness, the one from whom most would avert their eyes and withhold their affection.

Yet the beauty now radiant before the crowd is the same beauty then present in the one who was hungry, naked, sick, imprisoned. It is a beauty etched in the face of the carpenter's son by the mysterious interplay of light and shadow—the light that dances across the meadows and cities of the new creation, the shadow cast across the shoulders of the world by the Cross. The beauty of the Lord lies in its willing confinement in the ordinary, its persistent attraction to the wounded, its unflagging search for the lost, its tender suffering with the sorrowful.

In developing an eye for the unexpected appearance of God's beauty, we can respond to the perplexities of Christian community and contemporary life with a love that surpasses our native capacity for care.

—John S. Mogabgab, "Editor's Introduction," *Weavings* (May/June 2003)

◆ *Joy in Christ.* In prayer afterwards in private had a most precious view of Christ as a friend that sticketh closer than a brother. Oh, how sweet it was to pray to him! I hardly knew how to contemplate him with praise enough; his adorable excellence more and more seemed to open the longer I spoke to him. Who shall show forth all his praise? I can conceive it to be a theme long enough for eternity. The wonder is how I have not heretofore been swallowed up with admiration of Jesus Christ, and that I should be tempted hereafter to forget to praise and love him. Oh, that those happy seasons were continued, that the Spirit of truth would keep these things of Christ in the imaginations of the thoughts of my heart. I want no other happiness, no other sort of heaven. I sat down under his shadow with great delight, and his fruit was sweet to my taste. [*March 9, 1806*]

—Henry Martyn, *Selections from the Journal and Letters of Henry Martyn*

◆ *Behold* is a word we seldom hear and never use. I can't remember ever saying "Behold!" I can imagine a Shakespearian actor throwing out an arm and in a loud voice saying, "Behold (this or that)," but the place where it is used day by day is in the Bible and in our churches. "Behold the man" (John 19:5, KJV). "Say unto the cities of Judah, 'Behold your God'" (Isa. 40:9, KJV). *Behold* could well be a one-word summary of much of Christian theology and practice. It is always an invitation to pay attention, a near command to see beyond our feet. An out-thrust arm gives the word direction, and the word itself tolerates no delay.

Whatever the formal teachings of a religion, the common expression of that religion requires a personal language. The doctrine of sin becomes my sins and offenses. The doctrine of sanctification becomes imprecations to change, to do the right thing, the good thing, to shape up, to measure up to God's expectations. Christianity is no exception. But those of us whose lives have been shaped by a congregation and its worship, by the regular influence of biblical preaching, have been subject to Beholding. Behold the star, behold the Cross, the empty tomb, and see what *God* is doing. Behold the table set in our midst, behold "all sorts and conditions" kneeling with us, the table set in the midst of the valley. Behold the Samaritan, the widow and her penny, the water flowing from a rock, the tablets of the law, the mercy from the Cross.

Sometimes in our beholding an angel greets us: "Be not afraid; for behold, I bring you good news of a great joy" (Luke 2:10, RSV). These are the times when we are riding the subway and watch a man sway with the rhythm of the train as he brushes his cheek against the head of the child asleep in his arms. These are the times when we behold two ancient lovers walking hand in hand toward day's end. Behold the young man running just to feel the wind on his face, the woman in jacket and jeans turning the key of a tractor. Behold, a loved one calls from a faraway place, a long-ago friend writes a letter, our children come for a visit. Day by day the "dayspring from on high" (KJV) visits us in ways that are as ordinary as Bethlehem's child, and we behold the beauty of the Lord.

—John W. Vannorsdall, "Behold the Beauty of the Lord," *Weavings*

The Season after Epiphany
Sunday between February 4 and 10
(If this is the last Sunday after Epiphany, use Week 15.)

11. Be Still

Affirmation
Almighty God, you created us to rest in your peace.
May we be still and know that you are God.

Psalm: 46

Psalm Prayer
You are our very present help in times of trouble, O
God. Remind us that you are the ruler of the world,
and, as we wait in silent awe for your kingdom to
arrive in its fullness, inspire us to be harbingers of your
peaceable kingdom, living lives that break bows and
shatter spears. Amen.

Daily Scripture Readings

Sunday	A.	Isaiah 58:1-12; Psalm 112:1-10; 1 Corinthians 2:1-16; Matthew 5:13-20
	B.	Isaiah 40:21-31; Psalm 147:1-11; 1 Corinthians 9:16-23; Mark 1:29-39
	C.	Isaiah 6:1-13; Psalm 138; 1 Corinthians 15:1-11; Luke 5:1-11
Monday		Deuteronomy 8
Tuesday		Ecclesiastes 9:11-18
Wednesday		Psalm 4
Thursday		Mark 9:2-13
Friday		Luke 4:35-41
Saturday		Luke 12:22-32

Silence

Daily Readings for Reflection

Reflection: Silent or Written

Prayers: For the World, for Others, for Myself

Offering of Self to God
Holy God, we want to be still, experiencing and growing in your love so that we might shine on others with
the light of love. Amen.

Blessing
May the God who dwells in the most high place grant
us peace. Amen.

Readings for Reflection

ﳲ The people of God are always on the way to the
promised land. To be a follower of Jesus is to be a pilgrim, and it is to be on a journey that always leads
us toward God and God's goodness. The scriptures
remind us that God loves us and seeks to sustain us
in all of life. Therefore we can ask for guidance in the
confidence that God's way, the very best way, will be
made known to us.

The vision of the promised land comes from God.
The direction and strength to get there also come from
God. But if we are to see the vision and to make the
journey, we must be willing to give up what we have
for that which is not yet fully realized. We need a willingness and openness to discern, to see God's way and,
finally, a yearning to be led in that way alone.

"If you love me, you will keep my commandments. And I will pray the Father, and he will give
you another Counselor, to be with you for ever, even
the Spirit of truth, whom the world cannot receive,
because it neither sees him nor knows him; you know
him, for he dwells with you, and will be in you" (John
14:15-17, RSV).
—Rueben P. Job

❧ Solitude and silence are the essential conditions that favor deep retrieval for personal integration of all facets of the human-divine relationship. A supportive, praying community is the preferable context out of which we enter into the desert of solitude. The boundaries surrounding one's desert of solitude are the love of an intimate community.
—Norman Shawchuck, Rueben P. Job, and Robert G. Doherty, *How to Conduct a Spiritual Life Retreat*

❧ There is the first thing—the bringing of the inner life under the control of the Holy Spirit by the perpetual discipline which brings us back, day by day, to the remembrance and companionship of Jesus Christ. Upon that everything else depends, for if the inward life is not sound you cannot do much with the outer.
—William Temple, *Selections from the Writings of William Temple*

❧ You whom the Holy Spirit is urging to act that your soul may become the Bride of God, must . . . "sit alone and keep silence" as the prophet says. . . . Get away then I tell you, not physically but in mind and in intention, in spirit and devotion; for the Lord Christ is Himself a Spirit, and it is spiritual solitude that He requires of you, though bodily withdrawal is not without its uses, when it may be had, especially in a time of prayer. You have His own commandment in the matter, "thou when thou wilt pray, enter into thy chamber and when thou hast shut the door, pray." He Himself practiced what He preached. He would spend all night in prayer, not only hiding from the crowds but not allowing any even of His closest friends to come with Him. Even at the last, when He was hastening to His willing death, though He had taken three with Him, He withdrew even from them when He desired to pray. You must do likewise, when you want to pray.
—Bernard of Clairvaux, *Selections from the Writings of Bernard of Clairvaux*

❧ Too often the church is an enemy of our solitude. Too often the church is one more agent in the vast social conspiracy of togetherness and noise aimed at distracting us from encountering ourselves. The church keeps us busy on this cause or that, this committee or that, trying to provide meaning through motion until we get "burned out" instead and withdraw from the church's life. Even in its core act of worship the church provides little space for the silent and solitary inward journey to occur (sometimes filling the available space with noisy exhortations to take that very journey!). Studies show that the average group can tolerate only about fifteen seconds of silence before someone feels compelled to break it, and our Sunday services give little reason to doubt this finding. We fill the air with sounds which, however beautiful and moving, can easily divert us from the difficulties of being present to ourselves. If, as the philosopher Alfred North Whitehead once said, religion is what one does with his or her solitariness, the typical congregation leaves little room for religion.

—Parker J. Palmer, "Borne Again," *Weavings*

❧ At my local parish, a priest addressed a group of newly single adults who were struggling with the nauseating feelings of loss and grief that come with death or divorce. He cautioned us, "Be careful not to rush into new relationships just to fill the void in your lives. You have to learn to live with the emptiness. . . . Wait. Wait." But the waiting can be hard. Unwanted aloneness can cause agony. One night, very late, more recently than I'd like to admit, I was sitting at my small kitchen table. Alone and wrapped in my old terry cloth bathrobe, I believed my whole life had shriveled up into an endless parade of days. Having discovered a painful and unpleasant truth about a man I'd recently been dating, I'd been feeling very sorry for myself. And I wanted that sorrowful emptiness filled up—at almost any cost. . . . The desert of our weakness can be frightening, our emotional and spiritual emptiness starkly painful. We can choose to avoid this pain and fear, but the devil is in the avoidance. That was the wisdom of the priest who told us to "Wait. Wait." Many times my rushing to fill the vacuum has caused grief for me and others. Never once, however, have I been disappointed in waiting for the Lord. God is in the desert. God knows what I look like in my bathrobe, all alone late at night. And never once has God suggested that the sight is pathetic. Instead, in those empty hours, God says, "Talk to me. Then be still and know that I am God."

—Anne Marie Drew, "Brave Emptiness," *Weavings*

❧ Spiritual discernment asks us to pay attention. We need to attend to both what goes on around us and within us. Ideally, this attentiveness goes on much of the time, a sort of low level, constant spiritual sifting of the data of our experience. But there are times when discernment becomes much more focused, when a crossroad is reached or a choice called for. At times like these the cumulative wisdom of tradition tells us to pay attention on many levels: to consult scripture, to seek the advice of trusted advisors, to heed the *sensus fidelium* (the collective sense of the faithful), to read widely and deeply the best ancient and contemporary thinking, to pray, to attend to the prick of conscience and to the yearnings and dreamings of our hearts, to watch, to wait, to listen.

—Wendy M. Wright, "Passing Angels," *Weavings*

The Season after Epiphany
Sunday between February 11 and February 17
(If this is the last Sunday after Epiphany, use Week 15.)

12. Wonder

Affirmation
Triune God, you are wholly other, yet, in your love, you became incarnate of human flesh through Jesus Christ. As we behold this mystery, we desire to be drawn into your life of unity.

Psalm: 113

Psalm Prayer
Faithful and loving God, there is no one like you. When others fail us and are powerless to save, you act to rescue us. We give you praise for your steadfast love. Empower us to echo your life by lifting up the poor and being present with the brokenhearted. Amen.

Daily Scripture Readings

Sunday	A.	Deuteronomy 30:15-20; Psalm 119:1-8; 1 Corinthians 3:1-9; Matthew 5:21-37
	B.	2 Kings 5:1-14; Psalm 30; 1 Corinthians 9:24-27; Mark 1:40-45
	C.	Jeremiah 17:5-10; Psalm 1; 1 Corinthians 15:12-20; Luke 6:17-26
Monday		Exodus 15:1-18
Tuesday		1 Samuel 2:1-10
Wednesday		Luke 5:12-26
Thursday		Acts 3:1-10
Friday		John 5:19-29
Saturday		2 Corinthians 12:1-5

Silence

Daily Readings for Reflection

Reflection: Silent or Written

Prayers: For the World, for Others, for Myself

Offering of Self to God
Wondrous God, we give you praise for your steadfast love. May we live into your care for the poor, sick, and brokenhearted. Amen.

Blessing
May we be transformed into the likeness of the triune God, never ceasing to respond in wonder. Amen.

Readings for Reflection

❧ The dramatic change in the lives of people touched by the power and presence of God through the early church proved to be a nearly irresistible magnet, drawing many to believe in and follow Jesus Christ. Besides the miraculous healing of a lame beggar (Acts 3), many signs and wonders done among the people (Acts 5:12ff.) caught the attention of those outside and those inside this young church. It was clear to observers and participants: God was at work transforming individuals and communities through this new movement. It was also clear that many not only wanted to see what was going on but longed for such salvation, healing, and wholeness in their own lives.

Today people still look for evidence of God's transforming presence in the church and in the world. When they find that evidence, they often turn toward it, seeking to be close to the God who is obviously at work changing lives in such dramatic ways. They are drawn because they want to be close to God, and often they seek their own transformation and salvation. The congregation where signs and wonders are evident is the congregation that finds new people coming to be touched by that transforming presence of God.

In Acts we read of transformation that leads from sinfulness to holiness of life. The kind of transformation that leads from selfishness to sharing, from uselessness to usefulness, from sickness to health, and from death to life is the transformation many seek. This transformation is promised in the Gospels by the One who came that all might have life and have it abundantly.

Where are the signs and wonders of God's active and transforming presence most visible today? How can you and I make ourselves and the entire church more available, thus permitting those signs and wonders to occur within and through our lives? One way the early church made itself available was by always giving an unqualified yes when God invited obedience, witness, and service. Can we do as much?
—Rueben P. Job

ᵃ⁂ Every human being is of incredible worth regardless of the circumstance of race, gender, social distinctions, natural gifts of appearance, intelligence, or physical skills. You are loved, valued, and accepted just as you are and God looks upon you with favor because you are a part of God's magnificent creation.
—Rueben P. Job, *Spiritual Life in the Congregation*

ᵃ⁂ If you ever marvel at a tree laden with fruit and wonder about the secret of its fruitfulness, you soon begin considering the connection between the tree and its branches and the tree and the fertile soil which hides the tree's roots, holding the entire tree securely in its place. We can compare the life of the fruitful Christian with the fruit-laden tree. There is no fruitful life apart from a lively connection with Christ or apart from solid roots in a fertile "inner room" of prayer. This inner room provides us the necessary nutrition to sustain our deepest inner selves—a life "hidden with Christ in God" (Col. 3:3; *see also* Matt. 6:6; John 15:1-16).

And the greatest marvel of all is that such a life is fruitful without strain or worry. The tree itself did nothing to bear such a rich harvest of fruit. Just a few weeks ago it shivered, cold and lonely, in the winter. On the surface it seemed surely dead, never to bear fruit again. But the warm sun came to melt the snow and kiss the cold, frozen ground. A soft breeze gently shook the tree awake just in time to hear the song of a joyful bird. When the conditions were right, a little flower appeared and then its fruit.

So it is with the child of God. When the conditions are right we *will* bear fruit—for Christ has chosen us to bear fruit and has promised that our fruit will last (John 15:16). The conditions are made right in us when we develop the habit of retreating to be with God in meditation and prayer and then moving back into the world to give incarnational expression to the Word God has spoken to us there.

—Norman Shawchuck, Rueben P. Job, and Robert G.
Doherty, *How to Conduct a Spiritual Life Retreat*

❧ "Lord, let our eyes be opened" (Matt. 20:33). The blind men who cry out to Jesus along the Jericho road voice a desire that wells up from the deepest reaches of the human heart. Immersed in the darkness of life's hard certainties and tormenting uncertainties, we long to see a larger truth and more encompassing purpose illuminating our years. The cry of the people of Israel echoes our own yearning: "O that we might see some good! Let the light of your face shine on us, O LORD!" (Ps. 4:6). After a lifetime of walking past undetected meaning, unnoticed opportunity, unrecognized assistance, we are aware that often we look but do not perceive, observe but do not understand (Isa. 6:9). Drowsy with the weight of daily duties and cares, we can sympathize with Jacob when he awakens from sleep to

declare, "Surely the LORD is in this place—and I did not know it!" (Gen. 28:16).
—John S. Mogabgab, "Editor's Introduction," *Weavings* (November/December 1996)

❧ For certainly I see secrets within ourselves that have often caused me to marvel. And how many more there must be! Oh, my Lord and my God, how great are Your grandeurs! We go about here below like foolish little shepherds, for while it seems that we are getting some knowledge of You it must amount to no more than nothing; for even in our own selves there are great secrets that we don't understand.
—Teresa of Avila, *The Soul's Passion for God*

❧ You would hear from me then why and how God is to be loved? I answer, the cause of loving God is God; the manner is to love without measure. . . . I find no other worthy cause of loving Him, save Himself.
—Bernard of Clairvaux, *Selections from the Writings of Bernard of Clairvaux*

❧ Acknowledging God in adoring worship not only opens our spiritual eyes to the praises of the creation around us. It also awakens us to the reality that there exist beings of a higher order than we. These glorious creatures also worship God. Paul writes "that through the church the wisdom of God in its rich variety might now be made known to the rulers and authorities in the heavenly places" (Eph. 3:10). Our acknowledgment of the LORD I AM in worship actually bears witness to the heavenly beings! Our praise of God's grace proclaims to the Powers "the news of the boundless riches of Christ" and helps "everyone see what is the plan of the mystery hidden for ages in God who created all things" (Eph. 3:8-9).

In Revelation, we read of a door left open in heaven through which John peeked to see the deeper reality of the universe. Before the One on the throne are mighty,

living creatures: "Day and night without ceasing they sing, 'Holy, holy, holy, the Lord God the Almighty, who was and is and is to come'" (Rev. 4:8). When these creatures "give glory and honor and thanks to the one who is seated on the throne" (Rev. 4:9), twenty-four elders who have been on thrones around *the* throne fall down before the Lord God. They cast their crowns singing, "You are worthy, our Lord and God, to receive glory and honor and power, for you created all things, and by your will they existed and were created" (Rev. 4:11). So, in the heart of heaven, before the immediate presence of God, adoration is the lingua franca. As we speak the language of praise, we both summon the heavenly beings and heed their call to join them in this worship.
—Gerrit Scott Dawson, "Gathering Praise," *Weavings*

The Season after Epiphany
Sunday between February 18 and February 24
(If this is the last Sunday after Epiphany, use Week 15.)

13. Adoration

Affirmation
Holy God, you are worthy of praise because of your faithfulness to us. May we never cease to adore you.

Psalm: 100

Psalm Prayer
O God, you are indeed good. Therefore we desire to constantly make a joyful noise in your presence. Give us peace to know that in stillness you are present, and in chaos you are also with us. You are faithful to all generations, and you remember your people. For this we praise you. Amen.

Daily Scripture Readings

Sunday	A.	Leviticus 19:1-2, 9-18; Psalm 119:33-40; 1 Corinthians 3:10-11, 16-23; Matthew 5:38-48
	B.	Isaiah 43:18-25; Psalm 41; 2 Corinthians 1:18-22; Mark 2:1-12
	C.	Genesis 45:3-11, 15; Psalm 37:1-11, 39-40; 1 Corinthians 15:35-38, 42-50; Luke 6:27-38
Monday		1 Chronicles 16:8-36
Tuesday		Daniel 4:1-3
Wednesday		Psalm 99
Thursday		Mark 7:1-13
Friday		Romans 12:1-8
Saturday		Revelation 4:1-11

Silence

Daily Readings for Reflection

Reflection: Silent or Written

Prayers: For the World, for Others, for Myself

Offering of Self to God
O God, may we join with the never-ending chorus that sings, "Holy, holy, holy is the Lord," in both our words and deeds this day. Amen.

Blessing
May those who praise God, share God's peace. Amen.

Readings for Reflection

❧ Conversion is a journey. The Christian *is* saved and *is being* saved. Just as the child is not fully mature, so the Christian is not fully mature at the time of "birth" in Christ. As the Christian grows, the Spirit reveals attitudes and behaviors that frustrate the search for wholeness. For this reason the Christian will be aware of the conflict between resistance and acceptance of the will of God, between darkness and light.

As we grow in Christ, we will develop sensibilities that detect the slightest imperfection in desire or deed grievous to the Spirit. This growth process is experienced as an interior struggle between the kingdom of God and the kingdom of darkness (Rom. 7:14-25). It is important in the struggle to experience God's unconditional love as freedom (Rom. 8:1-14).
—Norman Shawchuck, Rueben P. Job, and Robert G. Doherty, *How to Conduct a Spiritual Life Retreat*

❧ Consider for a moment what, in practice, the word *adoration* implies. The upward and outward look of humble and joyful admiration. Awestruck delight in the splendor and beauty of God, the action of God and Being of God, in and for God's self alone, as the very color of life: giving its quality of unearthly beauty to the harshest, most disconcerting forms and the dreariest stretches of experience. This is adoration: not a difficult religious exercise, but an attitude of the soul. "To you I lift up my eyes, O you who are enthroned in the heavens!" I don't turn around and look at myself. Adoration begins to purify us from egotism straightaway. It may not always be easy—in fact, for many people it is not at all easy—but it is realism; the atmosphere within which alone the spiritual life can be lived. *Our Father in heaven, hallowed be your Name!* That tremendous declaration, with its unlimited confidence and unlimited awe, governs everything else. . . .

People who are apt to say that adoration is difficult, and it is so much easier to pray for practical things, might remember that in making this great act of adoration they are praying for extremely practical things: among others, that their own characters, homes, social contacts, work, conversation, amusements, and politics may be cleansed from imperfection, sanctified. For all these are part of God's Universe. God's Name must be hallowed in and through them if they are to be woven into the Divine world and made what they were meant to be.

—Evelyn Underhill, *The Soul's Delight*

❧ Adoration, as it more deeply possesses us, inevitably leads on to self-offering: for every advance in prayer is really an advance in love. "I ask not for thy gifts but for thyself," says the Divine Voice to Thomas à Kempis. There is something in all of us which knows that to be true.

—Evelyn Underhill, *Selections from the Writings of Evelyn Underhill*

❧ This first response of creation to its author, this awestruck hallowing of the Name, must also be the first response of the praying soul. If we ask how this shall be done within the individual life and what it will require of us in oblation and adjustment, perhaps the answer will be something like this: *"Our Father in heaven, hallowed,* revered, *be your* mysterious *Name* in my dim and fluctuating soul, to which you have revealed yourself in such a degree as I can endure. May all my contacts and relationships, my struggles and temptations, thoughts, dreams, and desires be colored by this loving reverence. Let me ever look through and beyond circumstance to you, so that all I am and do may become more and more worthy of the God who is the origin of all. Let me never take such words on my lips that I could not pass from them to the hallowing of your Name. (That one principle alone, consistently applied, would bring order and charity into the center of my life.) May that Name, too, be hallowed in my work, keeping me in remembrance that you are the doer of all that is really done; my part is that of a humble collaborator, giving of my best." This means that adoration, a delighted recognition of the life and action of God, subordinating everything to the Presence of the Holy, is the essential preparation for action. That stops all feverish strain, all rebellion and despondency, all sense of our own importance, all worry about our own success and so gives dignity, detachment, tranquility to our action and may make it of some use to God.

—Evelyn Underhill, *The Soul's Delight*

❧ Thou art holy, Lord God, who alone workest wonders. Thou art strong. Thou art great. Thou art most high. Thou art the Almighty King, Thou, holy Father, King of heaven and earth. Thou art the Lord God Triune and One; all good. Thou art good, all good, highest good, Lord God living and true. Thou art charity, love. Thou art wisdom. Thou art humility. Thou art patience. Thou art security. Thou art quietude. Thou art joy and gladness. Thou art justice and temperance. Thou art all riches to sufficiency. Thou art beauty. Thou art meekness. Thou art protector. Thou art guardian and defender. Thou art strength. Thou art refreshment. Thou art our hope. Thou art our faith. Thou art our great sweetness. Thou art our eternal life, great and admirable Lord, God Almighty, merciful Saviour.

—Francis of Assisi, *Selections from the Writings of St. Francis of Assisi*

❧ O most high, almighty, good Lord God, to Thee belong praise, glory, honour, and all blessing!

Praise be my Lord God with all His creatures; and specially our brother the sun, who brings us the day, and who brings us the light; fair is he, and shining with a very great splendor: O Lord, he signifies to us Thee!

Praised be my Lord for our sister, the moon, and for the stars, the which He has set clear and lovely in heaven.

Praised be my Lord for our brother, the wind, and for air and cloud, calms and all weather, by the which Thou upholdest in life all creatures.

Praised be my Lord for our sister, water, who is very serviceable unto us, and humble, and precious, and clean.

Praised be my Lord for our brother, fire, through whom Thou givest us light in the darkness; and he is bright, and pleasant, and very mighty, and strong.

Praised be my Lord for our mother, the earth, the which doth sustain us and keep us, and bringeth forth divers fruits and flowers of many colours, and grass.

Praised be my Lord for all those who pardon one another for His love's sake, and who endure weakness and tribulation; blessed are they who peaceably shall endure, for Thou, O most Highest, shalt give them a crown!

Praised be my Lord for our sister, the death of the body, from whom no man escapeth. Woe to him who dieth in mortal sin! Blessed are they who are found walking by Thy most holy will, for the second death shall have no power to do them harm.

Praise ye, and bless ye the Lord, and give thanks unto Him, and serve Him with great humility.
—Francis of Assisi, *Selections from the Writings of St. Francis of Assisi*

❧ Let us all, everywhere, in every place, at every hour, and at all times, daily and continually believe, truly and humbly, and let us hold in our hearts, and love, honor, adore, serve, praise and bless, glorify and exalt, magnify and give thanks to the most High and Supreme Eternal God, in Trinity and Unity, to the Father, and Son, and Holy Ghost, to the Creator of all, to the Saviour of all who believe and hope in Him, and love Him, who, without beginning or end, is immutable, invisible, unerring, ineffable, incomprehensible, unfathomable, blessed, praiseworthy, glorious, exalted, sublime, most high, sweet, amiable, lovable, and always wholly desirable above all forever and ever.
—Francis of Assisi, *Selections from the Writings of St. Francis of Assisi*

❧ God is the joy of their hearts, and the desire of their souls; which constantly cry out, *Whom have I in heaven but you? And there is nothing on earth that I desire other than you!* My God and my all! You are *the strength of my heart, and my portion for ever!*
—John Wesley, *A Longing for Holiness*

❧ Charles Wesley loved music. With two sons who were musical prodigies, Charles and Sally Wesley's home was always filled with the sounds of instruments and voices raised in song. Little wonder that Charles turned to the metaphors of music and song to describe the life of the community of faith—the people of God bound together by the love of Christ. For the believer, life is a concert of praise; indeed, one's whole life is a song to be sung, a melodious act of gratitude to the One who has given us life and redeemed us by grace. But while solos have their place, it is a chorus—the whole company of God's faithful people—that sings "Holy, holy, holy Lord, God of power and might. Heaven and earth are full of your glory." Wesley, in his hymn, describes a "rapturous song" of a "glorified throng" whose sacrifice of praise is the perfect harmony of lives tuned to the keynote of Christ's love. The Hebrew word *hallelujah*—[let us] praise God—captures the spirit of the choir and the nature of the song. According to Paul, more than anything else, thanksgiving and gratitude characterize life in Christ. If we surround ourselves with the love of Jesus—if the love of God envelops us in the same way that our clothes cover our bodies—then God gifts the community and the world with harmony. Peace rules. Unity prevails. All creation becomes a song of praise. What part do you play in this great harmony of the ages?

—Paul Wesley Chilcote, *A Life-Shaping Prayer*

The Season after Epiphany
Sunday between February 25 and February 29
(If this is the last Sunday after Epiphany, use Week 15.)

14. Grace Abounding

Affirmation
LORD, you have done so many things! You made them all so wisely! The earth is full of your creations! (Ps. 104:24).

Psalm: 105

Psalm Prayer
O Lord, we will remember your great deeds all our lives, and we desire to share the good news of your work with each new generation of your people. We thank you for guiding our spiritual fathers and mothers through deserts and into a home where they could rest in you. May we know a similar rest wherever we find ourselves by trusting in you and learning your precepts. Amen.

Daily Scripture Readings

Sunday	A.	Isaiah 49:8-16; Psalm 131; 1 Corinthians 4:1-5; Matthew 6:24-34
	B.	Hosea 2:14-20; Psalm 103:1-13, 22; 2 Corinthians 3:1-6; Mark 2:13-22
	C.	Isaiah 55:10-13; Psalm 92:1-4, 12-15; 1 Corinthians 15:51-58; Luke 6:39-49
Monday		Exodus 16:22-30
Tuesday		Psalm 34:1-10
Wednesday		Hosea 11:1-9
Thursday		John 1:1-18
Friday		Titus 2:11-15
Saturday		Matthew 5:13-16

Silence

Daily Readings for Reflection

Reflection: Silent or Written

Prayers: For the World, for Others, for Myself

Offering of Self to God
I will thank you, LORD, with all my heart; I will talk about all your wonderful acts. I will celebrate and rejoice in you; I will sing praises to your name, Most High (Ps. 9:1-2). Amen.

Blessing
May we be good stewards of the manifold grace of God, serving one another and preserving God's creation with whatever gifts of mind or heart we have received. Amen.

Readings for Reflection

❧ As we have said, the Christian life is possible only by the grace of God. Every awakening to God within us is the result of the Holy Spirit's action in and upon us. We are awakened to God and sustained in God by the initiative that the Holy One takes toward us and on our behalf. Just as life is pure gift, unrequested and beyond our power, so the spiritual life is offered to us from the heart of God long before we ever think of our walk with Christ.

The letter to the Ephesians proclaims that God's grace was flowing out to us before the foundation of the world. At the very beginning of creation we were chosen in Christ to live in love and peace with God (1:4). God's grace precedes, follows, surrounds, and sustains us. It is a constant and completely consistent gift. We cannot stop, alter, or change it. We are eternally cradled in God's abundant and life-giving grace.

While the initiative and the invitation to companionship are entirely God's, response lies with us. God gives us grace to respond to the awakening call of the Holy Spirit, but we can choose to turn away and refuse the invitation. Or we can choose, by the Spirit's help, to walk in faithfulness and harmony with God. By doing so we claim our true and full inheritance as children of God. Choosing to open ourselves to grace means receiving life's greatest gift and walking the path of spiritual abundance.

—Rueben P. Job and Marjorie J. Thompson, *Companions in Christ*

ew Defend me from all temptation, that I may ever accept the right and refuse the wrong. Defend me from myself, that in your care my weakness may not bring me to shame. May my lower nature never seize the upper hand.

Defend me from all that would seduce me, that in your power no tempting voice may cause me to listen, no tempting sight fascinate my eyes.

Defend me against the chances and changes of this life, not that I may escape them but that I may meet them with firm resolve; not that I may be saved from them but that I may come unscathed through them.

Defend me from discouragement in difficulty and from despair in failure, from pride in success, and from forgetting you in the day of prosperity.

Grant me this desire: that guided by your light and defended by your grace, I may come in safety and bring honor to my journey's end by the defending work of Jesus Christ my Lord. May it always be so!

—Norman Shawchuck

ew The poet theologian George Herbert exerted a tremendous influence upon Charles Wesley. His collection of poems entitled *The Temple* reveals his own personal quest for faith in and intimacy with God. In a poem built around the image of banquet, Herbert invites Christ to live and dwell in his heart and welcomes the delicious, sacred cheer that surpasses all other earthly joys. Using images common to the mystical tradition, he reflects upon the way in which God's sweetness surprises and deluges the soul. The psalmist describes God's speech—God's Law—in similar ways. God's words are "sweeter than honey to my mouth." What a phenomenal description of God and God's actions!

Recent studies demonstrate that most people conceive God as adversarial, critical, and distant. In terms of taste, it would probably be right to describe their concept—their taste—of God as bitter, sour, and acrid. But those who have come to know God in Jesus Christ have a very different conception. God's Word is sweet. God's law, God's commandments, God's words not only seem sweet but create sweetness. They sweeten everything they touch. In this unique way of thinking about our relationship with God, God delights in providing a banquet of sweet things for us. God invites all who are hungry and thirsty—all who seek mercy and salvation—to come, to drink, and to eat. God offers us the most nourishing food imaginable and shares the sweetness of Christ's mercy with us all.

O God, be sweetness to my taste.
—Paul Wesley Chilcote, *A Life-Shaping Prayer*

❧ Legend tells of a little girl who had an ugly hump on her back. The girl was so deformed that she was either ridiculed or pitied by everyone. When she died, it turned out that the ugly hump concealed angel's wings. Can it be that all the ugly things in our lives have in them angel's wings? Can it be that even our sin, our ugly sin, can be turned to good; could it conceal angel's wings?

This is the glorious promise of conversion: God is able to make all things work together for good. Even the sinful years, the ugly years, need not be wasted but can result in good. Is this not a most comforting assurance? For many of us our ugly years were numerous, and they cause deep remorse. They may have struck at the prime of our lives and ministries. For so long we have grieved them, feeling that many years of ministry were wasted. But the love of God dawns upon us, and with it comes a most amazing promise and a new hope: What we cannot redeem, God can; and what we cannot erase, God will.

—Norman Shawchuck

ֶ Grace works with mercy, raising, rewarding, endlessly surpassing what our loving and effort deserve, spreading abroad and showing the high, plentiful largesse of God's royal lordship in God's marvelous courtesy. This is from the abundance of love, for grace works our fearful failing into plentiful and endless solace. And grace works our shameful falling into high, honorable rising. And grace works our sorrowful dying into holy, blissful life.

—Julian of Norwich, *Encounter with God's Love*

ֶ *Cheap and Costly Grace.* Cheap grace is the preaching of forgiveness without requiring repentance, baptism without church discipline, Communion without confession, absolution without personal confession. Cheap grace is grace without discipleship, grace without the cross, grace without Jesus Christ, living and incarnate.

Costly grace is the treasure hidden in the field; for the sake of it a man will gladly go and sell all that he has. It is the pearl of great price to buy which the merchant will sell all his goods. It is the kingly rule of Christ, for whose sake a man will pluck out the eye which causes him to stumble, it is the call of Jesus Christ at which the disciple leaves his nets and follows him.

Costly grace is the gospel which must be *sought* again and again, the gift which must be *asked* for, the door at which a man must *knock*.

Such grace is *costly* because it calls us to follow, and it is *grace* because it calls us to follow *Jesus Christ*. It is costly because it costs a man his life, and it is grace because it gives a man the only true life. It is costly because it condemns sin, and grace because it justifies the sinner. Above all, it is *costly* because it cost God the life of his Son: "ye were bought at a price," and what has cost God much cannot be cheap for us. Above all, it is *grace* because God did not reckon his Son too dear a price to pay for our life, but delivered him up for us. Costly grace is the Incarnation of God.

Costly grace is the sanctuary of God; it has to be protected from the world, and not thrown to the dogs. It is therefore the living word, the Word of God, which he speaks as it pleases him. Costly grace confronts us as a gracious call to follow Jesus, it comes as a word of forgiveness to the broken spirit and the contrite heart. Grace is costly because it compels a man to submit to the yoke of Christ and follow him; it is grace because Jesus says: "My yoke is easy and my burden is light."
—Dietrich Bonhoeffer, *Selections from the Writings of Dietrich Bonhoeffer*

꙳ *Advice about Growth in Grace.* The sea is an excellent figure of the fullness of God, and that of the blessed Spirit. For as the rivers all return into the sea, so the bodies, the souls, and the good works of the righteous return into God, to live there in his eternal repose.

Although all the graces of God depend on his bounty, yet is he pleased generally to attach them to the prayers, the instructions, and the holiness of those with whom we are. By strong though invisible attractions God draws some souls through their intercourse with others.

The sympathies formed by grace far surpass those formed by nature.

The truly devout show that passions as naturally flow from true as from false love; so deeply sensible are they of the goods and evils of those they love for God's sake. But this can only be comprehended by those who understand the language of love.

The bottom of the soul may be in repose even while we are in many outward troubles, just as the bottom of the sea is calm, while the surface is strongly agitated.

—John Wesley, *A Longing for Holiness*

Last Sunday after Epiphany

15. The Time Is Ripe

Affirmation
Look, now is the right time! Look, now is the day of salvation! (2 Cor. 6:2).

Psalm: 126

Psalm Prayer
Ever-watchful God, you have done great things for us and every moment is ripe with your good purposes. Awaken us from spiritual drowsiness so that we may harvest the time you give us and reap the joy of your saving help. Amen.

Daily Scripture Readings

Sunday	A.	Exodus 24:12-18; Psalm 2; 2 Peter 1:16-21; Matthew 17:1-9
	B.	2 Kings 2:1-12; Psalm 50:1-6; 2 Corinthians 4:3-6; Mark 9:2-9
	C.	Exodus 34:29-35; Psalm 99; 2 Corinthians 3:12–4:2; Luke 9:28-36
Monday		Ecclesiastes 3:1-8
Tuesday		2 Chronicles 7:11-21
Wednesday		Isaiah 61:1-4
Thursday		Psalm 95:1-7
Friday		Luke 1:67-79
Saturday		Ephesians 5:8-15

Silence

Daily Readings for Reflection

Reflection: Silent or Written

Prayers: For the World, for Others, for Myself

Offering of Self to God

Even as you give yourself to us in the sacrament of time, so do we commend ourselves to you, Holy One, trusting that you will use not only our strengths but also our weaknesses in the work of realizing your new creation fully. Amen.

Blessing

May the Lord of all places and times, guide us beneath the world's veneer of breathless busyness to the deeps of every moment, where time swells with room to breathe the scent of eternity. Amen.

Readings for Reflection

❧ Hunger and thirst for God are universal. We have been created to yearn for God, our true home. And the Bible reminds us that God yearns for relationship with us, our coming home to God. Why then does our hunger and thirst so often go unsatisfied? If God does indeed yearn for us and we yearn for God, why does my life often feel unattached and empty?

My mother insisted that my two brothers and I be at the table before anyone began to eat. She always called me in ample time so that I could be washed and ready when the meal was prepared. But more often than she liked, I was late because I was preoccupied with catching frogs in the nearby spring, filling my stomach with chokecherries from a nearby grove, or just not listening.

God's yearning for us is more intense than any mother's desire for her children, and our world offers more enticing distractions than frogs and chokecherries. So how do we bring God's yearning and our hunger and thirst together? Jesus is our best example. Even though his journey toward God was without blemish, he found it necessary to go aside to rest and to pray again and again. And in the midst of the great needs of the people around them, Jesus called the disciples to come away by themselves to rest. From that time of rest they were thrust back into the ministry of caring for the needs of the crowds that followed Jesus.

Decide today to establish a way of life that includes time for daily prayer, reflection, and regular worship in a congregation. Set aside a day every month when you will "come apart" to read, reflect, and pray in a leisurely and concentrated way. John Wesley was right: don't wait, begin today!

—Rueben P. Job

᪣ Jesus aches with compassion for the hungry, the thirsty, the stranger, the naked ones, the sick, and the prisoners, so much so that he joins them to himself. He once told his followers that when they gave a drink "to one of the least of these who are members of my family, you did it to me" (Matt. 25:40).

Jesus longs to see his beloved Jerusalem repent its rebellion and return to the living God, sheltering once more under God's covenant love. He had lamented before crowds of people, scribes, and Pharisees . . .

Jesus knew that the healing of humanity required winning the battle from within the human condition. Healing could flow only through an entering into and a bearing of suffering and sin. When onlookers sneered, "He saved others; he cannot save himself," they could not see that only because he had *never thought of saving himself* could anybody be saved at all. And those who shouted, "If you are the Son of God, come down from the cross" could not see that it was precisely *because* he was the Son of God that he would not come down from the cross.

In the end, the deepest thirst of this Jesus—the thirst that held him to that cross—was the thirst of unrequited love. Jesus thirsts to see all people discover God's love for them through forgiveness and new life. His dying tells us, *God longs like this, thirsts like this, bleeds like this, always.*

No sponge of sour wine can slake that thirst. Only the assurance of our repentance and faith can do that.
—Peter Storey, *Listening at Golgotha*

❧ Paul wrote his letter to the Philippians from prison. He had endured much for the sake of the Lord. And yet, even in this circumstance, he learned to be content. The early Methodist people practiced the art of godly trust. They discovered profound mentors in Charles and Sally Wesley in this regard. The couple's home, filled with all the agony and ecstasy that is part and parcel of family life, glowed with a certain warmth and security born of trust in God.

One of Charles's hymns written for families reflects the spirit of their life together. In the midst of silent tears and boding fears, Christ proved his love and care, over and over again. Mercy flies to their rescue. Before the face of God, even death loosens its grip. Jesus offers no easy panacea for life's troubles, but, even in the midst of grief, the believer holds fast to Jesus' presence. God's perfect strength never fails; when we are weak, God's word of promise raises us above all fear and hopelessness in life. Full contentment depends upon relationships of trust—miracles of grace.
—Paul Wesley Chilcote, *A Life-Shaping Prayer*

❧ Deep in the substrata of our faith, in the vestige of ancient Israelite life we carry with us, is the notion of time as potentially both restful and reaping. We have, in fact, within our collective memory the knowledge that it is a good and right thing to honor the seventh day, the seventh year, and the seven-times-seventh year. We recognize, if only as dim remembrance, the significance of the Sabbath, the sabbatical, and the Jubilee year. We proclaim the injunction of Exodus 20:8, "Remember to keep the sabbath day holy" (NEB). On occasion we refer to Leviticus 25 with its insistence that in the sabbatical (seventh) year the land must lie fallow

and that in the Jubilee year (once in every fifty: the year following the seventh times seven), a general amnesty must occur, with captives freed and property redistributed. Somehow we know that time is not uniform, not only an entity to be used up or filled or an elusive substance that flies by too quickly and of which there is never enough. Time is potentially a sacred portal by way of which we enter briefly into eternity, a medium through which we are restored and made fruitful. In resting, reaping times, we can meet God.
—Wendy M. Wright, "Resting Reaping Times," *Weavings*

❧ The capacity to express vulnerability is a great human strength. We sometimes wish our vulnerabilities would disappear so we wouldn't have to worry about hiding them. Without these pesky vulnerabilities, we could convince the world that we have it all together, that we have no unsatisfied needs, that we can care constantly for others and never need care ourselves. It is hard to let people see our vulnerable parts—our fears and insecurities, our sadness and shame. To express vulnerability requires courage. Only in exercising this courage, in bravely showing our "weakness" to another, do we achieve a form of real power—the power to ask for help when needed.
—Sarah Parsons, *A Clearing Season*

❧ We have been given the freedom to choose what we see, what we pay attention to, what we rest our awareness on. There are zillions of things that can attract us, call us to themselves. Our task is to choose which ones we want to pay attention to, which ones we want to invest our energy in, for we cannot endure full consciousness of everything. We must focus on something more limited. On the other hand, we must not be too narrow in our awareness. We must be careful not to develop a preconceived idea of what we want the gift to be. Then it would not be gift, it would be something we went out and shopped for deliberately. (That's no fun; we have to do that on an almost daily basis, anyway!) No, we must always be expecting a surprise—a gift that is wrapped up in paper, hidden from immediate view. How do we come to a balance between total awareness and the too-limited view? It takes some practice. For most of us the difficulty will be in the widening of our vision. To do this we might start by spending a few minutes—no more than a couple at the beginning—just becoming aware of our surroundings. Most of the time we rarely see or hear what is actually within our range of perception. . . . We tend to have a preconceived notion of what we will find in our field of vision and hearing and sensing. This preconceived notion blocks out our awareness of other things. A truly spiritual task, a discipline actually, is to take the time as often as possible each day to stop, look, and listen to whatever is around and within us. Just a minute or so four or five times a day will gradually lead us into a heightened awareness of what is truly around us and within us.

—Jane Marie Thibault, *A Deepening Love Affair*

❧ The time is ripe for joy, and joy holds the universe together. I must find my joy in time, in the mighty rushing wind that pervades my work, in the Spirit's brooding over the waters of my eating and sleeping, in the crucifixion of wasted hours and the hope of resurrection for those who are redeemed. . . . The moments I have as a human being are shaping me for heaven on a day called "today."

—Kristen Johnson Ingram, "The Sacrament of Time," *Weavings*

❧ If we have given our whole heart to God and God's guidance and God's way of love, we have already become "a living sacrifice, holy and acceptable to God" (Rom. 12:1) in every small or great thing we do, whether in the home or out in the world. The ways of living this holy life are wide and varied.

Sometimes the opened gate does mean a different job, a different way of life, a different set of responsibilities and relationships. But at other times the opened gate may lead to a different way of doing our usual work, a new way of responding to others, an alternative way of praying, a transformed attitude toward ourselves, a different way of relating to God.

In any case, though, there will be a difference in our lives. A gate will open.

—Flora Slosson Wuellner, *Enter by the Gate*

The Season of Lent

The season of Lent may be the most emotionally charged season of the Christian year. It is a forty-day journey (not counting Sundays) when we watch the tight-knit community of Jesus and the Twelve form and grow in what it means to be faithful to the loving God Jesus tenderly called Abba. Jesus confronts and overcomes temptation in the loneliness of the desert. As he faces the cost of his mission of salvation, Jesus' prayer reveals both his agony and his trust: *My Father, if it's possible, take this cup of suffering away from me. However—not what I want but what you want* (Matt. 26:39). We see in Jesus the faithfulness we desire and the trust to practice it in good times and hard times.

There is practice and there is failure as the disciples face their own temptations and as they are sent out to serve, heal, teach, and proclaim the reality of God's kingdom on earth. Lent is a time of deep reflection as we consider the desert places of our own lives and the practice and failure that meet us in our own quest for faithfulness to the God of love, peace, and justice.

Growing conflict with religious leaders and the triumphal entry into Jerusalem on a beast of burden are but signs of what is to come in the days ahead. Moving from the exhilaration of crowds honoring him as Jesus rode into the city to the stark reality of his crucifixion is a whiplash of emotion. The highest hopes of the triumphal entry were completely crushed by the agony and brutality of the cross. Loud shouts of joy turn to cries of grief as the light born with Jesus is extinguished, plunging the world into the severity of utter darkness.

The season of Lent gives us time to remember our own humanity and our own mortality as we observe the lives of the Twelve, who were seeking to be faithful followers of Jesus in a world not unlike our own. But Ash Wednesday and the Crucifixion do not tell the entire story. There is more to come. And what is to come is so dazzling that the struggles in a troubled and violent world and the utter darkness of the crucifixion are rendered helpless. They are no longer the threat they once appeared to be.

16. We Shall All Be Changed

Affirmation

All of us are looking with unveiled faces at the glory of the Lord as if we were looking in a mirror. We are being transformed into that same image from one degree of glory to the next degree of glory. This comes from the Lord, who is the Spirit (2 Cor. 3:18).

Psalm: 30

Psalm Prayer

Gracious God, ever-present helper, we thank you that in the night of desperation and sadness over our separation from you, your steady hand is not far from us. As you lead us toward the dawn of new beginnings, may we join you and gather others in the bright dance that celebrates your desire to renew the face of the earth. Amen.

Daily Scripture Readings

Sunday	A.	Genesis 2:15-17, 3:1-7; Psalm 32; Romans 5:12-19; Matthew 4:1-11
	B.	Genesis 9:8-17; Psalm 25:1-10; 1 Peter 3:18-22; Mark 1:9-15
	C.	Deuteronomy 26:1-11; Psalm 91:1-2, 9-16; Romans 10:8-13; Luke 4:1-13
Monday		Genesis 32:22-32
Tuesday		Exodus 34:27-35
Wednesday		Isaiah 43:18-25
Thursday		Psalm 36:5-10
Friday		Luke 19:1-10
Saturday		Colossians 3:1-11

Silence

Daily Readings for Reflection

Reflection: Silent or Written

Prayers: For the World, for Others, for Myself

Offering of Self to God
Into your hands, O Lord, we place our whole selves, trusting that your vision for our lives and the life of the world is far richer than we could ever ask or imagine. Renew in us daily the choice to love and serve you without reservation. Amen.

Blessing
May the Lord who sets aside the former things to make space for the new, fashion us into worthy instruments of the peace and justice our world needs. Amen.

Readings for Reflection

❧ Christians see grace most clearly in God's act of self-giving through the person of Jesus Christ. In the suffering love and forgiveness of the cross, we perceive grace in all its fullness. Faith in Christ becomes the way we discover and apprehend this incredible gift (Rom. 5:1-2). From the beginning of creation we were meant to know ourselves as God's children, enjoying all of the benefits of our full inheritance (Eph. 1:5). Having lost our native inheritance through sin, we now receive these benefits through Jesus Christ. God's love and favor in Christ bestow them upon us.
—Rueben P. Job and Marjorie J. Thompson, *Companions in Christ*

❧ [W]e begin the Lenten season with our face pressed hard against the reality of our sin and our death. If we did not know how the story ends, this would be a dark and depressing journey. But we do know how the story ends and therefore in the midst of austerity and fasting we remember our faithful Savior and the

Easter declaration that life is always victorious over death, always!

A season that begins with ashes pressed upon our heads ends with the fragrance, sight, and touch of flowers racing through our senses and inviting us to join the triumphant song "Christ the Lord Is Risen Today!" Now we know as never before that our mortality will put on immortality (1 Cor. 15:53). Death and resurrection are now claimed as our own. Fear has given way to inexpressible joy, and doubt has given way to triumphant hope. Christ is risen!

—Norman Shawchuck and Rueben P. Job

❧ No creature, none of its actions and abilities, can reach or encompass God's nature. Consequently, a soul must strip itself of everything pertaining to creatures and of its actions and abilities (of its understanding, satisfaction, and feeling) so that when everything unlike and unconfirmed to God is cast out, it may receive the likeness of God. And the soul will receive this likeness because nothing contrary to the will of God will be left in it. Thus it will be transformed in God.

—John of the Cross, *Loving God through the Darkness*

❧ True delight in God's ways sometimes comes only after the discomfiting loss of various forms of ignorance, illusion, and innocence. Looked at this way, disillusionment can be seen as an event of purifying grace, an open door toward wisdom.

—Robert Corin Morris, "Disillusionment, Deliverance, and Delight," *Weavings*

❧ The worst things that happen do not happen because a few people are monstrously wicked, but because most people are like us. When we grasp that, we begin to realize that our need is not merely for moving quietly on in the way we are going; our need is for radical change, to find a power that is going to turn us into somebody else. That is what the Gospel offers to do; and it delivers us, once and for all, from the desperate folly of making experiments in the moral life. Always remember, when you experiment with your soul, that you can never judge the result. . . . As soon as we have done something that is nasty, . . . we have tarnished the mirror in which we are to look at our own reflection. If the standard by which we are going to try to judge and guide our lives is the mind of Christ, then we are going to try to live in constant fellowship with Him and in company with others who are seeking that fellowship with Him.

We shall make this the main business of our lives. It will become a bond of unity binding us to others who have the same aim, and communion with Christ in the fellowship of His servants will have become the means by which we try to apply the moral standard to ourselves.

O God our Judge and Saviour, set before us the vision of thy purity and let us see our sins in the light of thy countenance; pierce our self-contentment with the shafts of thy burning love and let that love consume in us all that hinders us from perfect service of thy cause; for as thy Holiness is our judgment, so are thy wounds our salvation.
—William Temple, *Selections from the Writings of William Temple*

❧ Growth is not always about getting through terrible pain. Most often it involves change, perhaps only a small shift in awareness or embracing a good part of you that got lost. Learning to love yourself and others more deeply, opening to the tender joy of pregnancy and birth, meeting the challenge of a new job, or being creative in retirement is most certainly growth too. So is surrendering a grudge, making room for forgiveness to take root, or learning to pray from your heart.
—Tilda Norberg, *The Chocolate-Covered Umbrella*

❧ Fully immersed in this world, Christians belong to no world. Instead, while teased by each hope and every vision, they know them to be only hints of the new heaven and new earth rooted in divine promises. And our yearning to become lost in God only intensifies our tears over the thought of leaving this life. Christian existence is joyful nonsense. In a culture of self-realization, the Christian's call is to renounce self; in the face of noise, silence is the preference; in a world of competition, the Christian's declaration is that the winners will be the losers and the losers winners; in a culture whose economy is intent on consumption, the Christian insists on simplicity; in a culture structured by possessions, the insistence is upon detachment; in a culture intent on a high standard of living, the Christian insists upon a high standard of life; and at every point, the Christian exposes the emptiness of fullness for the sake of the gospel's fullness of emptiness.

—W. Paul Jones, *The Art of Spiritual Direction*

17. Put a New and Right Spirit within Me

Affirmation
I'm weak and needy. Let my Lord think of me. You are my help and my rescuer (Ps. 40:17).

Psalm: 31

Psalm Prayer
Lord of all, may we honor you by remembering the great deeds of compassion through which you have released us from the weight of our sin and strengthened us to bless you with our whole being. Let our lives reflect your mercy toward all who are fragile and your justice for all who suffer oppression. Amen.

Daily Scripture Readings

Sunday	A.	Genesis 12:1-4; Psalm 121; Romans 4:1-5, 13-17; John 3:1-17
	B.	Genesis 17:1-7, 15-16; Psalm 22:23-31; Romans 4:13-25; Mark 8:31-38
	C.	Genesis 15:1-12, 17-18; Psalm 27; Philippians 3:17–4:1; Luke 13:31-35
Monday		Ezekiel 37:1-14
Tuesday		Joel 2:12-13
Wednesday		Psalm 51
Thursday		Luke 15:11-32
Friday		John 16:12-15
Saturday		Romans 6:1-14

Silence

Daily Readings for Reflection

Reflection: Silent or Written

Prayers: For the World, for Others, for Myself

Offering of Self to God
Lord of lords and King of kings, even as in the beginning dark deep waters awaited the form your Spirit would give to them, so today our souls wait for the freshening breeze of your love that will reanimate the dry bones of our faith. Amen.

Blessing
May the Lord, whose affection for us is limitless, deepen our fellowship with the Holy Spirit and increase our desire to be good citizens of the new creation. Amen.

Readings for Reflection

❧ Salvation is free, but the cost of discipleship is enormous. I try to hide from the truth, but when I read the Gospels and seek to live in communion with God, I discover both parts of the statement are dead-center truth. I can do nothing to earn my salvation. My redemption is a pure gift of grace, a gift offered to me without qualification or reservation. I am God's child, and no one or no thing can change that fact. Jesus Christ lived, died, and lives again to bring this gift of salvation to me in all its fullness. My faith can appropriate this gift, but even my greatest doubt cannot change its reality. I am God's beloved, embraced in God's love for now and eternity. All words are inadequate to describe the extravagance and grandeur of the gift of salvation. Our hymns of praise and gratitude fall lifeless before the immensity of this gift. We simply and humbly offer all that we are to the One who offers us the option of becoming more than we are.

In offering ourselves as fully as we can, we discover the cost of discipleship. For to bind our lives to Jesus Christ requires that we try to walk with him into the sorrows and suffering of the world.

Being bound to Jesus Christ, we see barriers broken down; we are led to places we have never been before and to carry loads we have not even seen before. Having offered ourselves to Jesus Christ, we may expect to become the eyes, ears, voice, and hands of Jesus Christ in the world and in the church. The cost of salvation? It is completely free and without cost. The cost of discipleship? Only our lives—nothing more and nothing less.
—Rueben P. Job

❧ Here, O God, I pray for a realization of my condition in your eyes. Help me to see and know myself as you see and know me. Give me clear insight into my relationship with you. Let me know myself as you know me.

Give me assurance that I belong to you. Remove from me those nagging doubts and needless fears that I may not be good enough to be numbered with the great company of heaven.

On the other hand, if I am living in separation from you, if I am more a creature of evil than a child of God, O Great Physician, use your convicting scalpel on me. Perform within me the surgery necessary to heal me of all soul-sickness.

Christ, I abandon myself to you. Do with me every necessary thing to assure my entrance into eternal life—and the heaven already prepared for me.
—Norman Shawchuck

❧ Pain is among the most powerful magnets for our attention. Surely a rupture in the deepest parts of our being, where our lives are knit together with God's by the tender tissue of divine love, must exert a forceful draw upon our thoughts and feelings. The wrenching words of Psalm 51 . . . are hardly those of a self-forgetful penitent: "For I know my transgressions, and my sin is ever before me. . . . Create in me a clean heart, O God, and put a new and right spirit within me" (Ps.

51:3, 10). Amidst the tumult of thoughts the world jars loose in us, does not the season of Lent quietly invite us to pause and take stock of ourselves?

—John S. Mogabgab, "Editor's Introduction," *Weavings* (May/June 1995)

❧ We should never desire to be above others, but ought rather to be servants and subject "to every human creature for God's sake." And the spirit of the Lord shall rest upon all those who do these things and who shall persevere to the end, and He shall make His abode and dwelling in them, and they shall be children of the heavenly Father, whose works they do, and they are the spouses, brothers and mothers of our Lord Jesus Christ. We are spouses when by the Holy God the faithful soul is united to Jesus Christ. We are His brothers when we do the will of His Father who is in heaven. We are His mothers when we bear Him in our heart and in our body through pure love and a clean conscience and we bring Him forth by holy work which ought to shine as an example to others.

—Francis of Assisi, *Selections from the Writings of St. Francis of Assisi*

❧ Really, there are no words to express the experience of the Holy Spirit. I have felt such religious joy several times, and I have had the joy of being immersed in light; there are no words to describe that joy. I have felt an absolute joy that cannot be tasted in such pleasures as fame or gain or the pleasures of the physical nature.

Christ said, "Receive the Holy Spirit": and at once he added, "If you forgive the sins of any, they are forgiven." That means the same as when he said, "Abide in my love." That is, the Holy Spirit, as the truth, gives the content of consciousness. As the Sanctifier, he gives a guarantee of our perfection. But that again is not separate from his atoning love. The realization of this love is altogether by the power of the Holy Spirit. Paul who experienced this love received the power to overcome all things with the joy of love.

Really the Holy Spirit and love cannot be separated. Christ came into the world to show the human race the love of God. All the teachings of Christ have relation to this love. Salvation means that God is love. Providence also means that we are kept by the love of God. Judgment means that God will weed out those who do not believe in the love of God. God is love. Christ is the crystal of God's love. The Holy Spirit is the Spirit of truth who reveals the atoning love of Christ.

This love is not the love that the world gives. It is the love that God gives. The love of the world is semiconscious. It only loves those whom it likes. But the love that is the fruit of the Holy Spirit is the full, conscious, atoning love that loves even those whom it dislikes.

When we thus think, all the teaching of Christ is love. Through the consciousness of the joy of this love, it flows out eternally like never-ceasing oil from a vessel. It is at this point the evangelist John says that the Holy Spirit and love are not to be separated. The mystical experience of the Holy Spirit is the intuitive recognition of the love of God. For that reason, those who have had a deep experience of the Holy Spirit, however poor they may be, whatever sickness they may suffer, however much they may be persecuted, rejoice in the unceasing love of God. Truly, in this meaning, the Holy Spirit is the Comforter, and we may say he is our Helper. The religion of the love of Christ is not a religion of fear. It is the fountain of love and joy and life. We must live forever in his love.

—Toyohiko Kagawa, *Living Out Christ's Love*

  ❧ We are known by God: wholly, deeply. God knows the best of us, the worst of us, the very parts we do not even understand about ourselves. And in Jesus Christ, we learn to know and trust that such knowledge aims not at our undoing but our renewing, not at our condemnation but our restoration. Set aside all fears of a God who waits to catch your every misstep. Rest in the knowledge and grace of a God who seeks you for your good.

—John Indermark, *The Way of Grace*

❧ Liturgical worship is not an end in itself. It is a portal into the heart, mind, and work of Jesus Christ by the power of the Spirit to the glory of God.

I can promise that you will meet Christ in daily prayer, in festal celebrations around the year, in the experience and remembrance of baptism, and in the celebration of the Eucharist. When Jesus talks with his disciples about how to handle fractures in the church, he concludes with this promise: "For where two or three are gathered in my name, I am there among them" (Matt. 18:20). I read that as both a promise and a yearning. The risen Christ yearns to be among us as a community of shared discipline and grace-filled worship. He promises to be present around font, book, and table. Your part is to include yourself in that community of open hands, hearts, and minds for the sake of Love.

—Daniel T. Benedict Jr., *Patterned by Grace*

❧ "Blessed are the poor in spirit," taught Jesus. Only when we understand that we are utterly needy because what we imagine we possess is not truly ours, regardless of appearances; only when we see that we cannot keep good health permanently and that our very being is rooted simply in God's creative love; only when we recognize that everything we call "our own" is but a constant, sustaining gift of the Spirit—only *then* are we free. Obedience consists in nurturing and living out such poverty of spirit. Freedom is the fruit—to give and receive in the same spirit of nonpossessive love God has given us.

—Marjorie J. Thompson, "Obedience," *Weavings*

꙳ Many conceive of the will of God as a track laid out before them which, if they will get on it and stay on it, will assure that their lives run smoothly, but, if they jump off the track, will bring only sadness and despair and lead to wreck and ruin. Others think of the will of God as a blueprint which, if properly read and followed, will help them build a sturdy house in which they may live safely and happily.

The Apostle to the Gentiles gave a different twist to this concept. In his letters, the will of God, what pleases God, or what is acceptable to God has to do with what kind of persons we are, with attitude and outlook. God wants us to be persons who live our lives from the vantage point of a covenant with God through and in Jesus Christ, conscientized and sensitized and tenderized by love, making the very best decisions we can make in the circumstances in which we find ourselves.
—E. Glenn Hinson, "Horizonal Persons," *Weavings*

18. *Vulnerability*

Affirmation
Listen to my prayer, LORD! Because of your faithfulness, hear my requests for mercy! Because of your righteousness, answer me! (Ps. 143:1).

Psalm: 125

Psalm Prayer
Like the mountains that surround Jerusalem, surround us, O Lord, in moments of weakness and vulnerability. Be with us always that we may never be shaken. Protect and comfort us with the assurance of your presence in times of deepest need. Amen.

Daily Scripture Readings

Sunday	A.	Exodus 17:1-7; Psalm 95; Romans 5:1-11; John 4:5-42
	B.	Exodus 20:1-17; Psalm 19; 1 Corinthians 1:18-25; John 2:13-22
	C.	Isaiah 55:1-9; Psalm 63:1-8; 1 Corinthians 10:1-13; Luke 13:1-9
Monday		2 Samuel 12:1-15
Tuesday		Ruth 1:1-18
Wednesday		Isaiah 53
Thursday		Matthew 4:1-11
Friday		Luke 22:63-71
Saturday		John 18:1-14

Silence

Daily Readings for Reflection

Reflection: Silent or Written

Prayers: For the World, for Others, for Myself

Offering of Self to God
In times of both weakness and strength we will place all our trust in you, O God. Amen.

Blessing
May the Lord of peace grant us peace this day and always in every way. Amen.

Readings for Reflection

❧ The Twelve all had a good beginning with Jesus. Their signs of loyalty, fidelity, and faithfulness came often in their brief time with Jesus. And yet in many of the crucial times for Jesus and for them, the truth is that they drifted astray. They lost sight of Jesus and his way and focused on themselves and their way.

A good beginning is wonderful to experience and to observe. Even more wonderful is to see a woman or a man full of years and still full of goodness and faith. To observe a marriage that is marked by fidelity and unqualified love after a half century of living brings hope and encouragement to all who desire strong families and strong communities. Faithfulness is a wonderful thing to experience and to observe.

Some congregations have remarkable and almost miraculous beginnings, beginnings that are marked by rapid growth and transformation of nearly every life that enters their sphere of ministry. These congregations' transforming ministry touches every part of their community, and that community is forever changed. Faithfulness is a wonderful thing to experience and to observe.

There are denominations that carry a precious part of the gospel's treasure in such faithful ways that the world is a better place because God has given them life. Their faithfulness in good times and bad, in wealth and poverty, provides direction and encouragement for all who choose to live a life of goodness and holiness.

Faithfulness is a wonderful thing to experience and to observe.

The bad news is that individuals, congregations, and denominations can drift astray. It happens so easily. It happens the moment we take our eyes off Jesus Christ. The moment we lose our center we begin to lose our way. We know it does not have to be that way because every day we can keep our eyes upon Jesus Christ and ask for guidance and grace to remain faithful. The good news Christians share is that Jesus Christ is able and willing to guide and enable us on our journey toward our true home with God.

—Rueben P. Job

❧ As I listen to myself and to other Christians, I notice that after some years of following Jesus we tend to suffer from various symptoms of drifting away.

When we were young in our faith, we were eager to give sacrificially of our time and resources to alleviate the pains of the poor; we were eager to take time for daily reading of the scripture and prayer. Fasting was a spiritual delight, and we would plow through snow up to our belt buckles to get to church on Sunday. Then, after some years, we began to drift away from the spiritual disciplines that sustained us in earlier times.

John labeled three deadly conditions that cause us to drift away from our earlier spiritual disciplines (1 John 2:16): lust of the flesh, lust of the eyes, and the pride of life (or, if you will, lustful desires, wandering eyes, and greedy eyes—a false sense of security in our material possessions). John insisted that if we follow in these ways, we certainly will come to spiritual and ethical shipwreck.

Most Christians, I suppose, don't come to such extreme conditions. But for many, after some years of faithful practice, spiritual rigor mortis sets in—and all is lost. Paul suggests an antidote for drifting away: " 'Sleeper, awake! Rise from the dead, and Christ will shine on you.' Be careful then how you live, not as unwise people but as wise, making the most of the time, because the days are evil. So do not be foolish, but understand what the will of the Lord is. Do not get drunk with wine, for that is debauchery; but be filled with the Spirit, as you sing psalms and hymns and spiritual songs among yourselves, singing and making melody to the Lord in your hearts, giving thanks to God the Father at all times and for everything in the name of our Lord Jesus Christ" (Eph. 5:14-20).

—Norman Shawchuck

&ebull; "No one has greater love than this, to lay down one's life for one's friends" (John 15:13). With these words Jesus adds specificity to the commandment that his disciples should love one another as he has loved them (John 15:12). Soon this specificity will become disturbingly concrete as Jesus lays down his life on the menacing altar of his enemies, entering the unfathomable agony of physical torture and spiritual abandonment. His ascent to Golgotha and descent into hell are culminating events in a life given wholly to the art of loving.

Even in the Incarnation, Christ lays down his life in order to enter and share ours. Though he was "in the form of God," he "did not regard equality with God as something to be exploited, but emptied himself, taking the form of a slave, being born in human likeness" (Phil. 2:6-7). Early theologians recognized that in Jesus God became fully human without either separation or confusion of God's being and human being. In the mystery of divine love that Jesus embodies, there is at once no distance and yet immeasurable spaciousness between God and humanity. God's love seeks the most profound intimacy with us but never in ways that encroach on our freedom.

To live in the paradox of no distance yet spaciousness in our own relationships is fundamental to laying down our life for others. Like Jesus we refrain from taking self-serving advantage of our status, knowledge, or power when we extend our love to others. Love constrains us from imposing on another our deepest convictions or our best intentions.

The spaciousness that opens when we set aside our own advantage permits us to take the risky initiative of reaching out to others. Once more we follow the pattern of divine love: "We love because he first loved us" (1 John 4:19). To love first requires us to shed the invulnerability of withholding ourselves from others until we think we know how they will respond. When we cease clinging to our supposed security, we lay down our life for our friends.

The initiative is risky because it opens us, as it does God, to the possibility of hurtful misunderstanding or rejection. If the cross is the most acute example of this in the history of God's relationship with us, it is not the only one. When Israel's infidelity pierces God's heart, pained divine anger flashes out in vengeful threats but finally softens into tender reconciliation (Hos. 2). Gazing out over Jerusalem, the holy city so hostile to him, Jesus laments, "How often have I desired to gather your children together as a hen gathers her brood under her wings, and you were not willing!" (Luke 13:34). Beyond this pain, however, lies the generosity of love that transcends and transforms conflict with the freedom to be for others. From such generosity and freedom flows a new creation.

—John S. Mogabgab, "Editor's Introduction," *Weavings* (July/August 2011)

❧ French philosopher and Talmudic scholar Emmanuel Levinas offers a perspective into the art of loving in the face of suffering. He writes about "the face" of "the other." In seeing the face of the other, especially the face of one who is vulnerable and in pain, Levinas maintains that a moral claim is made on us. In the face-to-face encounter the face of the other pleads, Do not hurt me. Do not kill me. Let me live!

While pondering, indeed playing with, Levinas's use of the word *face* I have come to recognize that there are three movements or moments in the art of loving, especially loving those who are wounded and weak, vulnerable and suffering.

The first movement in this art of loving is to look long enough *into the face* of another in order that we might read their pain and suffering. This entails lingering long enough to let the other, in all her brokenness and weakness, show forth in the light. This is the moment in which there is an epiphany of the face, a showing forth of the face of the other person in all its otherness. Often the other feels like nothing, reduced to invisibility by pain and diminishment. This first movement allows the face to speak, as if to say "I am here," so that the suffering person is given the chance to sense life possibilities that might be born beyond the nothingness that is felt beneath the suffering.

The second movement is to allow the other to look upon me as well, letting the nakedness of her face and my own be revealed. We must be willing to *go face to face* with the other. In this encounter we savor the earthly "enjoyment" as we forget ourselves in gazing upon the other.

The third movement in this art of loving is born out of our face-to-face encounter. It is a new way of looking together toward the horizon of what is beyond us both, a turning toward what will be, even if this does not mean a restoration to the state of well-being the other once enjoyed. In this posture, the art of loving calls us both to face up to whatever lies ahead, *to face up* to what is yet to come, to imagine how we will live *in the face* of what is not yet but will be, even and especially in the face of diminishment and death.

To risk face-to-face encounter with the other, to risk getting close enough to attend to the suffering, vulnerability, and pain we will see there and then to face up to what is yet to come in a shared future, is the dynamic of this art of loving. To look at each other in these ways involves more than just feeling the pain of the other and it prevents us from the knee-jerk reaction of offering shallow reassurances of improved well-being, and then going our way unchanged by the encounter. By looking long and lovingly into the face of suffering, we might learn to really see by a love that knows how to really look. And at the same time, by the same love, the suffering one—the other—might be fortified to endure the truth of the present and anticipate the possibility of what is yet to be.

—Michael Downey, "On Learning How to Look," *Weavings*

❧ Vulnerability before God means really believing in God's providential love for us and God's loving presence in the world. After years of obscurity, Jesus went into the desert at that moment when he felt God calling him to begin his public ministry. Where would all this lead? He didn't know, but he trusted God. Gradually he realized that his ministry meant a life of total economic insecurity—"Foxes have holes and the birds of the air have nests, but the Son of Man has nowhere to lay his head" (Matt. 8:20, JB). Further along it became clear that his journey was headed toward Jerusalem and a confrontation with the powers of his time. Later, in the garden of Gethsemane, with his closest friends sleeping, Jesus had to face his passion alone before God. So vulnerable was he that he sweat blood, begging for release and finally for the help to embrace that passion. He then rose to face his captors and the friend who would betray him. When the awakened disciples came to his rescue, he told them to put away their swords—"his hour" had come. As soon as Jesus was arrested, they fled in fear (Matt. 26:47-56). The "good shepherd" had become the sheep. Dragged before the high priest and then before Pilate, he remained silent (Matt. 26:63; 27:14). Condemned to death, the Lamb was led to the cross. His seed was about to fall into the

ground and die. Would it bear much fruit, as he had preached to others? Jesus dared to believe.
—James McGinnis, "Living the Vulnerability of Jesus," *Weavings*

❧ Jesus' intimate relationship with God flowed forth from prayer into his works of compassion. His life of healing can be summarized in his simple words to the centurion whose servant lay near death, "I will come and cure him" (Matt. 8:7). It was his will to be interrupted by the needs of others and to meet those needs with his healing, forgiving love. Constantly welcoming outcasts, Jesus declared, "I have come to call not the righteous but sinners" (Matt. 9:13).

Such obedience to God led Jesus into conflict. He said of the laws of Moses, "I have come not to abolish but to fulfill [them]" (Matt. 5:17). Yet Jesus' healing on the Sabbath and overturning the money table in the Temple scandalized the religious leaders. Although they sought his life, Jesus continued his ministry of love.

Jesus' willing obedience continued even though betrayal and death lay ahead. Several times, we read that he predicted his death. And praying in the garden of Gethsemane, Jesus acknowledged the end he was facing. In his true humanity, he hoped to avoid the suffering; but as Immanuel, God with us in radical availability, he gave himself to God: "My Father, if it is possible, let this cup pass from me; yet not what I want but what you want" (Matt. 26:39). The essence of abandonment followed as Jesus gave his life on the cross.
—Gerrit Scott Dawson, *Companions in Christ*

❧ When it was noon, darkness came over the whole land until three in the afternoon" (Mark 15:33). In Mark's Gospel an overwhelming darkness cloaks the land midway between the time of Jesus' crucifixion and the moment of his death. The agonizing hours of that terrible afternoon stretch out between two definitive marks of our tortured human condition: the crucifixion, through which a world delirious with fear and confusion immobilizes the incarnate God on the wooden crossbeam of its own alienation, and then death, that cosmic affront to the Creator of life. The immovable solidity of the cross and the irrevocable silence of death frame a vision of God's most profound vulnerability. Yet precisely here on bare Golgotha, where God's vulnerability is so starkly visible, it is also most deeply concealed, engulfed in a darkness that obscures even the most prominent features of the land. What is this darkness? Perhaps it is the mystery of divine vulnerability. In the secret depths of this mystery a new work of immeasurable proportions is underway, a new destiny is forming for the creation which hitherto had been condemned to death: "On him lies a punishment that brings us peace, and through his wounds we are healed" (Isa. 53:5, JB).

—John S. Mogabgab, "Editor's Introduction," *Weavings* (July/August 1993)

&. In God's life with us vulnerability is the fount of healing. In our life with God this is true as well. We are hidden with Christ in God (Col. 3:3), our wounds swathed in the darkness of God's vulnerability, our hearts gently prepared to offer others the silent sanctuary of a spacious vulnerability. Vulnerability as a healing gift offered to others—this is not usually the first thing that comes to mind in our culture. Recently a workshop leader invited participants to voice their associations with the word *vulnerability*. Responses included adjectives such as meek, intimidated, naive, inferior, ugly, and foolish. Vulnerability is not seen as a gift to be given but a weakness to be overcome. Not vulnerability but security is the ideal that most often governs our national, communal, and personal decisions. Perhaps one of the greatest sources of loneliness in contemporary life is that our vulnerability, which unites us in a common humanity and enables us to be

woven together in love, now is cause for our isolation in fear-filled cells of spiritual solitary confinement.
—John S. Mogabgab, "Editor's Introduction," *Weavings* (July/August 1993)

❧ Look at Jesus on the cross. Totally bound, weak, and broken, yet whispering God's forgiveness to those around him. What a picture of both vulnerability and power. The most transforming power we see in the Gospels is the power of crucified, vulnerable, suffering love. God's power is revealed in vulnerability.
—Trevor Hudson and Stephen D. Bryant, *Transforming Discipleship*

Fourth Sunday in Lent

19. The Gift of Tears

Affirmation

For everything there is a season, and a time for every matter under heaven . . . a time to weep, and a time to laugh (Eccl. 3:1, 4, NRSV).

Psalm: 38

Psalm Prayer

Gracious God, you know the sighs confined and hidden within the depths of our hearts, sighs for which there are often no words. Do not be far from us, O God, when we cry out unto you. Hear our prayers today. Amen.

Daily Scripture Readings

Sunday	A.	1 Samuel 16:1-13; Psalm 23; Ephesians 5:8-14; John 9:1-41
	B.	Numbers 21:4-9; Psalm 107:1-3, 17-22; Ephesians 2:1-10; John 3:14-21
	C.	Joshua 5:9-12; Psalm 32; 2 Corinthians 5:16-21; Luke 15:1-3, 11-32
Monday		Genesis 43:16-34
Tuesday		Luke 19:29-44
Wednesday		Philippians 3:12-21
Thursday		1 Samuel 24:8-22
Friday		Luke 22:47-62
Saturday		John 11:17-44

Silence

Daily Readings for Reflection

Reflection: Silent or Written

Prayers: For the World, for Others, for Myself

Offering of Self to God
O God, we give ourselves over to your care, trusting only in your infinite mercy and love. We will continue to give thanks to you, O Lord, for all that we have and all that we are. We will rest assured in the knowledge that when we cry to you in sadness or in joy you will hear our cry and make reply. Amen.

Blessing
May the God of love and peace, who gives us both tears of joy and sorrow, comfort us when we mourn, soothe us in our distress, rejoice with us when we are glad, and be with us always. Amen.

Readings for Reflection

❧ A prince is identified with privilege, rank, and special benefits, but Jesus, the Prince of Peace, comes into Jerusalem riding on a donkey, a symbol of lowliness. His entrance is greeted with affirmation and acclamation. There is a joyous mood in the crowd as the people anticipate the promise of the prophets before them.

"Rejoice greatly, O daughter of Zion! Shout aloud, O daughter Jerusalem! Lo, your king comes to you; triumphant and victorious is he, humble and riding on a donkey, on a colt, the foal of a donkey. He will cut off the chariot from Ephraim and the war horse from Jerusalem; and the battle bow shall be cut off, and he shall command peace to the nations; his dominion shall be from sea to sea, and from the River to the ends of the earth" (Zech. 9:9-10).

The promise of peace for a people plagued by war and strife was wonderful news. Perhaps now their long agony would come to an end. The promise of peace is enough to make any suffering people celebrate. Do you suffer today? Sometimes the wars within are as devastating as the wars without. At some time in our lives, most of us will know the darkness of loneliness, disappointment, and despair. When the Prince of Peace comes to offer release, redemption, help, and hope, we are also filled with joy and the "hosannas" burst from our lips as well.

Jesus chose the way of peace in a violent world. He taught his disciples to do the same. Just for a moment Peter forgot, and because of that, one in the arresting party lost an ear. But still Jesus rebuked Peter and courageously continued his journey as the Prince of Peace on the way to his own death.

—Rueben P. Job

ﻼ The realization of God's love for us comes as a life-changing, liberating moment. Jesus announced his ministry as one of setting persons free from the effects of sin and darkness to enjoy a life of complete freedom and full salvation.

The "inhabitants" of the dark recesses of our conscious and subconscious selves are often so fear—or guilt—producing that we go to almost any length to avoid admitting or confronting their existence. But once the realization of God's unconditional love is secure, we begin to look into the dark side of life's experiences in order to be led from that darkness into the light (Col. 1:13-14). God's love for us means we need not stay as we are, for the Holy Spirit is with us to help us face ourselves and to go from where we are to where God wants us to be.

—Norman Shawchuck, Rueben P. Job, and Robert G. Doherty, *How to Conduct a Spiritual Life Retreat*

ﻼ Tears are deemed a gift by many ancient masters of the spiritual tradition, a gift not merely in the sense of something given, but in the biblical sense of a *charism*, a gift of the Spirit, belonging on the list that Paul enunciates in his first letter to the Corinthians. Tears were, for the ancient church, given to some along with wisdom, knowledge, faith, healing, prophecy, and the like, for the life of the entire community.

It seems to have been Athanasius, the great fourth-century bishop of Alexandria, who first spoke of tears as such a gift. But other notable early Eastern Christian writers expounded on them as well. Assuming that inner dispositions had a corresponding outer expression, the Eastern church writers most often saw tears as the outward manifestation of the spiritual experience of *penthos*, a term we might translate as "compunction." Compunction literally means "to puncture with" and refers to the spiritual pain due not only to a shocked recognition of sin and human weakness, but the simultaneous awakening dissatisfaction with sin and longing for God. To have our hearts thus "punctured" is both the beginning and the dynamic of the journey.

—Wendy M. Wright, "Tears of a Greening Heart," *Weavings*

❧ The ancient East understood there to be different types of tears, some of spiritual origin and import, others not. Spiritual tears in themselves were variously categorized and described. They could have purifying power. They might function differently for those just beginning on the spiritual journey and for those far along. They could be provoked by memory of sin as well as consideration of the goodness of God, the desire for heaven, the fear of hell, or the thought of judgment.

Overwhelmingly, tears were understood as a gracious God-given gift, a wonderful physical sign that the inner world of a person was being transformed. There is in these ancient Eastern masters a sense of the ongoing cleansing taking place as a person draws nearer to God. Tears thus become, in a sense, a sign of the continuing power of the baptismal waters to redeem the created world.

—Wendy M. Wright, "Tears of a Greening Heart," *Weavings*

❧ When we find Mary standing outside the tomb, she is weeping. Two days earlier, she had seen the person whom she loved dearly, the one who had released her from her torment, put to death on a cross. She had followed him around Galilee. She had been at the foot of the cross and accompanied his crucified body to the tomb in Joseph's garden. Then early on Sunday morning she had gone with a small group of women to the tomb. To their great distress, they found the stone rolled away and the body of Jesus gone. Soon afterward Peter and John arrived, only to depart and leave Mary alone in the garden, standing beside her pool of tears.

The longer I think about Mary's tears, the more I recognize the need for her to cry. She needed those tears to express the deep grief of her heart. They were necessary to ease the intensity of her inner pain. They were necessary to relax those raw nerves rapidly reaching the breaking point. They were necessary to lighten the weight of sorrow bearing heavily down upon her spirit. They were necessary for the processes of healing and transformation to begin. Indeed, I believe that without her tears, Mary may have failed to recognize the shining figures inside the tomb. After all, tears can help us to see things differently. They clear the dust from our eyes and give us fresh insight and vision.

—Trevor Hudson, *Hope Beyond Your Tears*

❧ Tears of grief and tears of joy often mingle together in a single moment of enhanced vision, endowing us with new eyes that discern traces of the God who suffers with us silently in the pure vulnerability and power of divine love. There is comfort in such tears. They bring fresh understanding that God is nearby, sharing to the full our humanity in all its bitterness and blessedness.

—John S. Mogabgab, "Editor's Introduction," *Weavings*
  (March/April 2000)

❧ If obsessing on news reports is not the best of all responses to violence and tragedy, what is? While better responses include comforting the afflicted, joining a cleanup crew, donating money, or getting involved in settings that promote reconciliation, there is another important response in which off-site folks can participate: the ongoing weeping with God, whose heart throbs when humans harm and oppress each other. Whether the violence is directed at us, surrounds us, or even rises up within us, we can train our heart to grieve on a regular basis in order to release our claim on vengeance because we are children of God.

Such weeping is, I believe, an ongoing discipline for those in whom God dwells. Sandwiched between scripture's difficult biddings to "bless those who persecute you" and "live in harmony with one another," is the command: "weep with those who weep" (Rom. 12:14-16). . . .

In Christian spiritual tradition, certain kinds of weeping are a *charism*, or gift of the Spirit. Captured in the Greek word *penthos*, such weeping involves a broken and contrite heart and inward godly sorrow. Stories of the Desert Fathers often include the bidding to stay in one's cell and weep for one's sins. "Useful" grief included "weeping over one's own faults and weeping over the weakness of one's neighbours." It is this latter action—weeping over others' bent lives and the evil phase they have chosen, and even for the redemption of their lives—that helps us respond to tragedy and disaster without vengeance.

—Jan Johnson, "Weeping with God as a Spiritual Discipline," *Weavings*

Fifth Sunday in Lent

20. Letting Go

Affirmation

LORD, you are my God. I will exalt you; I will praise your name, for you have done wonderful things, planned long ago, faithful and sure (Isa. 25:1).

Psalm: 55

Psalm Prayer

Sometimes life seems unbearable. Our hearts and minds are weighed heavily upon, and we struggle to let go of all that burdens us for fear of losing the illusion of control we have over our lives. We call upon your name today, O God, that you may free us from worry and all that troubles our minds, bodies, and spirits. We put our trust in you, O God, this day and always. Amen.

Daily Scripture Readings

Sunday	A.	Ezekiel 37:1-14; Psalm 130; Romans 8:6-11; John 11:1-45
	B.	Jeremiah 31:31-34; Psalm 51:1-12; Hebrews 5:5-10; John 12:20-33
	C.	Isaiah 43:16-21; Psalm 126; Philippians 3:4-14; John 12:1-8
Monday		Isaiah 41:10-13
Tuesday		Proverbs 3:3-8
Wednesday		Matthew 6:25-34
Thursday		Romans 8:31-39
Friday		Philippians 4:10-13
Saturday		Hebrews 12:1-2

Silence

Daily Readings for Reflection

Reflection: Silent or Written

Prayers: For the World, for Others, for Myself

Offering of Self to God
O Lord, we all have things we need to release. With your help we will lay aside all in life that burdens us, leaving behind those things that do not matter and clinging only to the things that do. Amen.

Blessing
The LORD remembers us and will bless us: God will bless the house of Israel; God will bless the house of Aaron; God will bless those who honor the LORD— from the smallest to the greatest (Ps. 115:12-13). Amen.

Readings for Reflection

❧ There is a necessary *metanoia* in each breakthrough into further spiritual growth, a necessary change of heart that will lead to a new conversion of one's attitudes and behaviors. There must be a "letting go" of something in our lives in order to make room for the "laying hold" of a new and higher consciousness of the presence and claims of God.

At this point the necessary change of heart is to become willing to accept the wonder that God already loves us just as we are and to surrender to the consequences of that love—both to God and to ourselves.

God's love flows like a river into our life situations and, like a river, its benefits can be dammed up behind the human tendency to resist unconditional love and the very idea that we are lovable.

The change of heart at this stage involves a willingness to let go of the very things that cause us most hurt—our sin and the psychic prisons in which we have locked away our most cherished dreams, potentialities, and spontaneities, as well as the darkness that causes us to stumble in our efforts toward new dimensions in life.

We cling to our resistances simply because it seems too good to be true that we are being invited through God's love to surrender our sin for salvation, our prisons for freedom, and our darkness for light. But when we are able finally to break through our resistance we find ourselves in a new dimension of life and relationship (John 10:10).

—Norman Shawchuck, Rueben P. Job, and Robert G. Doherty, *How to Conduct a Spiritual Life Retreat*

☙ Remember for whom you work: Whether you work for a private company, the government, a large corporation, or yourself, the true disciple understands that he or she ultimately is working for God in that place. "Whatever your task, put yourselves into it, as done for the Lord and not for your masters, since you know that from the Lord you will receive the inheritance as your reward; you serve the Lord Christ" (Col. 3:23-24).

—Norman Shawchuck

☙ Don't grit your teeth and clench your fists and say, "I will! I will!" Relax. Take hands off. Submit yourself to God. Learn to live in the passive voice—a hard saying for Americans—and let life be willed through you. For "I will" spells not obedience.

—Thomas Kelly, *The Sanctuary of the Soul*

☙ The spiritual life is a journey out of Egypt into the Promised Land, by way of the wilderness. There is nothing in the desert. I am alone with my thoughts in the desert. I am alone with my sin in the desert. The desert is also a place of quiet and rest. It is a place to get away. It is the place to know how much God cares for me—that God wants me to rest in and be attended by God. The desert is a place of devotion to God with no distractions, the place where all is forsaken for the love of God. Poverty and detachment have their value as they are prompted by God's love for me and are expressions of my love in return. God has brought me into this desert

so I can know of the love God has for me. I thought it was to hurt me, to make me feel bad, to teach me self-control, but it has been so that I can hear and feel how much God loves me. It is not a question of how much I *must* depend on God, but how much I *can* depend on God. . . . God has taken me into the desert not to separate me but to love me. The desert is being alone with God. I can let go of everything because I am held by God. I claim nothing because I am claimed by God.
—Fred B. Cunningham, "Excerpts from a Pastor's Journal," *Weavings*

❧ Contrary to the contemporary slogan proclaiming the one with the most stuff wins, it seems that the closer to God one becomes, the less one needs or even desires material goods. This sense of needing less is closely connected with one particular attribute: trust in God.

Whether it was Saint Francis or the Desert Mothers and Fathers or the pilgrim or Julian of Norwich, the closer each came in relationship to God, the more he or she trusted in God for everything. So as we pray with and into our material situation in the world, we confront the question: Do we really trust God with our lives—our literal, physical lives? This is a very challenging question. Maybe we trust God with our thoughts and feelings but what about the material stuff that keeps us fed and housed? And what about our attention and our priorities? As we pray into our lifestyle, we encounter the issue of materialism. What is it that holds our attention—God or stuff?
—Daniel Wolpert, *Creating a Life with God*

❧ One of the myths of our culture is that control of ourselves and others is what gives us freedom. If we are in control, then obviously we can make decisions, and that leaves us free. But that is a myth. The paradox is that as we give up control to God, we actually live in a deeper freedom. The freedom of God may call us to turn all of our most precious definitions of faithfulness on their heads. It may be that the most difficult call for us to respond to is not a call that demands of us great sacrifices but a call that offers to us great gifts.

—Judith E. Smith, "The One Thing Necessary," *Weavings*

❧ Letting God work in our lives to bring into order our unruly wills and affections means relinquishing the lofty expectations we cherish that we can achieve equilibrium in our soul life. We need to allow for seasons of the spirit and to recognize that we are not disembodied beings but people made to serve God with our full humanity. Christ, as the Word, "became flesh and lived among us" (John 1:1-14), affirming our humanness, experiencing the full range of human need and emotion yet remaining openhearted in his response to God. Though stretched to breaking point in Gethsemane, he did not harden his heart; he remained *stable* in his commitment and faithfulness in the present, painful moment; he allowed for *conversion* by setting aside his own desire for the success of his mission; and in his "yes" he expressed unquestioning *obedience* to the One he addressed intimately as "Abba." This was a truly dark season for Christ. The struggle took place at nighttime, reflecting the experience of not knowing, waiting, letting be that is a necessary element in the process of growth. In this story we find reflected the universal experience of loss that plunges us into anguish, evokes cries for help in our weakness, and invites trust in God who is in, under, and beyond the present affliction. The alternative to trust and letting go is a hardness of heart that refuses the grace available to us in our ordeal.

—Elizabeth J. Canham, "Listen with the Ear of Your Heart," *Weavings*

Palm Sunday or the Passion of Christ

Palm Sunday is a day of drama. We again see the ambiguity that confronts Jesus as his life and ministry unfold before the world. This day marks the clearest announcement of a new leader different from any the world has ever seen. His leadership stands in stark contrast to the religious and secular culture of the day, and of ours as well.

In Jesus we see a leader who is humble and self-less, unbelievably courageous yet gentle, incredibly truthful yet unimaginably loving. Here we see a completely fearless leader who faces the consequences of being a different kind of leader. Matthew reports that the "whole city was stirred up," asking, "Who is this?" (Matt. 21:10). And we know that the loud shouts of acclamation will soon turn to loud cries of "Crucify."

In this drama we see our own ambiguity about Jesus. We too praise him and declare our desire and commitment to follow him everywhere and always. This is easy to do as children carry palm branches in our processions and we sing songs of praise to our faithful Savior.

However, when the trials and testing times come we, like the crowds in Matthew's Gospel, often waver. And sometimes, God forgive us, we turn away and even turn against the very words and actions that define the life of Jesus. Palm Sunday is the perfect introduction to Holy Week. We see the disciples and the crowds experiencing what we experience as we seek to walk with the God made known to us in the life, death, and resurrection of Jesus Christ. Yes, the days can be dangerous and difficult but thanks be to God, Easter is almost here.

21. *Impasse*

Affirmation
O God, you go before us and are with us in difficult moments. Turn our eyes to you for help.

Psalm: 43

Psalm Prayer
Holy God, when deceitful people assail our character, remind us of just virtues that you yourself practice in your dealings with humanity. Bring us to a more intimate knowledge of your joyous righteousness so that we may hope in you with all our being. Amen.

Daily Scripture Readings

Sunday	A.	Isaiah 50:4-9*a*; Psalm 118:1-2, 19-29; Philippians 2:5-11; Matthew 21:1-11
	B.	Isaiah 50:4-9*a*; Psalm 118:1-2, 19-29; Philippians 2:5-11; Mark 11:1-11
	C.	Isaiah 50:4-9*a*; Psalm 118:1-2, 19-29; Philippians 2:5-11; Luke 19:28-40
Monday		Exodus 14:1-19
Tuesday		Haggai 2:1-9
Wednesday		Psalm 53
Thursday		Lamentations 4
Friday		John 10:22-33
Saturday		James 4:1-10

Silence

Daily Readings for Reflection

Reflection: Silent or Written

Prayers: For the World, for Others, for Myself

Offering of Self to God
O God, you have freed your people from exile. Inspire us to accept that freedom achieved by your Son, our Lord, who humbly rode into Jerusalem on a road paved with palm branches to finish your work of salvation. Amen.

Blessing
May the God who acts to protect God's people be with us this day and always. Amen.

Readings for Reflection

  Jesus' life gives us a supreme example of spiritual life as journey. Like us, Jesus began his earthly sojourn as a helpless, vulnerable infant, completely dependent on the nurture of his parents and the providential grace of God. He grew from childhood to the maturity of adulthood, all the while coming to fuller consciousness of his identity in relation to the One he knew as Father. Even at age twelve, he was at home in his Father's house among the elders of Jerusalem. He was firmly "oriented" in his unique relationship with God and received divine affirmation for his vocation specifically in his baptism and at his transfiguration. Jesus knew intensely personal communion with God. He knew many high and holy moments of divine power manifested in and through himself; he knew the joy of community with his disciples and with the crowds who revered him. But he was not immune to struggle, disappointment, or the sting of rejection from friend and foe alike. Surely the experience of temptation in the wilderness was one of disorientation and reorientation for Jesus. On more than one occasion, Jesus expressed his frustration with disciples and others who repeatedly misunderstood his teachings and his basic purpose. Even more the agony of Gethsemane, the experience of betrayal and denial by his closest human companions, and the ultimate horror of feeling abandoned even by God reveal a depth of disorientation in Jesus' life journey that defies our comprehension. Yet Jesus pioneered for us the ultimate reorientation to God's loving purpose in the glory of his resurrection. God's final word is life, not death; communion, not separation!

—Rueben P. Job and Marjorie J. Thompson, *Companions in Christ*

❧ God loves me—all of me. Not only my good side but also my bad side. He sent Christ to save the world because He loved it—all of it, and I will be saved, all of me because God loves the whole world and God loves all of me. What a wonderful gift.

—Norman Shawchuck

❧ In Goethe's *Faust*, Mephistopheles offers a description of theological studies that also applies to the formation of Christian identity: "The way is hard to find, wrong roads abound, and lots of hidden poison lies around which one can scarcely tell from medicine." Sometimes the way is more than hard to find; it seems impassable. Today many seekers are encountering impasses in personal life. Overtaken by old inner wounds, recently gnarled relationships, unexpectedly unstable finances, they have come to the end of the tether, stumbled into the heart of darkness (Joseph Conrad). Moreover, impasses snake out beyond the personal sphere. Social and political life, ever tormented by the ancient question of how we can live together well, seem regularly and alarmingly to become exhausted in places of no exit (Jean-Paul Sartre). Weariness grows. Hope collapses.

"What we all dread most," observes G. K. Chesterton's amateur sleuth Father Brown, "is a maze with *no* centre. That is why atheism is only a nightmare" (*The Complete Father Brown,* Chesterton 1981, 235). Throughout the Bible, a recurring pattern discloses the true center of humanity's most intractable mazes, the wholly unexpected but always trustworthy passage through life's most unyielding impasses. In story after story, it is God who makes passable what is impassable by the world's reckoning, who leads us through a bewilderment of stubborn dead ends into the gracious center of God's own purposes. For Sarah, Hannah, Elizabeth, and Mary there are impossible births, which defy the biological impasse to conception posed by age, infertility, or virginity (Gen. 17:17-22; 1 Sam. 1:2-20; Luke 1:5-25, 57-60; Luke 1:26-37). For Naaman, the woman with a hemorrhage, and a man born blind, there are impossible healings, where terrifying diseases and lifelong conditions surrender to the well-being God intends for all creation (2 Kings 5:1-14; Matt. 9:20-22; John 9:1-7). For the people of Israel, backed to the sea by Pharaoh's troops, and Peter, imprisoned under heavy guard, there are impossible breakthroughs, where barriers of geographical or institutional place give way to a larger, more compelling reality (Exod. 14:9-22; Acts 12:6-11). And finally, for Jesus there is the impossible triumph. Sealed in the tomb, he sheds death's seamless shroud and comes forth mantled in the life of a new creation (John 20:1-18). Everywhere the pattern is the same: The most daunting impasse cedes a passage to God; the most impenetrable maze has a Center.

—John S. Mogabgab, "Editor's Introduction," *Weavings* (March/April 1996)

❧ The risen Christ doesn't float ethereally above his tomb, clean and neat and unscarred. His resurrection has been a struggle. Something happened. Something fierce and world-altering. Something costly. He smiles for he has conquered, really conquered, finally and definitively conquered the last enemy, death.

It never fails that every year following the Palm/Passion Sunday service in the church I serve, at least one person will remark to me or to some member of the staff that the service moved too quickly from a high moment of Palms to the agony of the Cross. The observation is of how disconcerting it can be to move from "Hosanna, loud hosanna" to "Beneath the cross of Jesus." The move, however, is intentional. Jesus suffered. Jesus died. He really did. It was a ferocious death with all the powers of hell amassed against the one good and loving person who ever lived. But without that struggle on Friday, without the pain of his loving us to death, there is nothing to celebrate today. It's simply a warm blanket. "Dear Teacher." No struggle. Nothing happened. Nothing has changed.

If there is no death, then God's got nothing to do on Easter. But if there is a death, then Easter morning is a ferocious moment when life triumphs over death, and what God did on Easter for Jesus and for us is the most radical and important truth that any of us can know or believe.

Carlyle Marney, in one of his greatest sermons, says of Judas that the ultimate tragedy of his life was not his betrayal of Jesus but that he did not hold on until Sunday to see what God would do with his betrayal and despair. What a tragedy that Judas wasn't at the tomb on Sunday to see that there is forgiveness even for his sin and relief even from his deep despair. He then would have known that we are not on our own, not in this life alone. He would have known what Mary was discovering, that there is One who is with us in death and in life. Not just anyone, but the very One who raised Jesus from the dead and who has the power to do that for you and me as well.

It is not warm faith we celebrate. It is not "Dear Teacher" who greets us on Easter morn. It is the risen Christ. Easter Sunday we celebrate that ferocious moment when, by the grace and power of God, the agony and the death of Friday is overcome. Good is stronger than evil. Love triumphs over hate. Life conquers death. Easter is that ferocious moment when

Christ tramples down death by death, and upon those in the tombs bestows life.

—K. C. Ptomey, "This Ferocious Moment," *Weavings*

❧ A strange life-giver, the Holy Spirit, for the life given is compassed about by desolation. The story of Jesus bears stark testimony to this unsettling truth. At the birth of Jesus the Spirit-guided words of Simeon prophesy desolation for Israel and for the heart of Mary as well (Luke 2:34-35). Immediately after his baptism, during which God calls Jesus "my Beloved," the Spirit drives him into the wilderness of isolation, vulnerability, and temptation (Mark 1:12-13). And at the end of a life exquisitely responsive to every subtle rhythm of the Spirit's leading, Jesus chokes out the unthinkable words, "My God, my God, why have you forsaken me?" (Matt. 27:46).

Christian tradition teaches that there are times when we, like Jesus, are led into arid soulscapes that bruise and disorient us. These places seem bereft of God's presence and filled with temptations to lose heart in God's goodness, care, and sovereignty. In this harsh "winter of abandonment" (Johannes Tauler), Jesus' anguished cry of desertion becomes our own. Desert and cross—places of excruciating separation from the God we have come to know but equally unbearable intimacy with the God we are yet to know, places barren of all human possibilities but pregnant with grace. "Lord," exclaims the scorned and ill young priest in *The Diary of a Country Priest* by Georges Bernanos, "I am stripped bare of all things, as you alone can strip us bare, whose fearful care nothing escapes, nor your terrible love." [There are] riches hidden in the poverty of desert and cross, symbols of God's "terrible love." In the "fearful care" of the Holy Spirit we are stripped bare but not left naked and exposed in desert wastes.

—John S. Mogabgab, "Editor's Introduction," *Weavings* (September/October 1993)

❧ If we picture all the obstructions between us and God as a wilderness, Lent presents us with time to clear and cultivate a part of that wilderness, to create an open space in it. In this newly opened space, we may live more freely and commune more closely with the divine. We can transform this wilderness and make it our home, our garden, a place that invites God in and asks God to stay.
—Sarah Parsons, *A Clearing Season*

❧ And the well runs dry. It's one of the most common experiences in the spiritual life. A practice that we have cherished, a habit that has deepened us and drawn us closer to God, a discipline that we perhaps have engaged in for years, no longer seems to work. Gradually over time or overnight with no warning, its familiar contours turn foreign, dull, perhaps even painful.

Pondering the questions that lie at the bottom of a dry well offers a journey of its own. What I know is this: to find the answers, we have to pay attention to the dryness. This is a desert place. As uncomfortable as it may be, there is no substitute for these desert places in the spiritual life. They offer a wisdom that we cannot get any other way.
—Jan L. Richardson, *In the Sanctuary of Women*

❧ Yet for Christ to become our light, we must do one thing: "Repent." Repentance always requires us to turn around, change directions, quit walking away from God and begin walking the walk of faith toward him who is God-with-us. Our continued efforts to stay on God's side and to go in God's direction encourage us in our living until that way of life becomes as natural as breathing. Our life in Christ takes a lifetime both to learn and to live out.
—Bonifacio B. Mequi Jr., "Faith in the Balance," *The Upper Room Disciplines 1999*

The Season of Easter

Now we see clearly the rest of the story. Death is not the end. Violence is not victorious. Death and darkness are overcome for all time and for all people! The Lord is risen. Death loses its sting, and God's light permanently overcomes the darkness of evil. This is the new world in which the Christian now lives—the kingdom of God on earth as it is in heaven, life abundant and eternal. This is the news that brings hope to every Christian in every age and circumstance. It is the truth that gives courage and hope in the darkest hour and brings comfort, joy, and peace for all time. Cries of grief turn to songs of joy that have continued since that first Easter morning encounter with the risen Christ. Even the strongest doubts surrender as Christ's living presence makes itself known to the followers of Jesus.

Now we join the mighty chorus and proclaim Christ—crucified, dead, buried, and risen from the dead—as the Lord of all things and Savior of all humankind. We celebrate the completion of the salvation story and offer our lives once again to walk in constant companionship with the risen Christ. We anticipate the outpouring of God's Spirit upon us to enable us to live faithfully and joyfully as redeemed and beloved children of God. We realize now as never before the extravagant mercy and love of God for us and for all creation. This boundless and contagious love moves us day by day to live as Jesus lived, offering love, mercy, peace, and compassion to all we meet. This love sends the faithful to visit the prisoner, heal the sick, feed the hungry, rescue the lost, and provide for the poor. For now we better understand what it means to say, "God so loved the world that he gave his only Son, so that everyone who believes in him won't perish but will have eternal life" (John 3:16).

The season of Easter is set within the fifty days following our Lord's resurrection. This season includes the Lord's ascension and leads us to the season of

Pentecost. Pentecost reminds us that we are never alone as faithful followers of Jesus Christ. The Holy Spirit is sent to instruct, guide, and comfort us; to give us hope and joy and companionship through this life and into the next.

Now we do know the rest of the story. Now we can make the gospel story our own.

22. *Mystery*

Affirmation

God of new life, you have brought your reign into the world through the resurrection of your only Son, our Lord.

Psalm: 80

Psalm Prayer

O Lord, at times we feel like the Israelites in Exile. Hear our cry for help and restore us so that we might be saved. Stay near to us when we try to wander from you, and guide us safely with your mysterious love. Amen.

Daily Scripture Readings

Sunday	A.	Acts 10:34-43; Psalm 118:1-2, 14-24; Colossians 3:1-4; John 20:1-18
	B.	Isaiah 25:6-9; Psalm 118:1-2, 14-24; Acts 10:34-43; Mark 16:1-8
	C.	Acts 10:34-43; Psalm 118:1-2, 14-24; 1 Corinthians 15:19-26; Luke 24:1-12
Monday		Genesis 18:1-15
Tuesday		Isaiah 6:1-7
Wednesday		Psalm 64
Thursday		Daniel 2:24-45
Friday		John 20:1-18
Saturday		1 Corinthians 15:35-58

Silence

Daily Readings for Reflection

Reflection: Silent or Written

Prayers: For the World, for Others, for Myself

Offering of Self to God
God of new creation, we want to live a life that bears witness to the reconciliation you have brought through Jesus' resurrection. Inspire us to follow Jesus' way so that your Kingdom may be known even now. Amen.

Blessing
May the God who brings life into places where death once ruled give us calm assurance for the future this day. Amen.

Readings for Reflection

❧ Jesus' journey is in some sense a model for each of his followers, although each will experience the particular pattern of the journey in a different way. We have glimpses of that pattern for the twelve disciples who began their journey by accepting Jesus' call to follow him. Along with many days of wearying travel, punctuated by ridicule and rejection from some, came stunning moments of revelation and wonder: impossible healings, the miraculous feeding of the multitudes, the calming of a sudden storm on the lake. The disciples learned only gradually and imperfectly who Jesus was. Whatever certainties they had about him were thrown into crisis at their last Passover supper and in the devastation of the crucifixion. Yet beyond this profound disorientation came experiences of the risen Lord. One of the most powerful stories is the one of two disciples on the road to Emmaus. Here, two little-known men discovered the risen Christ as companion and teacher on their path of confusion and sorrow. The completely new orientation to life and meaning those disciples received remains a powerful promise for our own experience of life in faith.
—Rueben P. Job and Marjorie J. Thompson, *Companions in Christ*

❧ Lord, how mysterious is your manner of courtship with me. In the morning when I do not come alone with you, you call to me from your place, you awaken an emptiness within me that I know only you can fill. So I go to the place of our meeting, knowing that I miss much by failing to answer your call.

—Norman Shawchuck

❧ The other day I watched a cloud form very suddenly and cover the summit of a great mountain, and hide its exalted glory. I could see the track, which had been made by the feet of many generations, winding up the mountain, and I could see where it was lost in the lowering cloud. The cloud itself was bright and radiant. It concealed, and yet it was luminous. It had its deep secrets, and yet it was lucent. It was a home of light, and yet it acted as a veil. The summit of the mountain was hid, but the minister of concealment was also a minister of grace and glory.

And there are bright clouds which often overshadow the lives of the devoted friends of the Lord Jesus Christ. Secrets are hid from our gaze. We cannot trace even the outlines of our Father's will. Meanings are shrouded in mystery, but in the very mystery there is a certain radiance. The Presence that is hid is shining. The secrets are love secrets. The veil is there, but within the veil is the home of God.

The atonement itself is a bright cloud. The ordinary roads are lost in the vast mystery, and the mountain peaks are hid, but the cloud is not black and cold and chilling; it is warm and radiant with eternal love. The Lord is within the cloud, in the unfathomable wonders of perpetual sacrifice. Our understandings are not yet finally enlightened, but the heart is kindled and sustained. We can rest in the Lord and wait patiently for Him. When the veil is lifted we shall see "Jesus only."

And in Christ Jesus even death itself is a bright cloud. It is a great mystery, but it is lit up from within. The fitting symbol of a Christian's death is not midnight but dawn; not blackness but greyness, for greyness is just blackness made luminous with an indwelling whiteness. Within the mystery of death the Sun of Righteousness is arisen and there is healing in His radiant wings. The veil has not yet been lifted; but death is like a house in the night-time, whose shades are drawn, and whose door is closed, but whose windows are bright with the comforting cheer of fire and light within. Our Lord is in the house and the mystery is radiant.

And so it is with many other mysteries which confront us in life's way. In Christ Jesus there are bright clouds. Tomorrow is one of them. Yes, and when we look back, yesterday is another of them. We need not fear to enter the cloud. The transfigured Saviour is within. It is the dwelling-place of the Lord.

—John Henry Jowett, *The Friend on the Road*

৯ It may be objected, that, by this method, we shall have no mysteries imprinted on our minds: but it is quite the reverse; for it is the peculiar means of imparting them to the soul. JESUS CHRIST, to whom we are abandoned, and whom *"we follow as the way, whom we hear as the truth, and who animates us as the life"* (John 14:6) in imprinting Himself on the soul, impresses the characters of His different states; and to bear all the states of JESUS CHRIST is far more sublime, than merely to reason concerning them. S. Paul bore in his body the states of JESUS CHRIST: *"I bear in my body,"* says he, *"the marks of the Lord Jesus"* (Gal. 6:17), but he does not say that he reasoned thereon.

In our acts of resignation, JESUS CHRIST frequently communicates some peculiar views or revelations of His states: these we should thankfully receive, and dispose ourselves for what appeareth to be His will. Indeed, having no other choice, but that of ardently reaching after Him, of dwelling ever with Him, and of sinking into nothingness before Him, we should accept indiscriminately all His dispensations, whether obscurity or illumination, fruitfulness or barrenness, weakness or strength, sweetness or bitterness, temptations, distractions, pain, weariness, or doubtings; and none of all these should, for one moment, retard our course.

GOD engages some, for whole years, in the contemplation and enjoyment of a particular mystery; the simple view or contemplation of which gathers the soul inward, provided it be faithful: but as soon as GOD is pleased to withdraw this view from the soul, it should freely yield to the deprivation. Some are very uneasy at feeling their inability to meditate on certain mysteries; but this disquietude hath no just foundation, since an affectionate attachment to GOD includes every species of devotion: for whosoever, in repose and quiet, is united to GOD alone, is, indeed, most excellently and effectually applied to every divine mystery: the LOVE of GOD comprehends, in itself, the love of all that appertains to Him.

—Jeanne Guyon, *Short and Easy Method of Prayer*

ॐ   Once-still leaves now flutter,
    thanks to you, O breath of life.
    Once-set stone now shifts,
    by the power of your love.
    Once-hard hearts now soften,
    thanks to you, O flame of Spirit.
    Come quickly, come now.
    Alleluia,
    Amen.
    —Pamela C. Hawkins, *The Awkward Season*

ॐ Our journey toward abundant living is like walking a spiritual labyrinth repeatedly, from an ever deepening inner space. We walk toward the center to be transformed by God's love; then we walk outward to transform our small space in the world by reflecting God's love. There is no intention to trick us or get us

lost along the journey. But there is mystery. Always mystery. And awe. And amazing grace.
—Marilyn Brown Oden, *Abundance*

❧ God speaks to me through creation. Throughout the year I watch God's creation from my breakfast table. During the winter months, the birds visit my bird feeder and birdbath. The birds "neither sow nor reap nor gather into barns" (Matt. 6:26), yet they trust and do not worry. . . . Take some time today to notice the beauty of God's earth and to join its living mystery. Creating God, you created the birds, the mushrooms, the sea monsters of the deep—and you created me. Open my eyes, my ears, and my senses today that I may become one with your living mystery. Amen.
—Beth A. Richardson, *The Uncluttered Heart*

❧ [Christ's] is a call that frees . . . The call is not an ending but a beginning. The birth of the baby invites us into a search. I think the simple truth that is being held out . . . is not so much a life lived as though all the answers were given, but a life lived as though all our answers are only gateways into deeper levels of answering, which in turn lead us into mystery where all answers give way to bended knee and adoration and praise.
—Wendy M. Wright, *The Vigil*

23. Count It All Joy

Affirmation
O God, you remain near to us, inviting us always to know your joy.

Psalm: 47

Psalm Prayer
Lord, we shout with joy for your goodness today. Remind us that you are the Sovereign of the earth and that you alone are worthy of our praise. Gather us to you and let the entire world know the peace of your reign. Amen.

Daily Scripture Readings

Sunday	A.	Acts 2:14, 22-32; Psalm 16; 1 Peter 1:3-9; John 20:19-31
	B.	Acts 4:32-35; Psalm 133; 1 John 1:1-2:2; John 20:19-31
	C.	Acts 5:27-32; Psalm 118:14-29; Revelation 1:4-8; John 20:19-31
Monday		Nehemiah 8:1-12
Tuesday		Isaiah 65:17-25
Wednesday		Psalm 63
Thursday		John 15:1-11
Friday		James 1:2-18
Saturday		2 Corinthians 8:1-15

Silence

Daily Readings for Reflection

Reflection: Silent or Written

Prayers: For the World, for Others, for Myself

Offering of Self to God
When we feel overwhelmed by life, Lord God, direct us into the knowledge of your joyful peace so that we can show your goodness to those we encounter from day to day. Amen.

Blessing
May the God of joy bless us and keep us, stirring up desire for God's kingdom alone. Amen.

Readings for Reflection

❧ O Lord of life, we thank you that the day of resurrection has dawned upon us. In its clear light, help us now to step from whatever sign of darkness there may be in ourselves into the true light and life, which is now yours—and which you long to share freely and fully with us.

Come to us—tune our heart and mind to give abundant thanks and praise to God—that on every Sunday we may solemnly celebrate the day of our Lord's resurrection. Give us in this day quiet peace and special gladness, that being protected night and day by your mercy, we may rejoice always in the gift of life given to us by our faithful Savior.
—Norman Shawchuck

❧ God loves lavishly, soaking creation with life, and the joyful freedom of God's love traces the horizon of our joy. That is why the joy we know in the company of God is not dependent on immediate circumstances such as good health, fair wealth, or amiable fellowship. Joy reflects a divine care so broad it enfolds the whole creation, yet so sensitive it registers the fall to earth of a single sparrow (Matt. 10:29). Joy draws its color and intensity from a palette of grace far more splendid than the muted hues that dapple the surface of daily experience.

It is acquaintance with this palette that prompts James to say, "Count it all joy" (James 1:2, RSV). This robust embrace of all facets of experience reveals that the spiritual life is a journey into the fullness of joy, a joy as complete as the love between Jesus and his Father (John 15:9-11; 16:16-24). The author of Hebrews reminds us that "for the sake of the joy that was set before him [Jesus] endured the cross" (Heb. 12:2). So encompassing is this joy that, like a desert sunset, it sheaths in gold every stony hour of suffering, every bony tree of our endurance. Paul recalls an experience among the Christians in Macedonia that graphically portrays the power of joy to transfigure a human landscape: "during a severe ordeal of affliction, their abundant joy and their extreme poverty have overflowed in a wealth of generosity on their part" (2 Cor. 8:2). Our companion, guide, and comforter on the great journey into joy is the Holy Spirit. At the outset, it is the Spirit who inspires joy when grace has opened us to receive God's word (1 Thess. 1:6). Across the years, when life's perplexities impoverish us, it is the Spirit who, working through the gift of joy, removes all boundaries to our hope (Rom. 15:13).

—John S. Mogabgab, "Editor's Introduction," *Weavings* (November/December 1993)

❧ In the opening chapter of his letter, James gives us hope by reminding us that our life's difficulties, trials, and temptations give us an opportunity to grow. However, we need to stop and reflect on our situation: Are our present difficulties of our own doing? In what ways might these circumstances build our character? We cannot accomplish life's purpose through the attainment of ease or luxurious comfort. We accomplish life's purpose only in the achievement of Christlike character.

Christians can count it all joy when we encounter various trials. These test the mettle of our faith in God's purpose; when met with courage, these trials produce steadfastness of character. Everything that we have learned through our suffering, hardship, and related experiences rests on our assured conviction that God supports our lives.

—Costa Stathakis, "God's Purpose for Our Lives," *The Upper Room Disciplines 1999*

❧ God alone, the eternal and infinite, satisfies all, bringing comfort to the soul and true joy to the body.
—Thomas à Kempis, *A Pattern for Life*

❧ Joy is, by its very nature, an ecstatic experience. By that I mean that it comes more from beyond us than from within us. . . . Yet not only does joy *come from* beyond us, it also *goes out* beyond us, including more than ourselves in its scope. While happiness may stop at my doorstep, joy cannot be so easily contained. Joy broadens its reach to embrace others with its disposition. It is this ecstatic or "from-beyond-us-to-beyond-us" quality of joy that comes to expression in worship.

When Dante was making his ascent to heaven in the *Divine Comedy*, he heard what sounded like "the laughter of the universe" (Dante 1948, 176). Such sublime laughter—the joy of a world completely transformed by the healing, reconciling work of God—is beyond our ability to comprehend, or even fully imagine. It is a joy that, in J. R. R. Tolkien's words, lies "beyond the walls of this world."

And yet worship gives us a window upon this joy, a moment for getting caught up, even if only slightly, in that universal laughter. Sometimes we call this a "proleptic" experience, that is, participation in something that is still largely anticipated. In this instance, what we are anticipating is the joy of our complete reconciliation with God and with creation.

—Paul Lynd Escamilla, "Something Bigger than All of Us," *Weavings*

᷍ Why is this word *joy*, so frequent in scripture, so absent in our modern vocabulary? Probably because the experience itself is so strange. Joy is not at all synonymous with familiar words such as *cheerfulness, enjoyment, pleasure, satisfaction, fun,* or even *happiness.* So strange is it that scripture tries to plumb joy's depths by linking it with apparently antithetical words. Thus at Jesus' birth, the shepherds were "terrified" when they heard the "great joy" (Luke 2:9-10). At Jesus' death, Mary Magdalene departed quickly from the tomb with "fear and great joy" (Matt. 28:8). In confronting the resurrection, the disciples disbelieved for joy (Luke 24:41).

It is not surprising, then, that early Christians experienced their mission similarly. When Paul and Barnabas were persecuted and expelled, they shook the dust from their feet while being "filled with joy" (Acts 13:50-52). Thus the writer of James insisted that every Christian should "count it all joy . . . when you meet various trials" (James 1:2, RSV). Paul agreed, "I find joy in my sufferings" (Col. 1:24, AT).

Puzzling as this life of joy appears to be, we dare not dismiss it as peculiar to the early church. Jesus himself modeled this strangeness. Jesus, "for the joy that was set before him endured the cross, despising the shame" (Heb. 12:2, RSV).

This linking of joy with negative experiences such as fear, persecution, and suffering connects the Good News deeply with the Hebrew scriptures. The prophets understood well that joy is for those who mourn (Isa. 66:10). The psalmists likewise insisted that morning joy is for those who mourn in the night (Ps. 30:5). In fact, so linked are sorrow and joy that the psalmists insisted that both are the doings of God: "Fill me with joy and gladness; let the bones which thou hast broken rejoice" (Ps. 51:8, RSV).

—W. Paul Jones, "Joy and Religious Motivation," *Weavings*

❧ Reflecting on joy, however, may inspire us to alter the status quo and to anoint each other with the oil of gladness with more readiness, consistency, and regularity than before. Maybe we owe it to each other to do just that. Maybe we owe it to ourselves to survey our culpability as squelchers of joy in others and of being part of systems and institutions that do not tolerate, let alone encourage, joy. Maybe we need to redress the balance of somberness by gladdening others with support, kind words, encouragement, laughter, hope, time, and the simple gift of self. It wouldn't hurt. It could heal. And it would point to that kingdom first heralded by angels who proclaimed the "good tidings of great joy" that went hand in hand with "peace on earth."

—Doris Donnelly, "Good Tidings of Great Joy,"
  Weavings

❧ Joy is so precious that a person alive with delight glows. So it is with the church. Evangelism is gross salesmanship unless at the center of the church there are those whose lives themselves testify "that neither death, nor life, nor angels, nor principalities, nor things present, nor things to come, nor powers, nor height, nor depth, nor anything else in all creation, will be able to separate us from the love of God in Christ Jesus our Lord" (Rom. 8:38-39, RSV). When the church is a community of joy, evangelism occurs as contagion. It has little to do with forcing decisions about things invisible. It is the sharing of a joy rendered visible by our joyousness. We are drawn toward faithfulness as shared joy—with one another and with the whole creation— by the intuition that union with God alone can satisfy our deepest yearning. It is here, in Calvin's words, that our living has as its primary end a glorifying of God which is an enjoyment forever.

—W. Paul Jones, "Joy and Religious Motivation,"
  Weavings

24. In the World but Not of It

Affirmation

So then, if anyone is in Christ, that person is part of the new creation. The old things have gone away, and look, new things have arrived! (2 Cor. 5:17).

Psalm: 120

Psalm Prayer

Great God of peace, we live in a world wracked by every kind of discord. We thank you that in Jesus Christ you have shown us how to live as witnesses to your new creation. Guide us as we seek to speak words of reconciliation where there is division and to act creatively where ancient habits press humanity toward an old future. Amen.

Daily Scripture Readings

Sunday	A.	Acts 2:14, 36-41;
		Psalm 116:1-4, 12-19;
		1 Peter 1:17-23;
		Luke 24:13-35
	B.	Acts 3: 12-19; Psalm 4;
		1 John 3:1-7; Luke 24:36-48
	C.	Acts 9:1-6; Psalm 30;
		Revelation 5:11-14; John 21:1-19
Monday		Exodus 14:21-31
Tuesday		Leviticus 26:9-13
Wednesday		Joshua 24:13-18
Thursday		Luke 6:39-49
Friday		John 17:10-23
Saturday		Ephesians 2:1-10

Silence

Daily Readings for Reflection

Reflection: Silent or Written

Prayers: For the World, for Others, for Myself

Offering of Self to God
Lord of ever-new beginnings, it is all too easy for us to slip comfortably into the familiar passions and priorities of the world, forgetting that you have brought us out of the world so we could be in it as bearers of your light. Remembering your love, I join my voice with Joshua's and affirm once more that today "my family and I will serve the LORD" (Josh. 24:15). Amen.

Blessing
May the Lord whose love gave us hope when we were hopelessly submerged in the cares of the world clothe us with that same love for the life of the world. Amen.

Readings for Reflection

❧ We are born and we shall all die. The person who is in communion with God wears mortality comfortably. To be with God is to be at home in this world and the next.
—Rueben P. Job

❧ If we are to learn what God promises, and what God fulfills, we must persevere in quiet meditation of the life, teaching, deeds, suffering, and death of Jesus. It is certain that if we live close to Jesus and follow his way, nothing will be impossible for us because all things are possible for God.
—Norman Shawchuck

❧ In John's Gospel, Jesus' High Priestly Prayer (ch. 17) reveals that there are indeed two worlds in which we must learn to live. One is the world both John and Paul understand to be marked by division, confusion, and hostility. The other is the realm of Christ characterized

by reconciliation, understanding, and peace. We are called to live in the first in a manner that reveals that we belong to the second. Specifically, we are sent into the world to show forth the truth of God's kingdom already present in Christ (John 17:16-23). We belong *in* the world, but not *to* it.
—John S. Mogabgab, "Editor's Introduction," *Weavings* (March/April 1987)

ᴥ The Church is in the world to save the world. It is a tool of God for that purpose; not a comfortable religious club established in fine historical premises.
—Evelyn Underhill, *Selections from the Writings of Evelyn Underhill*

ᴥ This is truly the work of God that you are doing. This is Love working in you, with you, through you, as the essence of you—filling the world with wisdom and beauty, delight and compassion. . . .

This work, this "yes" to Love, is not for jesting at all. It is for the life of the world. It is the labor pains in the birthing of the kingdom. It may include generous measures of jesting and pleasure and joy. But it remains the means by which God's kingdom will come to fruition on earth. And until the kingdom is here completely, it is not for the purpose of jesting that we are being invited to do this work. It is for loving. The author of *The Cloud of Unknowing* says of this work: "All of mankind living on earth will be helped by this work in wonderful ways of which [we] are not even aware. . . . For this is a work . . . that man would have continued to do if he had never sinned. And it was for this work that man was made, as all things also were made to help him and further him in this work, so that by means of it man shall be made whole again."
—Jane Marie Thibault, *A Deepening Love Affair*

ᴥ Mystical experiences are not limited to those who have a measure of freedom to choose lives that help foster these experiences. We read accounts of mystical experiences during and after the time of slavery in the United States. These accounts remind us that God seeks out God's people in every circumstance and that God's power is available in conditions of oppression and horror.

In the visions that came to those living in slavery, we see God assuring them of the presence of another landscape, a terrain of hope at hand. This landscape does not merely exist in another place in some distant future; rather, with these visions God offers the possibility of healing and freedom in *this* world, in *this* circumstance, in *this* life, not just for the recipient of the vision but for the community as well.

—Jan L. Richardson, *In the Sanctuary of Women*

When we know we have locked off areas of pain that are not ready for change or healing, Christ's love does not assault us. It is enough for a while to think of loving light quietly shining on our defended areas. It is enough for a while to think of the Christ gently touching the fear and pain hiding there, reaching into our depths for the crying ones who are buried so deep we do not consciously hear their cries. We do not have to go there and look at them ourselves until we feel ready. Deep gifts are also being touched and released in those hidden places. The pain is being transformed into new, undreamed-of powers within us. It is enough for a while just to give consent to the deep, transforming healing that is taking place.

In time, the locks will melt, the doors will be healed, and we will be able to look at the pain we have hidden for so long. We do not have to look by ourselves. The risen Christ looks and understands with us. In time, new power and beauty will come forth from those shadows.

—Flora Slosson Wuellner, *Miracle*

Fourth Sunday of Easter

25. *Creativity*

Affirmation

But now, LORD, you are our father. We are the clay, and you are our potter. All of us are the work of your hand (Isa. 64:8).

Psalm: 8

Psalm Prayer

How majestic are your works, O Lord, that spring forth from your boundless love. From mysterious stars burning silently in the night sky to a passion for the possible that burns steadily in the human heart, your creativity inspires and invites our own creative energies. May the songs we sing and the plans we make honor your plans for us, "planned long ago, faithful and sure" (Isa. 25:1). Amen.

Daily Scripture Readings

Sunday	A.	Acts 2:42-47; Psalm 23; 1 Peter 2:19-25; John 10:1-10
	B.	Acts 4:5-12; Psalm 23; 1 John 3:16-24; John 10:11-18
	C.	Acts 9:36-43; Psalm 23; Revelation 7:9-17; John 10:22-30
Monday		Genesis 1:1-5
Tuesday		Job 26:5-14
Wednesday		Isaiah 45:16-19
Thursday		Luke 1:26-38
Friday		Matthew 28:1-10
Saturday		1 Peter 2:2-9

Silence

Daily Readings for Reflection

Reflection: Silent or Written

Prayers: For the World, for Others, for Myself

Offering of Self to God
Loving Source of all creativity, you have formed us to join you in the work of shaping a world that reflects your design for unity in diversity among all your creatures. I gladly give myself to this great charge and ask that you inspire in me holy creativity greater than I could ask for or even imagine. Amen.

Blessing
We are offspring of the Creative One, whose overflowing love manifests itself in a thousand expressions of beauty. As true sons and daughters, may we receive and live our spiritual heritage with wise-hearted artistry. Amen.

Readings for Reflection

ᨀ Words cannot describe the "knowing" that God is with us and neither can that presence ever be confused or misapprehended when once that visitation comes into one's room. Oh, that I might lay hold of it and live each moment in the realization of this ineffable presence and knowing.

It is in silence and stillness and waiting that God comes. A vacuum is always needed for God to fill—no vacuum, no visitation! We must create a vacuum by creating a time of no-thing and then wait in stillness.

And God is the great vacuum Cleaner. He comes into our momentary vacuum of activity and mental work, and from that place he vacuums clean our hearts, minds, and spirits. He cleans us of the dust, lint, and crust of our lives so that He may enter more crevices of our soul and that we may be more holy and happy in living. We can't clean ourselves—God can. My Lord, Father, everlasting God, you brought me into life and have sustained me to this very moment; your breath, even now in my nostrils, a thread connecting me with

you—and when this thread is broken I shall away to
be forever with you.
—Norman Shawchuck

❧ Let it be
that you will ever
turn yourself Godward.
In clarity
and in confusion,
in distress
and in delight,
may your mind
find its home and its rest
in the One whose thoughts
are ever stayed on you.
—Jan L. Richardson, *In the Sanctuary of Women*

❧ I have a conversation with God when I write or
paint. Sometimes I loudly voice strong opinions as
the Divine Listener allows me to get things off my
chest. Other times, God does the talking and my job
is to listen. When God talks, the part of me that pon-
tificates—my ego-self—eavesdrops on a conversation
between the Divine Creator and my soul. In the face
of such wisdom, my ego-self is rendered speechless;
it can add nothing substantial to the illuminating discourse it hears.

As a pilgrim searching for the place of my own
resurrection, I believe God continuously converses
with my soul-self, the part of me that God has always
intended for me to be. This truest part remains hidden
away, safe in Love's arms, until I am ready to let it shine
through me completely. My soul's conversation with
the Holy One continues in ceaseless communion like
a sonnet spoken by two lovers—though most of the
time I know nothing about it. Only through the gift
of creative expression, in eavesdropping moments of
grace, do I sense a conversation occurring at all. With
a flash of insight I am privy to truth so universal and

simultaneously so intimately personal that it meets my exact need while meeting the needs of the world. The insight I receive in a moment of illumination, imbued with vitality and healing, contains God's truth. In such moments, moisture soaks into the parched places of my life. What was dying regains energy. Whenever I am privileged to overhear a conversation between God and my soul, the art I make conveys more universal meaning than the creative works of my dumbstruck ego. This deeply meaningful art comes wrapped up in the Creator's creativity and blessed into being in ways I could not manage on my own.

Unfortunately, not all my creative endeavors contain divine wisdom; much that I have written and painted has been solely the product of my own ego and its shadow side. Some of it may be considered good art but not great art. The truth contained within these creations distinctively differs from the wisdom that emerges out of my soul's conversation with the Divine Creator; the truth is smaller and less universal. Making ego-centered art feels labor-intensive with no sense of ease or flow about the work. The illuminating moment is absent, and art making becomes like jack-hammering through concrete with a nail file. I think I am allowed to have times like these in order to remember from whom the deeper creativity comes.

—Karla M. Kincannon, *Creativity and Divine Surprise*

&. All Christians need to pray. We are by nature prayers. Prayer is like the air we breathe. Without prayer we quickly become less than what God created us to be. But it is also beneficial for us to grow in prayer. Jesus' disciples acknowledged their need for growth and instruction in this area of their lives. On one occasion when Jesus had spent time in prayer and returned to his followers, the disciples said to him, "Lord, teach us to pray, as John taught his disciples" (Luke 11:1). Jesus responded with what we now call the Lord's Prayer. This model prayer gave those who yearned to cultivate a deeper spirituality a pattern into which they could grow. It is not enough to pray. We need to grow in prayer; otherwise, our human potentialities will remain undiscovered and undeveloped. Prayer creates intimacy with God and reveals to us who we really are.

—Paul Wesley Chilcote, *Changed from Glory into Glory*

❧ The need to rediscover our creativity is more urgent than we might think. When we exile creativity to distant corners of our existence, our ability to perceive the things of God in our life and in the life of the world radically diminishes. Without creativity we are deaf to God's call; what we are to be and do remains a conundrum. The truth of our existence lies in the heart of God, and if we cannot perceive the Divine Presence, we cannot make meaning of our days. Like the pearl of great price in Matthew's Gospel, our creativity is priceless and beyond measure.

Creativity fine-tunes our listening. By focusing our full love and attention on the creativity buried within, we train our awareness to see the Spirit's subtle stirrings over the waters of that which wants to be created in us. As we engage our creativity in the service of our spirituality, we discern the frequency of our soul's yearnings and the deeper currents of life. We hear the cries of our neighbor and know the meaning under the silence. Knitting together the known and the unknown, the seen and the unseen, our creativity helps us make something whole and beautiful out of the pieces of our existence. It reveals to us the truth of our soul in the place of our own resurrection.

—Karla M. Kincannon, *Creativity and Divine Surprise*

❧ Though typically associated only with artists and children, creativity partially reflects the image of God within each of us. It is one strand of our divine DNA. The other strand is love, which is enormously creative. Woven together in a double helix, creativity and love compose the soul's purpose in life while providing the tools to mirror our Creator. They are the means as well as the end of the journey, the path as well as the purpose. We need both on the spiritual path: it takes creativity and love to heal the worst parts of ourselves and to live fully into the best parts. These tools of transformation carry us to union with the divine Creator, the goal of the spiritual life. Whenever we embrace creativity and love, we come closer to embodying the person God intends us to be. Though most of us acknowledge some ability to love, many think we possess no capacity for creativity. In my ministry, I meet individuals who think they lack creativity because they cannot make art; but they can create a satisfying meal from a nearly empty pantry or conduct a business meeting in which opposing constituents work out a compromise. Creativity is so much more than art making. It is a tool for navigating through everyday experiences to find the sacred in the God-given moment. Those who believe they lack creativity have relegated it to remote regions of their life, burying it under the need for security, approval, and control. However, like love, which is stronger than death, creativity does not die; it simply waits to be unearthed and set free.

—Karla M. Kincannon, *Creativity and Divine Surprise*

26. Singleness of Heart

Affirmation
You must love the Lord your God with all your heart,
with all your being, with all your strength, and with all
your mind, and love your neighbor as yourself (Luke
10:27).

Psalm: 26

Psalm Prayer
God of all that is good and just, grant us courage to
walk the path of faith with integrity and wisdom to
rely on you to guide our feet toward the level ground
of vital Christian community. Test us where we think
we are strong, and strengthen us where we know we
are wavering. Above all, create in us pure hearts given
fully to love of your truth. Amen.

Daily Scripture Readings

Sunday	A.	Acts 7:55-60; Psalm 31:1-5, 15-16; 1 Peter 2:2-10; John 14:1-14
	B.	Acts 8:26-40; Psalm 22:25-31; 1 John 4:7-21; John 15:1-8
	C.	Acts 11:1-18; Psalm 148; Revelation 21:1-6; John 13:31-35
Monday		Deuteronomy 10:12-22
Tuesday		1 Chronicles 28:1-10
Wednesday		Jeremiah 29:8-14
Thursday		Luke 18:18-30
Friday		John 15:12-17
Saturday		2 Timothy 4:1-8

Silence

Daily Readings for Reflection

Reflection: Silent or Written

Prayers: For the World, for Others, for Myself

Offering of Self to God
Ever-gracious God, we know that you weave all things together for good when love for you shapes our desires. Gather and cleanse the motivations of our hearts so that they may work in concert with the new creation you have sown among us through your beloved Son, Jesus Christ. Amen.

Blessing
We have been knit together in the womb of God's mercy and birthed anew as brothers and sisters of Jesus Christ. May the tapestry of our lives display ever more clearly the pattern of humanity colored by love of God and textured by love of neighbor. Amen.

Readings for Reflection

❧ Lord, may neither time nor circumstance alter your call to me. Lead me through storm and trial, times of ease and times of difficulty, and grant grace that I may always be faithful to you and to your call. May I go gladly where you send me, even to that task so difficult and unappealing that no one else will go. All I ask is that you go with me and remind me that I am where you have asked me to be. And one more thing, if it is possible, may some good come of my call, not to me, but to your people, your kingdom, and the world you love. Amen.
—Norman Shawchuck

❧ To live the life of prayer means to emerge from my drowse, to awaken to the communing, guiding, healing, clarifying, and transforming current of God's Holy Spirit in which I am immersed. But to awaken is not necessarily to return. Awareness, no matter how vivid, must be accompanied by "a longing aye to dwell within the beauty of his countenance," and until prayer

knows and is the expression of this longing, it is still callow and is likely to melt away at the first sharp thaw.
—Douglas V. Steere, *Dimensions of Prayer*

❧ Do not allow yourself one thought of separating from your brothers and sisters, whether their opinions agree with yours or not. Do not dream that anyone sins in not believing you, in not taking your work; or that this or that opinion is essential to the work, and both must stand or fall together. Beware of any impatience of contradiction. Do not condemn or think harshly of those who cannot see just as you see, or who judge it their duty to contradict you, whether in a great thing or a small. I fear some of us have thought harshly of others merely because they contradicted what we affirmed. All this tends to division; and by everything of this kind we are teaching them an evil lesson against ourselves.
—John Wesley, *A Longing for Holiness*

❧ *That they may be one.* The Lord is going away. In the whole world His cause will be represented by his little handful of disciples. If they fall apart, the cause is lost. What is most of all essential is that they be united. We see in the *Acts of the Apostles* in how many ways the infant Church was tempted to disunity—as for example in the doctrinal difference concerning the authority of the Law for Gentile Christians (Acts 15:1-29) or the personal difference between Paul and Barnabas concerning John Mark (Acts 15:36-41). Such division at that stage would have been fatal; it has been sufficiently disastrous coming later, as it did. So the Lord's prayer was, and (we cannot doubt) still is, that His disciples may be one.

But the unity of the Church is precious not only for its unity in strengthening the Church as an evangelistic agent. It is itself in principle the consummation to which all history moves. The purpose of God in creation was, and is, to fashion a fellowship of free spirits knit together by a love in all its members which answers to the manifested love of God—or, as St. Paul expresses it, to "sum up all things in Christ" (Eph. 1:10 ASV) . . . . The unity of the Church is something much more than unity of ecclesiastical structure, though it cannot be complete without this. It is the love of God in Christ possessing the hearts of men so as to unite them in itself—as the Father and the Son are united in that love of Each for Each which is the Holy Spirit. The unity which the Lord prays that His disciples may enjoy is that which is eternally characteristic of the Triune God. It is therefore something much more than a means to any end—even though that end be the evangelisation of the world; it is itself the one worthy end of all human aspiration; it is the life of heaven. For His prayer is not only *that they may be one;* it is *that they may be one as we.*

—William Temple, *Selections from the Writings of William Temple*

❧ *O Lord Jesus Christ, thou Word and Revelation of Eternal Father, come, we pray thee, take possession of our hearts and reign where thou hast right to reign. So fill our minds with the thought and our imaginations with the picture of thy love, that there may be in us no room for any desire that is discordant with thy holy will. Cleanse us, we pray thee, from all that may make us deaf to thy call or slow to obey it, who, with the Father and the Holy Spirit art one God, blessed for ever. Amen.*

—William Temple, *Selections from the Writings of William Temple*

❧ Great theology evokes great praise. Great praise flows from the deep well of the faith once for all delivered to the saints. In prayers of adoration, we tune our thoughts to what the blessed Triune God has revealed. Such alignment with the One who is true, good, and beautiful sets joy flowing through us. To say all this more simply, we're wired for God. When we plug in to "the grace of God in truth" (Col. 1:6, RSV), the music of adoration sings through our wires. We worship.

—Gerrit Scott Dawson, "Gathering Praise," *Weavings*

❧ Most of us grew up saying prayers, reading prayers, or listening to others praying. Few of us were challenged to *be* prayer. There is a difference between a person who says prayers and a prayerful person. It is the difference between something we do and someone we are.

Do you know someone who *is* a prayer? He or she is probably someone who views life in a different way than most—someone who seems to have found a way to be aware of God's presence in an ongoing way.

We are called as Christian people to be present in each moment in order to experience that God's time and our time have intersected. We are called to practice the presence of God. It is this for which our hearts yearn.

—Ron DelBene, "A Simple Way to Pray," *Weavings*

❧ To know the Creator—not merely to affirm that there is one, but to *know* the Creator who truly is—is joy and enchantment and peace. Once we have encountered this Creator, we will always (no matter how often we forget or how determinedly we ignore the experience) have a recollection of who we truly are, what we truly owe, and how glad the knowledge of this obligation makes us. Returning to this knowledge after a long absence or on a daily or an hourly basis, reacquaints us with this gladness, with the depth of love that echoes between our inmost selves and the Self who made the universe.

—David Rensberger, "Adoring the Creator," *Weavings*

27. For the Life of the World

Affirmation
But I have sure faith that I will experience the LORD's goodness in the land of the living! (Ps. 27:13).

Psalm: 146

Psalm Prayer
God of our best hopes, you keep watch over all that you have created to nourish it with the vitality of your loving care. Where human intentions go astray, your faithfulness shows us the way to life in abundance. Where human institutions falter, your kingdom endures forever. You regard with kindness all who are lost, ill, oppressed, disregarded, or trodden down by any form of adversity. And in Jesus Christ, you became one with us in suffering so that we might become one with you in commitment to the life of the world. Therefore it is right that we should praise you with our whole being. Amen.

Daily Scripture Readings

Sunday	A.	Acts 17:22-31; Psalm 66:8-20; 1 Peter 3:13-22; John 14:15-21
	B.	Acts 10:44-48; Psalm 98; 1 John 5:1-6; John 15:9-17
	C.	Acts 16:9-15; Psalm 67; Revelation 21:10, 22–22:5; John 14:23-29
Monday		Exodus 16:1-15
Tuesday		Deuteronomy 5:1-22
Wednesday		Jeremiah 31:1-13
Thursday		Mark 1:35-39
Friday		John 6:48-51
Saturday		1 John 4:9-12

Silence

Daily Readings for Reflection

Reflection: Silent or Written

Prayers: For the World, for Others, for Myself

Offering of Self to God
May the words of our mouths and the thoughts that guide our actions be in accord with your continuous and costly commitment to justice, peace, and health in the world you love so much. In the name of your beloved Son, Jesus Christ, the bread of heaven who gives life to the world. Amen.

Blessing
May the Lord and giver of life create in us a desire to be servants of love for the life of the world. Amen.

Readings for Reflection

❧ Have you ever been extremely thirsty? If you have experienced deep thirst, you know how wonderful and refreshing cool water can be. We can live for many days without food but only a short time without water. When the Samaritan woman encountered Jesus at Jacob's well, she was searching for that which would quench her body's thirst for life-giving and life-sustaining water. In the presence of Jesus she recognized a deeper thirst, the thirst for God. And it was to this thirst that Jesus offered living water and the promise that her thirst for God could be satisfied.

The thirst for God is universal because we have been created with a longing for the Creator. This desire to know and be known by the One who made us and loves us is often ignored, denied, and finally buried under a multitude of pursuits and interests. But then some event in life invites or forces us to pause, and the desire for God comes rushing back to our awareness. And once again we know that real life is impossible without the companionship of the One who first gave us the gift of life and who sustains us even now. We know for certain that we need living water; we need what only God can give if we are really to live.

Today Jesus continues to offer living water, a way, and a companionship that can quench our thirst for God. Our part is to recognize the deep need for God within us and to offer hospitality to the One who seeks to fill and satisfy that need. Like the psalmist, our souls thirst for God. The good news we share is that through Jesus Christ our thirst can be satisfied.
—Rueben P. Job

❧ Spirituality is a growing awareness of our receptivity of the spirit of God in our lives, and the means by which we can keep that receptivity alive and vital as we are formed into the image and nature of Jesus. Now we are able to serve others even as Jesus offered himself as servant to all. This is Jesus' spirituality, and it is his gift to all who bind their lives to him.
—Norman Shawchuck

❧ He who knows and understands Christ's life, knows and understands Christ Himself; and in like manner, he who understands not His life, does not understand Christ Himself. And he who believes on Christ believes that His life is the best and noblest life that can be, and if a man believe not this, neither does he believe on Christ Himself. And in so far as a man's life is according to Christ, Christ Himself dwells in him, and if he has not the one neither has he the other. For where there is the life of Christ, there is Christ Himself, and where His life is not, Christ is not, and where a man has His life, he may say with St. Paul, "I live; yet not I, but Christ liveth in me (KJV)." And this is the noblest and best life; for in him who has it God Himself dwells with all goodness. So how could there be a better life? When we speak of obedience, of the new man, of the true Light, the true Love, or the life of Christ, it is all

the same thing; where one of these is, there are they all, and where one is wanting, there is none of them, for they are all one in truth and substance. And whatever may bring about that new birth which makes alive in Christ, to that let us cleave with all our might and to nothing else; and let us forswear and flee all that may hinder it. And he who has received this life in the Holy Sacrament, has verily and indeed received Christ, and the more of that life he has received, the more he has received of Christ, and the less, the less of Christ.
—*Theologia Germanica*

❧ We are the agents of the Creative Spirit in this world. Real advance in the spiritual life, then, means accepting this vocation with all it involves. Not merely turning over the pages of an engineering magazine and enjoying the pictures, but putting on overalls and getting on with the job. The real spiritual life must be horizontal as well as vertical; spread more and more as well as aspire more and more. It must be larger, fuller, richer, more generous in its interests than the natural life alone can ever be; it must invade and transform all homely activities and practical things. For it means an offering of life to the God of life, to whom it belongs; a willingness—an eager willingness—to take our small place in the vast operations of God's Spirit instead of trying to run a poky little business on our own.
—Evelyn Underhill, *The Soul's Delight*

❧ If repentance requires our turning around and changing direction, clearly the divine expectation is to follow Christ, to respond to his call, and to throw our lot in with him. As the early disciples did, so must we. We are not an especially gifted people, either with wealth or power or influence. Jesus' first disciples certainly were not. Jesus called them from the ordinariness of their lives as fishermen so that, by giving themselves to him, he could do something extraordinary with them.

Current times are no different. God in Christ calls us from the ordinariness of our lives, expecting to do something extraordinary with us. We must actively participate so the light of the world may overcome life's darkness. The world may perceive that there is no greater fool than God who expects to win the world with weaklings like ourselves. Yet that has been God's curious way as revealed in Jesus Christ, a carpenter in a workshop, a peasant teacher putting God's mind into the many to make them fish for people. "And I," said Jesus, "when I am lifted up from the earth, will draw all people to myself" (John 12:32).

So it is. Jesus calls; we respond. Jesus chooses us; we choose him and say with Paul, "I belong to Christ." We lift Christ up when we help remove the sting of shame or abuse or prejudice inflicted upon people, and they retain their human dignity and sense of worth. We lift him up when we side with the outcast or the lonely, overcoming boundaries that divide people from one another. Belonging to Christ is not a matter of feeling warm and fuzzy; it is a way of living and acting as Christ-called people. So be it.

—Bonifacio B. Mequi Jr., "Faith in the Balance," *The Upper Room Disciplines 1999*

❧ In his prayer, Jesus cites a specific purpose for the relationship of loving union with God. He notes a vital intention for being restored in the glory of God: "that the world might believe that you sent me" (John 17:21, AT) and "that the world might know that you sent me" (John 17:23, AT). The world will not believe and know that God sent Jesus because our theology is true, our doctrine correct, and our liturgy proper. The world will know and believe *when it sees Jesus in us*.

The Word becomes flesh *in* us so that God's transforming love might touch a broken and hurting world *through* us. We are to be those in whom God's life touches people enmeshed in the deadly illusions of the world; those in whom God's light illumines the darkness of persons blinded by the world's false values; those through whom God's healing touches the wounds of people crippled by the corrosive lifestyle of the world; those in whom God's wholeness touches persons broken in body, mind, or spirit by the pernicious perspectives of the world; those through whom God's cleansing touches people stained by sin; those through whom God's liberating grace frees people held in the bondage of dehumanizing attitudes, habits, and addictions; those through whom God's transforming love challenges social, cultural, political, and economic systems that disfigure human communities.

—M. Robert Mulholland Jr. and Marjorie J. Thompson,
The Way of Scripture

❧ Were you to ask what prayer at the heart of the spiritual journey looked like, I would say that prayer is, or at least begins with, the human hunger for companionship. It is, on a deeper level than anticipated, the answer to our need for intimacy and friendship. Like all relationships, this one with God begins with curiosity: the ability to consider this, to think about that, to collect data (usually from the scripture), and to analyze the person of Jesus of Nazareth. In our best relationships curiosity eventually gives way to wonder, and wonder is a necessary ingredient in the composition of prayer. Wonder enables us to let the great mysteries of Christ's life dwell within us. The flow of prayer seems to demand that God direct us, form us, mold and inspire us. This is what we allow to happen when we take our eyes from ourselves and turn them to God, who then becomes the center of our loving attention. And in this process of God's becoming the center of our lives, it becomes possible for us to become what we love.

—Doris Donnelly, "Is the Spiritual Life for Everyone?"
Weavings

28. The Things That Make for Peace

Affirmation

Because of our God's deep compassion, the dawn from heaven will break upon us, to give light to those who are sitting in darkness and in the shadow of death, to guide us on the path of peace (Luke 1:78-79).

Psalm: 85

Psalm Prayer

Ever-patient God, you have indeed been kind to us. Your forgiveness opens the way to a new future, your goodness brightens our days, and your truth shows us the things that make for peace. Thank you that in Jesus Christ your salvation has come near to us, for he is the peace that heals our wounded world. Amen.

Daily Scripture Readings

Sunday	A.	Acts 1:6-14; Psalm 68:1-10, 32-35; 1 Peter 4:12-14, 5:6-11; John 17:1-11
	B.	Acts 1:15-17, 21-26; Psalm 1; 1 John 5:9-13; John 17:6-19
	C.	Acts 16:16-34; Psalm 97; Revelation 22:12-14, 16-17, 20-21; John 17:20-26
Monday		Deuteronomy 30:15-20
Tuesday		Psalm 34:11-13
Wednesday		Micah 6:1-8
Thursday		Matthew 5:38-42
Friday		John 14:21-27
Saturday		Ephesians 2:11-22

Silence

Daily Readings for Reflection

Reflection: Silent or Written

Prayers: For the World, for Others, for Myself

Offering of Self to God
We desire to receive the peace that Jesus offers all his disciples. Faithful God, help us to overcome fear, anger, envy, and all other states of mind and heart that stand as obstacles to our maturing into ambassadors of your peaceable kingdom. Amen.

Blessing
Let the LORD give strength to his people! Let the LORD bless his people with peace! (Ps. 29:11). Amen.

Readings for Reflection

 There are those times in our lives when nothing seems to go as we planned. Times when day after day we are faced with difficulties and darkness no matter how much we long for lighter loads and light for our pathway. There are other times when we come from a spectacular high moment and suddenly find ourselves hanging on to hope by our fingernails. While such a situation can be distressing, it is good to remember that we are not the first to experience darkness, difficulty, or disappointing surprises in the midst of faithful and sunny days.

Chapter 6 in Mark's Gospel reports the rejection Jesus encountered in his hometown, the first missionary venture of the Twelve, the death of John the Baptist, feeding the five thousand, Jesus' walking on the water, and the healing in Gennesaret. In this one chapter we are confronted with the widest range of human emotion and experience, great miracles as well as great disappointment.

Our lives may be a bit steadier and the peaks and valleys a little more subdued than what Jesus and the Twelve experienced. However, we do live through those periods when nothing seems to go our way, when the winds of life seem to be against us, when we are working hard but getting nowhere. So it was with the disciples as they strained at the oars against an adverse wind. Then Jesus appeared to them and uttered the words we all want to hear in the terror of our personal storm: "Take heart, it is I; do not be afraid" (Mark 6:50). The storm was over the moment Jesus was recognized by the disciples, and soon the men found themselves at their destination.

One of the best times for us to cultivate the nearness of God emerges when nothing is going our way. Such an experience may sharpen our ability to see God at work in our midst and in our lives. Remember that we are not alone when things are not going our way, as we are not alone when things are going our way. Each situation gives us opportunity to pay attention to God's presence and call for God's help.
—Rueben P. Job

☙ Concern for peace lies at the very heart of biblical tradition. Peace is the great promise and hope of the Hebrew scriptures. The New Testament offers a number of images that express the fulfillment of this promise and hope in Jesus Christ: to be born again from above through the Spirit (John 3), to live according to the Spirit instead of according to the flesh (Rom. 7), to move from slavery to freedom (Gal. 5), from hostility to reconciliation (Rom. 5), from darkness to light (1 Pet. 2), from death to life (Rom. 6).

The theme of peace, therefore, points to the center of the gospel of Jesus Christ, which Paul expressed with typical directness: "He is the peace between us" (Eph. 2:14, JB). Paul perceived that Christ's death on the cross had inaugurated the reign of God's peace for which Israel had waited so long. The spell of religious and political antagonism that divided the world between Jews and Gentiles had been broken. In its place, embodied in Jesus Christ and visible in those who gathered in his name, was a new humanity united in community and reconciled with God. For this reason, Paul was convinced that practicing the art of peace was essential to the meaning of the church: "May the peace of Christ reign in your hearts, because it is for this that you were called together as parts of one body" (Col. 3:15, JB).

When strangers greet one another in the name of Jesus, when enemies embrace because of Jesus, when congregations seek truth in remembrance of Jesus, then the peace of Christ is reigning in human hearts. Diversity then ceases to divide and instead begins to enrich a deeper unity in Jesus Christ. So fundamental and comprehensive is this unity that Paul could say, "There is neither Jew nor Greek, there is neither slave nor free, there is neither male nor female; for you are all one in Christ Jesus" (Gal. 3:28, RSV).

—John S. Mogabgab, "Editor's Introduction," *Weavings* (March/April 1988)

   All desire peace, but they do not care for the things that pertain to true peace.

     A peaceable man doth more good than he that is well learned.

     Peace consisteth rather in true humility, than in self-exaltation.

A good and peaceable man turneth all things to good. He that is in peace is not suspicious of any. But he that is discontented and troubled is tossed with divers suspicions: he is neither quiet himself, nor suffereth others to be quiet. He often speaketh that which he ought not to speak; and leaveth undone that which it were more expedient for him to do. He considereth what others are bound to do, and neglecteth that which he is bound to do himself.

O how good is it, and how it tendeth to peace, to be silent about other men, and not to believe at random all that is said, nor eagerly to report what we have heard. How good it is to lay one's self open to few, and always to be seeking after thee who art the searcher of the heart. Nor should we be carried about with every wind of words, but we should desire that all things both within and without, be accomplished according to the pleasure of thy will.

—Thomas à Kempis, *The Imitation of Christ*

Think not therefore that thou hast found true peace, if thou feel no heaviness; nor that all is well, when thou art vexed with no adversary; nor that all is perfect, if all things be done according to thy desire. Neither do thou think at all highly of thyself, nor account thyself to be specially beloved, if thou be in a state of great devotion and sweetness; for it is not by these things that a true lover of virtue is known, nor doth the spiritual progress and perfection of a man consist in these things. Wherein then, O Lord, doth it consist: In giving thyself up with all thy heart to the divine will, not seeking thine own interest, either in great matters or in small, either in time or in eternity. So shalt thou keep one and the same countenance, always giving thanks both in prosperity and adversity, weighing all things in an equal balance.

—Thomas à Kempis, *The Imitation of Christ*

He that gives alms to the poor takes Jesus by the hand; he that patiently endures injuries and affronts, helps him to bear his cross; he that comforts his brother in affliction, gives an amiable kiss of peace to Jesus; he that bathes his own and his neighbor's sins in tears of penance and compassion, washes his Master's feet. We lead Jesus into the recesses of our heart by holy meditations; and we enter into his holy heart when we express him in our actions.

—Jeremy Taylor, *Selections from the Writings of Jeremy Taylor*

❧ As people of peace who live in the house of love, we need to resist our culture's fascination with violence, might, and death. Video games, TV shows, and movies are filled with images of combat and destruction. Some have suggested a new discipline of fasting from the violent images in entertainment as a method of noncooperation with evil. . . .

God speaks the language of love and affirms life. In your prayer, ask God to show you where to resist the world's fascination with violence and death. Ask God to guide you in living with love and peace.
—Larry James Peacock, *Openings*

  Peacemaking must not be reduced to recruitment for and prosecution of particular political perspectives on specific issues. How many well-intentioned, often zealous peacemakers have taken one step forward and three steps backward by equating a commitment to peacemaking with voting in a particular way on a referendum.
—Jim Antal, "Peacemaking in the Congregation," *Weavings*

  Where there is charity and wisdom there is neither fear nor ignorance. Where there is patience and humility there is neither anger nor worry. Where there is poverty and joy there is neither cupidity nor avarice. Where there is quiet and meditation there is neither solicitude nor dissipation. Where there is the fear of the Lord to guard the house the enemy cannot find a way to enter. Where there is mercy and discretion there is neither superfluity nor hard-heartedness.
—Francis of Assisi, *Selections from the Writings of St. Francis of Assisi*

  In my experience, grace always appears in the profound return to the center of one's self, and often occurs in pain as well as in relief. Gratitude is a deep part of grace, but grace is an even more encompassing current in the flow of life. Long ago, while pastoring in the Northeast, I gave up on the notion of grace as rescue or grace as the God version of the knight suddenly riding in on the white horse to save the princess. Instead, I came to know grace as the ingredient of welcome in the midst of exile. Grace, I realized, is the substance of love, forgiveness, and hope, or one might say the molecular structure of all that returns us to the center of our selves in affirmation and resurrection power. Resurrection power is what creates and recreates the essence of our selves as testimony in the universe to God's unique fingerprint in every living thing. Indestructible and filled with light, we see the face of Jesus in all the faces of those who claim this energy.

—Mary L. Fraser, "Grace," *Weavings*

The Day of Pentecost

The day of Pentecost marks the descent of the Holy Spirit and reveals to the followers of Jesus that everyone can now know God's presence everywhere and at all times. Pentecost comes after Easter on the church calendar because historically Pentecost followed the experience of the risen Christ. Pentecost transformed the defeated followers of Jesus into courageous, fearless, bold, and eloquent witnesses through the power of the Holy Spirit.

The second chapter of Acts gives a firsthand account of the amazing transformation of ordinary people into extraordinary witnesses in what has come to be known as "the day of Pentecost." The following chapters of Acts report the results of this face-to-face experience of God's presence and grace. A frightened gathering of disciples became a thriving, learning, growing, sharing, and winsome community. Observers were drawn to them. Each day more people chose to join them in the new and diverse community given to a life of loving and serving both God and their neighbors. Wonders and signs of God's activity were plentiful. Awe and amazement continued to encourage these dissimilar people, drawing them into a unified and life-giving community.

Today we too wait in expectation that wind and fire from God will sweep across church and world to usher in a new day of unity, peace, justice, compassion, love, and faithfulness. Now and then we do see signs of God moving among us—those of us who offer ourselves without reservation as holy vessels to be called, sent, and used by the God of love. This is our God who sent Jesus Christ and the Holy Spirit to enable each of us to live as beloved children and to be part of God's beloved family.

Today we celebrate the fulfillment of the angel's promise to Joseph and Mary that she would give birth to a son whose name, Emmanuel, means *God with us*.

Our fear of the present and future is erased as we invite God's presence not only to guide and direct, teach and lead, protect and defend us but also to dwell within us and be our constant and redeeming companion for all time.

29. Power from On High

Affirmation

The one who is high and lifted up, who lives forever, whose name is holy, says: I live on high, in holiness, and also with the crushed and the lowly, reviving the spirit of the lowly, reviving the heart of those who have been crushed (Isa. 57:15).

Psalm: 91

Psalm Prayer

Almighty God, we desire to take our refuge in you. Keep us from the snares of the world and protect us. Give us faith to trust you like the psalmist, who knew of your saving help. We thank you for the witness of those who have gone before us in the knowledge that you were their protector. May we sense that same feeling of security in you. Amen.

Daily Scripture Readings

Sunday	A.	Acts 2:1-21; Psalm 104:24-34, 35*b*; 1 Corinthians 12:3*b*-13; John 20:19-23
	B.	Acts 2:1-21; Psalm 104:24-34, 35*b*; Romans 8:22-27; John 15:26-27; 16:4*b*-15
	C.	Acts 2:1-21; Psalm 104:24-34, 35*b*; Romans 8:14-17; John 14:8-17
Monday		Exodus 2:15-25
Tuesday		2 Kings 2:1-22
Wednesday		Micah 3
Thursday		Psalm 68:28-35
Friday		Luke 24:36-53
Saturday		Ephesians 3:14-21

Silence

Daily Readings for Reflection

Reflection: Silent or Written

Prayers: For the World, for Others, for Myself

Offering of Self to God
Holy God, we desire to show your loving power to the world. Draw us nearer to you, and fill us with your Holy Spirit so that we might shine with your love. Amen.

Blessing
May we be empowered this day to embody God's love and justice. Amen.

Readings for Reflection

❧ What are you planning to do that you cannot achieve without help from beyond yourself? What is God calling you to be and do that requires God's intervention? These questions move us quickly to the realization that we often live our lives on the easy path of the least faith and effort. To observe the church is to see that we are not alone in choosing the easy path. Yet we know there is a better way and a higher calling for us as individuals, as congregations, and as denominations.

The early disciples were told to wait upon God until the power came. They waited and the power did come. The book of Acts is a brief record of how the early church carried on its life and ministry with power from beyond itself. The record of individuals and Christian movements that have transformed the world within and around them testifies to the capacity to receive power from beyond to fulfill their calling. This power was given to ordinary people who were called to live in an extraordinary way. Could that be your calling today?
—Rueben P. Job

❧ The scripture reading for today said, "You may ask me for anything in my name and I will do it" (John 14:14, NIV). I am sure I do not fully understand this passage. Does God give only that which will make God known? Are there really no limits to my asking? At first this seemed too much to understand. Then as I reflected upon this passage and my life, the truth became clear to me. God made known in Jesus has given me everything I have ever asked for. Simply stated, God has left no request unanswered. Perhaps it is the simplicity of this statement that I do not understand, not its complexity. God has been so very generous to me and to my family. I have come to rely upon the truth that God will act generously to me and to all who seek his face. God's loving care has been remarkably predictable, even those times when I was totally unaware of that love and care.

—Norman Shawchuck

❧ "You are the light of the world" (Matt. 5:14). How bewildering this bold assertion must have been to the band of followers who heard Jesus speak that day on a mountain far removed from the magnificence and power of imperial Rome. From the Eternal City peace and prosperity had spread like dawn across the Middle East and Europe. Yet Jesus, facing his disciples, could already see them enveloped in a power so formidable that in comparison the luminous achievements of Rome flickered like a mere candle. He knew that the power of God, the "power from on high" he promised to his adherents (Luke 24:49), accomplishes what no other power on earth can do. Through those who receive it, God's power offers light to the world, a world swathed in the turbulent gloom of contending lesser powers.

   Still more bewildering is the Christian conviction that God's power flows from the cross of Christ. Yet there, on a dead tree planted in a barren hill, the fury of every destructive power foundered on the power of God's unquenchable love for us. In the unimagined depths of creation spiritual tectonic plates groaned and shifted, reconfiguring the foundations of human existence. If the crucified man Jesus is a horrifying image of our inability to save ourselves from the crushing weight of powers and principalities, the risen Lord Jesus is the resplendent reality of a new humanity suffused with the light of God's good purpose.

The reservoir from which we receive God's world-illuminating power is intimate companionship with the crucified and risen Lord, whose presence is mediated by the Holy Spirit. From this inexhaustible reservoir flows the spiritual authority of the martyrs. An early letter from the persecuted church in Smyrna reports, "The noble martyrs of Christ attained such towering strength of soul that not one of them uttered a cry or groan. They proved to all of us that in the hour of their torture they were free of the body, or rather that the Lord himself stood by them and talked with them" (*The Early Christians in Their Own Words*). Indeed, so close is this companionship with Jesus that to render it appropriately Paul must say, "I have been crucified with Christ; and it is no longer I who live, but it is Christ who lives in me" (Gal. 2:19-20).

—John S. Mogabgab, "Editor's Introduction," *Weavings* (May/June 1999)

✍ After Jesus told his followers all that they would one day do in his name, he gave them a single piece of counsel. They were to continue in Jerusalem until clothed with power from on high (Luke 24:49). This was it. Hold. Stay put. Wait on the power. Nothing more. And absolutely nothing less. In the midst of a people who did talk about spiritual things, they were actually, and single-mindedly, to wait on the Spirit.

—Stephen V. Doughty, "Why Are They, Well, So . . . ?!", *Weavings*

❧ Intercessory prayers often go hand in hand with action to address problems. In times of injustice and social oppression, when the gap between the rich and the poor widens, prayers of intercession for change become linked with letter-writing campaigns, marches and sit-ins, and the creation of alternative models.

Today lift up to God a situation of pain or hurt in the world. Pray for leaders who could make a difference. Pray for people who are hurt, oppressed, and ignored. Pray for those whose actions contribute to the pain. Pray for the church to involve itself as an agent of change, a voice of reconciliation, and a partner in healing.

—Larry James Peacock, *Openings*

❧ God's power, love power, works in any human vulnerability. That perspective is one that many in our age and culture have difficulty understanding. We know a lot about power. Some say that our culture is obsessed with power. We want more power to run bigger electric generators so that we can have more comforts and conveniences or more power to put up bigger payloads into space to terrify our enemies so they will not dare to threaten us. But our power logic, Paul would point out, is not God's power logic. Our power logic runs, "The weak are weak. The strong are strong. In weakness is weakness. In strength is strength." God's power logic runs, "In your human weakness you may find my power."

—E. Glenn Hinson, *Spiritual Preparation for Christian Leadership*

❧ When we anchor our hope in God's steady love and good plans for us, hope becomes a permanent part of us. We have hope not because we are powerful or smart or resourceful but because of who God is.

—Mary Lou Redding, *While We Wait*

The Season after Pentecost/Ordinary Time

The season after Pentecost is the least structured season of the Christian year. It continues to remind us of the central truth of the gospel. This is made abundantly clear by the fact that the season begins with Trinity Sunday and ends with Reign of Christ Sunday.

However, each Sunday has its distinct message shaped by the lectionary readings of the day. The Gospel readings focus on teachings about the kingdom of God and also include the social concerns present in the epistle and Old Testament readings of the season.

The season after Pentecost is a time for Christians to reflect deeply on the meaning of God's kingdom as they seek to live as faithful followers of Jesus Christ. But the call and demand of the scriptures of the season ask for much more than reflection. Clearly, this season of the year calls for a faithful response to the gospel, a response that goes beyond reflection and takes the believer where Jesus has gone before. The faithful find themselves being led to humanity's wounds, where Jesus is already at work welcoming, loving, and healing the lost.

The season after Pentecost invites us to recall Jesus' words, "Healthy people don't need a doctor, but sick people do" (Mark 2:17). It also calls to mind that as Christians we are the Body of Christ and are sent to offer Christ's loving presence, redemption, healing, companionship, and hope to the wounded of the world.

This is an overwhelming calling. We cannot do it on our own. But we remember Pentecost and that the promise of *God with us* has been fulfilled. We then find courage, insight, wisdom, strength, grace, and God's loving presence to guide and uphold us as we say yes to the call of God. So we continue our faithful and joyful walk with the ever-present One to comfort, guide, and sustain us.

Trinity Sunday: First Sunday after Pentecost

Trinity Sunday is the first Sunday of the season of Pentecost. The day of Pentecost revealed the Holy Spirit at work with the early Christian community, demonstrating the intimacy of our relationship with God. It was the presence of God the Holy Spirit that breathed life and power into the first Christians and the newly born Christian church. Jesus had promised the Holy Spirit as guide, comforter, sustainer, and teacher who would reveal everything these early disciples and the church needed to know (John 14:25-26). Thankfully this promise holds true today for the church and for individual Christians.

It is appropriate that Trinity Sunday follows Pentecost Sunday as the church seeks to understand more fully the mystery and magnificence of the God of love made known by Jesus Christ. The triune God, who is forever beyond our comprehension, will always remain a mystery. Nevertheless, the Holy Spirit discloses to the church, to disciples of Jesus, and to every seeker in search of a relationship with God the truth that God is Father, Son, and Holy Spirit.

The simple confessions to God in the New Testament offer further revelation of the God known most clearly in the life, death, and resurrection of Jesus. Early Christians and the young church clung to such texts as John 14:15-16 ("If you love me, you will keep my commandments. I will ask the Father, and he will send another Companion, who will be with you forever") and John 14:21 ("Whoever has my commandments and keeps them loves me. Whoever loves me will be loved by my Father, and I will love them and reveal myself to them").

The church later formulated creeds to carry the holy mystery of the triune God for all to see, hear, and confess. These creeds were defined and refined during vigorous debate and examination of Old and New Testament texts. The two most common confessions of faith, the Apostle's and the Nicene Creeds, attempted to bring light and understanding to those who sought to follow Jesus. The Nicene Creed is the most explicit in its definition of the triune God and continues to be widely used.

Perhaps it is time again to take seriously the beautiful revelation of God in three Persons given us in biblical texts, creeds, and Christian experience. Today, we seek a way of faithfulness for ourselves and for all who desire to walk the path of life in the company of our promised divine Companion. That life-giving path will be made known to us as we respond to the Spirit's invitation and assistance. In the good company of the Holy Spirit, may we be led to an ever-deepening relationship with this magnificent God of love.

Trinity Sunday: First Sunday after Pentecost

30. The Freedom of the Christian

Affirmation
The Lord is the Spirit, and where the Lord's Spirit is, there is freedom (2 Cor. 3:17).

Psalm: 40

Psalm Prayer
O Lord, you have delivered us from trouble when we were on the cusp of destruction. Embrace us, and give us your secure freedom. Make us ready to tell of your goodness and receive your gifts. In you, we rejoice. Amen.

Daily Scripture Readings

Sunday	A.	Genesis 1:1-2:4*a*; Psalm 8; 2 Corinthians 13:11-13; Matthew 28:16-20	
	B.	Isaiah 6:1-8; Psalm 29; Romans 8:12-17; John 3:1-17	
	C.	Proverbs 8:1-4, 22-31; Psalm 8; Romans 5:1-5; John 16:12-15	
Monday		Daniel 3:8-18	
Tuesday		Psalm 32	
Wednesday		John 10:1-18	
Thursday		1 Corinthians 10:14-33	
Friday		Galatians 5:1-15	
Saturday		1 Peter 2:9-25	

Silence

Daily Readings for Reflection

Reflection: Silent or Written

Prayers: For the World, for Others, for Myself

Offering of Self to God
This day, we want to embrace your loving freedom, O God, knowing that only in your freedom can we find an abundant life. Empower us to be slow in casting judgment but quick in loving. Amen.

Blessing
May we love and serve the Lord and those around us in peaceful freedom. Amen.

Readings for Reflection

❧ God is near to us, loves us, and awakens our love for God. Today I give thanks for God's call and assignment to duty. I have been led to great challenge and diversity, but always I have been sustained. God never fails or disappoints and is always faithful, even when I foolishly forget my call and my constant companion. God's presence is indefinable but unmistakable. Today I give thanks for that holy and sustaining Presence within my life and within all of creation.
—Norman Shawchuck

❧ We live in a world convinced that security is the most reliable context for freedom. The bitter irony of this conviction is that the havens of security we create are unable to provide the freedom we seek. The quest for national, economic, or personal security too often generates compulsive patterns of life at the expense of genuine freedom. Christian tradition offers an alternative. In biblical perspective, it is obedience rather than security that forms the proper context for freedom. Thus, the Christian vision of freedom is focused through the lens of a paradox: "Whoever cares for his own safety is lost; but if a man will let himself be lost for my sake, he will find his true self" (Matt. 16:25, NEB).
—John S. Mogabgab, "Editor's Introduction," *Weavings* (May/June 1988)

❧ Freedom is, at its roots, not about options. At least in the Christian context, freedom is about love, what we love, how we love. Multiplicity of choices might in fact hinder love from having the context, the time, the room, the struggle requisite for growth and deepening. We forget sometimes that the Paschal mystery, dying in order to allow new life to emerge, is fundamental to all of creation, including human beings. We may rightly want to live as expansively as possible, but in fact, we are limited, we can't have it all, we have to close some doors. To focus our energies, to suffer imperfection, to work things out, to wait out a storm—all these are essential ingredients in commitments that last. My own experience and that of partners in marriages that work leads me to believe that authentic freedom, as well as love and joy and peace, can be the fruit of freely chosen constraint. We need, I think, to be a bit suspicious of our culture's infatuation with options.

—Roberta L. Bondi, "Practicing: A Second Flute," *Weavings*

❧ It appears to me that great freedom and great exactness should be united. Exactness makes us faithful, and freedom makes us courageous. If you are very strict without being free, you will become servile and scrupulous. If you are free without being strict, you become negligent and careless. Those who have little experience of the ways of God think they cannot unite these two virtues. They understand, by *being exact*, living in constraint, in sorrow, in a timid and scrupulous unquietness that destroys the repose of the soul; that finds sin in everything, and that is so narrow-minded that it questions about the merest trifles, and dares hardly to breathe. They define *being free*, having an easy conscience, not regarding small things, and to be content with avoiding great faults, and not considering any but gross crimes as faults, and saving these, allowing whatever flatters self-love, and any license to the passions that does not produce what they call great evil.

It was not thus that St. Paul understood things when he said to those whom he endeavored to make Christians: "Be free, but with the liberty that Jesus Christ has given you. Be free, for the Savior has called you to liberty; but let not this liberty be an occasion or pretext for evil."

—Francois Fenelon, *Selections from the Writings of Francois Fenelon*

⁂ In man God creates his image on earth. This means that man is like the Creator in that he is free. Actually he is free only by God's creation, by means of the Word of God; he is free for the worship of the Creator. In the language of the Bible, freedom is not something man has for himself but something he has for others. No man is free "as such," that is, in a vacuum, in the way that he may be musical, intelligent or blind as such. Freedom is not a quality of man, nor is it an ability, a capacity, a kind of being that somehow flares up in him. Anyone investigating man to discover freedom finds nothing of it. Why? Because freedom is not a quality which can be revealed—it is not a possession, a presence, an object, nor is it a form for existence—but a relationship and nothing else. In truth, freedom is a relationship between two persons. Being free means "being free for the other," because the other has bound me to him. Only in relationship with the other am I free.

—Dietrich Bonhoeffer, *Selections from the Writings of Dietrich Bonhoeffer*

⁂ The God we worship not only fixed the borders of the sea and rested on the Sabbath but also voluntarily chose the confines of the flesh so that every one of its limitations might become the dwelling place and doorway to abundant life. The Infinite was confined in swaddling clothes and subjected to the same path of bridling and taming the wilderness of desire as we are.

His Way is one of disciplined body and soul, of desire restrained only so it may find its deeper and more life-giving goal. This Way opens our souls to grow into the likeness of the Love and Justice, the Courage and Patience, the Wisdom and Radiance in whose image we are made. Such love, in the end, learns to desire only the Good, and is free from hindrance to choose it.

—Robert Corin Morris, "This Far and No Farther," *Weavings*

ᏍᎭ Resurrection goes far beyond simply life after this life; it is life here and now; life not shaped, limited, or destroyed by the awesome powers of death. In spite of all that appears to be true, in spite of all who say they are in control, in spite of all the powers that be and their attempts to define who we are and how we live, Jesus Christ risen means we have been set free!

—Janet Wolf, "Chosen For . . . ," *The Upper Room Disciplines 1999*

ᏍᎭ It appears to me that true fidelity consists in obeying God in everything and following the light that points out our duty, and His spirit that prompts us to do it; with the desire of pleasing Him, without debating about great or little sins, about imperfections or unfaithfulness; for though there may be a difference in fact, to the soul that is determined to do *all* His will there is none. It is in this sense that the Apostle says that the law is not for the upright; the law constrains, menaces, if I may so speak, tyrannizes over us, enslaves us. But there is a superior law that raises us above all this, and introduces us into the true liberty of the children of God. This ever desires to do all that it can to please its Father in heaven, according to the excellent instructions of St. Augustine. Love God and then do all you can. To this sincere desire to do the will of God we must add a cheerful spirit that is not overcome when it has failed, but begins again and again to do better; hoping always to the very end to be able to do it; bearing with its own involuntary weakness, as God bears with it; waiting with patience for the moment when it shall be delivered from it; going straight on in singleness of heart, according to the strength that it can command; losing no time by looking back, nor making useless reflections upon its falls, which can only embarrass and retard its progress. The first sight of our little failures should humble us, but then we must press on, not judging ourselves with a Judaical rigor, not regarding God as a spy who watches for our least offence, or as an enemy who places snares in our path, but as a father who loves and wishes to save us; trusting in His goodness, invoking His blessing, and doubting all other support; this is true liberty.

—Francois Fenelon, *Selections from the Writings of Francois Fenelon*

❧ The signs are unmistakable. Those who place their trust in Christ receive his peace, a peace that is unspeakable and unknown. We are thankful first and foremost for what Jesus Christ has done for us. It is by the Holy Spirit that "we know the things of God" and experience God's power in our lives. And the fruit of the Spirit is "the meek and lowly heart." Thankfulness for the activity of the Spirit in our hearts and lives marks the true Christian.

—Paul Wesley Chilcote, *Changed from Glory into Glory*

The Season after Pentecost/Ordinary Time
Sunday between May 29 and June 4
(If the Sunday between May 24 and 28 follows Trinity Sunday, use
Week 14, then return to the regular sequence.)

31. Many Gifts

Affirmation
Now we have received not the spirit of the world, but
the Spirit that is from God, so that we may understand
the gifts bestowed on us by God (1 Cor. 2:12, NRSV).

Psalm: 23

Psalm Prayer
God of abundant generosity, you desire to fill our lives
with good gifts that bring us joy and strengthen the
common life of your people. Those who dwell in your
house, opened to all by your beloved son, Jesus Christ,
truly lack nothing. May the table you set before us be
one around which we celebrate the rich unity in diversity that is a sure sign of your kingdom. Amen.

Daily Scripture Readings

Sunday	A.	Genesis 6:9-22; 7:24; 8:14-19; Psalm 46; Romans 1:16-17; 3:22-28; Matthew 7:21-29
	B.	1 Samuel 3:1-10; Psalm 139:1-6, 13-18; 2 Corinthians 4:5-12; Mark 2:23-3:6
	C.	1 Kings 18:20-21, 30-39; Psalm 96; Galatians 1:1-12; Luke 7:1-10
Monday		Genesis 2:15-24
Tuesday		Exodus 4:10-17
Wednesday		Numbers 11:10-17
Thursday		Isaiah 42:1-9
Friday		Mark 1:1-11
Saturday		1 Corinthians 12:4-11

Silence

Daily Readings for Reflection

Reflection: Silent or Written

Prayers: For the World, for Others, for Myself

Offering of Self to God
All that we have and all that we are is from your hand,
O Lord. Receive what is yours and do with us what
best serves the full arrival of your reign on earth. In the
name of Jesus and the power of the Holy Spirit. Amen.

Blessing
May the Lord grant us unity of spirit, sympathy, love
for one another, a tender heart, and a humble mind.
Amen.

Readings for Reflection

&. The author of Ephesians begins by blessing the God
who has gifted us "with every spiritual blessing" in
Christ [1:3]. It is really quite awesome to think that God
"chose us in Christ before the foundation of the world
to be holy and blameless before him in love" [1:4]. The
rich blessings that come with this gift are many: We are
forgiven and redeemed from sin, adopted as children
of God, given the inheritance of salvation and knowledge of the mystery of God's will. This is our destiny,
chosen not by us but by God for us. And all this abundance of grace is a sheer expression of God's goodwill
toward us in Christ. We are being drawn irresistibly to
the purpose for which we were made: to praise God
with joy!

 The book of Ephesians gives us here a sweeping
and convincing portrait of God's tremendous goodwill
toward us. It pictures a comprehensive plan for all creation, gathered up in Christ, the Word made flesh. The

mystery of this plan is Christ's sacrificial love: Though we have fallen far from grace by sin, in him we are forgiven, reconciled, restored to holiness. God's greatest desire and good pleasure are to bless us in Christ Jesus! Nothing will be withheld from those who live in him by faith. The single word that sums up the central truth of this passage is *grace*.

—Rueben P. Job and Marjorie J. Thompson, *Companions in Christ*

❧ Why would God choose to gift us so lavishly when all of us have been disobedient—sometimes willfully and sometimes unknowingly? As the letter explains, it is simply "so that in the ages to come [God] might show the immeasurable riches of his grace in kindness toward us in Christ Jesus" (Eph. 2:7). It is God's nature to love with overflowing kindness. Indeed, in a deeper sense, grace is the gift of God's own presence with us, "freely bestowed on us in the Beloved" (Eph. 1:6). Jesus is the Beloved, a name revealed in his baptism (Matt. 3:17). Every spiritual gift—love, purity, mercy, peace, truth, fidelity, simplicity, joy—is an offering of God's own nature to us in Christ Jesus. Such grace is given for our comfort, healing, guidance, and transformation. It is given so that we might have life in abundance.

—Rueben P. Job and Marjorie J. Thompson, *Companions in Christ*

❧ I am carrying in my Bible two wonderful pictures of my grandsons, Alex and Ali. I gaze at the pictures and ache to be with them, to hold them, to hear their voices, and to watch their movements.

Their pictures cause me to yearn to be with them—a yearning that almost hurts—so much do I love them and want to be with them.

Today I read Colossians 1:15, "He is the image of the invisible God . . ." and beside this verse I have written "a picture of God." Jesus is a picture of God, and as I gaze upon Christ, I yearn to see God, to be with God, to hear God's voice, to see God's movements. I yearn for some of the mystery of God to dissolve so that I may see and experience God more fully.

But for now, I have Jesus, the image of God, and I must gaze on him in the Gospels. For when I gaze upon the words of Jesus I hear the voice of God; and when I gaze upon the activities and actions of Jesus I see God; when I observe the suffering of Jesus, I know God's deep, aching love for me; and when I reach out and touch Jesus in the Gospels, I lay my hand upon God. Thanks be to God for the gift of Jesus and a clear and beautiful picture of God.

—Norman Shawchuck

❧ "Now you are the body of Christ and individually members of it" (1 Cor. 12:27). Paul's striking metaphor for Christian community conveys the intricate web of relatedness that unites us in the risen Body of Christ. We are bound together in an interdependence and mutuality analogous to the systems and structures of a healthy human body (1 Cor. 12:12-31). And the animating energy of our life in Christ is God the Holy Spirit, who bestows upon various members the capacities needed in the community for its growth and strength. "To each is given the manifestation of the Spirit for the common good" (1 Cor. 12:7). In the world and often in the church, gifts distinguish us from others and place us above or below them. In Christ and only by the grace of the Holy Spirit in the church, gifts draw us to one another and place us side by side, a unique corporate witness to the new creation inaugurated in the life, death, and resurrection of Jesus.

"Now there are varieties of gifts, but the same Spirit" (1 Cor. 12:4). Something vast and mysterious confronts us in Paul's conviction that the potentially centrifugal diversity of the church is contained by a deeper unity rooted in Christ and enlivened by the Spirit. We catch glimpses of a fresh reality in which affirmation of spacious unity does not collapse into expectation of smothering conformity, and esteem for diversity unravels into neither relativistic individualism nor strife over rank, rights, and privileges. The vital tension of unity in diversity, which can only remain vibrant and vivifying by committed practice of the love Paul describes in 1 Corinthians 13, is tangible proof of the new social relations that characterize God's creation now healed and whole in Christ.

"But we have this treasure in earthen vessels, to show that the transcendent power belongs to God and not to us" (2 Cor. 4:7, rsv). Creation is indeed healed and whole in Christ, but this truth has not yet been fully realized in the world or the church. The many gifts that constitute Christian community point to the time when God will be "all in all" (1 Cor. 15:28), but today they reside in the frail receptacle of our common humanity. How susceptible we are to cultural forces that press us swiftly and subtly toward individualistic frames of reference and foster decreasing tolerance of diversity in some Christian bodies and in society as a whole.

—John S. Mogabgab, "Editor's Introduction," *Weavings* (May/June 2008)

❧ Our identity as God's beloved children, then, embraces both who we are and who we are becoming. We are infinitely loved. We are, with all our vastly varied gifts, being renewed in the divine image, and we bear this image back into the world. We each do this in our own way—a thousand different ways, indeed a million ways and infinitely more. Our core identity comes with particular gifts. Unique gifts and graces are an expression of God's personal love for us, a confirmation of our belovedness. No two of us act, think, or serve alike. And God's love sets each one of us wholly free, free to be ourselves and free to be for others the image of the loving God.

—Stephen V. Doughty and Marjorie J. Thompson, *The Way of Discernment*

❧ When Paul enumerates various gifts in 1 Corinthians 12:4-11—wisdom, knowledge, faith, healing, miracles, prophecy, discernment, tongues, interpretation—he reminds his readers of two important truths, lest they descend into petty prestige competitions: that all these gifts are from the same Spirit and that all are for "the common good" (1 Cor. 12:6-7). The work to which we are called as worshiping communities—fostering the common good—requires that we understand the needs of the whole body, take prayerful stock of the resources among us, pray for those that are lacking, watch in hope for gaps to be filled and needs to be met, and allow everyone a share in the work of the kingdom, even those who seem to themselves or to others to have little to offer.

—Deborah Smith Douglas, "Pilgrims, Strangers, and the Hope of the Poor," *Weavings*

❧ Holiness is a gift of grace. Its qualities cannot be imitated or faked. If we try to act them out, people will sense our inauthenticity, for such gifts come from deep intimacy with God.

How can we cultivate such gifts in our own lives? It would be nice if we could take a course guaranteed to produce personal holiness or find some exercise or technique that would make us saints. But, of course, it is not that simple. It is not a matter of technique; it is a matter of values, of commitment, and, more than anything else, of love—love for the God who created us and has called us to discipleship.

—William O. Paulsell, "Ways of Prayer," *Weavings*

❧ Imagine yourself on a journey toward loving and knowing God through the liturgy of the church at worship. Imagine that others have already discovered this pathway of holiness and eagerly wait to share this journey with you. I start by telling you about one of those people. Her name was Marion.

Marion displayed a passion for ritual and the church's liturgy. A faithful soul, she would bear with "low church" worship, but if you wanted to see her face light up with excitement, just don the vestments, light the incense, and use the great ritual of the church to its full measure. Then Marion would roll her eyes, press her hands together, and say, "Wonderful, wonderful. It was just glorious!" She seemed at a loss for words, almost transported by some beatific vision.

Some love Christ best in silence, in compassionate service to others, or in devotional readings of scripture; but Marion loved and knew Christ best in the liturgical life of the church.

She died during Holy Week. Her funeral was held on Easter Monday. What more fitting time could there be for her friends and family to gather around Word and Table to sing and say a triumphant "alleluia" and commend her to God in the hope of resurrection? While I could not attend, I heard that Marion's funeral was a glorious liturgy filled with laughter, love, and faith. . . .

What is it that Marion loved? Ultimately, it was Christ, but penultimately it was the ways of worship, the experience of the community engaged in ritual, song, prayer, and praise. For Marion the communal worship of the church—its liturgy—was what Jacob called "the gate of heaven" (Gen. 28:17).

—Daniel T. Benedict Jr., *Patterned by Grace*

The Season after Pentecost/Ordinary Time
Sunday between June 5 and June 11
(If after Trinity Sunday; otherwise turn to next Sunday.)

32. Ambassadors of Reconciliation

Affirmation
Father in heaven, you have reconciled the world through your Son, and you have filled us with your Holy Spirit so that we might bear witness to your love as ambassadors of reconciliation. Amen.

Psalm: 41

Psalm Prayer
O God, our God, may we be counted among the blessed who remember those in the margins of society. And, as we work to bring news of your reconciliation to the poor, the orphan, the widow, and the alien, may those who speak ill of us also come to know your healing restoration.

Daily Scripture Readings
Sunday	A.	Genesis 12:1-9; Psalm 33:1-12; Romans 4:13-25; Matthew 9:9-13, 18-26
	B.	1 Samuel 8:4-11, 16-20; Psalm 138; 2 Corinthians 4:13-5:1; Mark 3:20-35
	C.	1 Kings 17:8-16; Psalm 146; Galatians 1:11-24; Luke 7:11-17
Monday		Leviticus 25:8-22
Tuesday		Hosea 2:14-23
Wednesday		Psalm 94
Thursday		John 18:15-18, 25-27; 21:15-19
Friday		Galatians 6:1-10
Saturday		2 Corinthians 5:11-21

Silence

Daily Readings for Reflection

Reflection: Silent or Written

Prayers: For the World, for Others, for Myself

Offering of Self to God
As Jesus identified his vocation, so also may we identify ours: "To preach good news to the poor, to proclaim release to the prisoners and recovery of sight to
the blind, to liberate the oppressed, and to proclaim the
year of the Lord's favor" (Luke 4:18-19). Amen.

Blessing
Let us go forth with the good news of reconciliation,
bringing those who alienate into right relationship with
those who are alienated so that all may know the reconciling love of God. Amen.

Readings for Reflection

&. We have seen it in athletes and politicians and now
and then in religious leaders such as Mother Teresa,
Martin Luther King, Billy Graham, and Dorothy Day.
A driving passion is a joy to behold when it is given to
a noble and righteous cause. It is unlikely that a noble
or righteous cause will succeed without the driving
passion of those who share the ideals of the mission.

However, it is not only the well-known athletes,
politicians, religious leaders, and celebrities who need
or demonstrate a driving passion. We can thank God
that every day countless men and women give themselves fully to bringing a vision of the world inspired
by Jesus Christ to reality. These men and women place
God at the center of their lives and place God's will at
the top of their priority list. Most often these heroic
servants of Christ are not recognized and are invisible
behind the scenes doing what they do best—loving

God and neighbor with a pure love expressed in their actions every day of their lives.

A driving passion can be destructive to the person driven and to those in the way of that passion unless it is grounded in Jesus Christ. We can each fall prey and victim to a driving passion for the wrong purpose or goal. Our only safety net is a life given completely and without reservation to God in Christ. When we can say that it is indeed Christ who lives and rules within us, we can be free of worry about the results of our driving passion. That passion will be directed, as was the passion of Jesus, only for good and noble ends. What is the driving passion of your life? Where will it lead you if you follow it for the rest of your life?

—Rueben P. Job

❧　I love you, Lord, and so I always will;
　　For through the decades you have led and helped;
　　And so you continue still.

　　I serve you, Lord, and so I always will;
　　For you did call, I abandoned all;
　　And so I always will.

　　Spirit gives light and power,
　　beyond my capacities to go;
　　For when you open wide the door,
　　Spirit energies flow;
　　And so they always will.

　　I bless you, Lord, in you all life is full;
　　For every need you supply;
　　My greatest need to fulfill;
　　And so you always will.

　　Lead on! O Source of Light;
　　And compass true;
　　Lead on! I follow you!
　　No other Guide will do.
　　—Norman Shawchuck

❧ From the scriptures we get a glimpse of reconciliation far more profound than patching up differences, or making a private peace with what's wrong with the world, or putting a bandage over hurts inflicted in the course of living. Paul, for one, had something else in mind. Reconciliation for Paul begins "within," when we hear (and believe) God's words of acceptance and mercy. That realignment of the heart spills across all of our relationships, closing the gaps that distance us. Eventually, those who minister reconciliation, as well as those affected by it, create the world heralded by the angels at the birth of Jesus where peace and goodwill prevail. It is a place where lions and lambs live together and children play with poisonous snakes (Isa. 11:6, 8). It is a place, still a-borning, where the peace that surpasses human understanding becomes normative. And it is a place where war and violence are the stuff of fiction and make-believe.

When Paul passes the mantle of ambassadorial rank to each of us, we may surmise two things: First, that God's intention for the world is unity, and second, that the mission to gather the world as one that was begun by Jesus was left incomplete by him. That mission was delegated to the community of believers gathered in his name.

Each of us is an ambassador in the service of a leader who deputizes us to spread news of peace, restoration, and collaboration to a world sorely in need of this news. There are few things about which God is more persistent than this—that each of us engage in this ministry of reconciliation and bring it to completion. It is nothing less than our meaning, our historical destiny, and our corporate identity.

—Doris Donnelly, "Ambassadors of Reconciliation,"
Weavings

❧ Forgiveness stands at the heart of the Christian life—God's forgiveness of us and our forgiveness of others, God, and ourselves. We pray Jesus' prayer with the whole of God's church, "Forgive us our sins as we forgive those who sin against us." Often, even for very painful offenses against us, we find forgiveness easy. At other times, however, no matter how we try we cannot forgive. We cannot change our hearts, nor does God's grace seem to have the power to touch them. Sometimes this is because we fear that in the very act of forgiving we would acknowledge the right of the other person to take our selves away and treat them as worthless. At other times, when we are not sure why we cannot forgive or know ourselves to be forgiven, I believe it is because we do not allow ourselves to *have a self* to forgive or be forgiven. If this is true for specific acts of forgiveness, how much more does it apply to reconciliation, that fundamental posture of life Paul associates with the new creation.

In order to receive and offer reconciliation, we need to be able to claim a self whose very identity lies in God, a self which we know can neither be given away nor stolen. Many of us have a hard time claiming our identity in God. We believe that the call to love the neighbor sacrificially means pouring ourselves out for others like water into sand until there is nothing left of us. And yet, where can God's forgiving and reconciling grace touch me if not in my very self? How can I share that grace with others if I cannot acknowledge that I have a self to be transformed by that grace? How can I afford to offer forgiveness and seek reconciliation if I believe that doing so means giving others the power to decide whether I ought to have a self at all?
—Roberta L. Bondi, "Becoming Bearers of Reconciliation," *Weavings*

 One body. One spirit. That appealing goal is our mission as reconcilers who push forward frontiers of peace through the following commitments.

As ambassadors of reconciliation we take the splits we observe very seriously. In a culture that supports rugged individualism and privatism, caring about divisions and wanting to put the pieces back together again is not normal procedure. On the contrary, there is a tendency to accept separations and losses as a way of life and ascribe them to the way things are. Reconcilers work against the current trend: they spot divisions, grieve over them, and treat them with the seriousness they deserve.

As ambassadors of reconciliation we bring the ruptures to public attention. It is not enough to weep silently over the losses sustained in child abuse, divorce, AIDS, torture, health care for the indigent elderly, and violence that divide families and nations. It is also important to draw these collisions among persons, positions, and within systems to everyone's attention.

A curious paradox occurs when this is done. Even though our primary goal as ambassadors of reconciliation is peace, the path of reconciliation is frequently routed through conflict and confrontation. To raise issues of justice in the public forum is to risk upsetting the status quo. We ruffle feathers when we speak the truth without evasiveness. We run the risk of peeving the power brokers who have much to lose if their unilateral power base is brought into question. But that is precisely what the reconciler is willing to do, unpopular as the task is.

As ambassadors of reconciliation we urge a sense of responsibility among all parties and encourage involvement toward reconciliation. It is not enough that we simply bring injustice, suffering, and unreconciled relationships, positions, and systems to public attention. It is also important to help people assume responsibility for things as they are and things as they ought to be.

—Doris Donnelly, "Ambassadors of Reconciliation," *Weavings*

❧ The ultimate aim of forgiveness is reconciliation—restored relationship, the joy of renewed trust and communion. Reconciliation is the final goal, even if we are not emotionally ready for it. Certainly we should not force it if we are not ready. Some may feel that they will never be ready to meet an abuser again this side of the grave. Such feelings are to be respected. But whether in this world or the next, we must eventually come to terms with one another. God's intention is reconciliation for all.

—Marjorie J. Thompson, *The Way of Forgiveness*

The Season after Pentecost/Ordinary Time
Sunday between June 12 and June 18
(If after Trinity Sunday; otherwise turn to next Sunday.)

33. Turning the World Upside Down

Affirmation
[God] has shown strength with his arm. He has scattered those with arrogant thoughts and proud inclinations. He has pulled the powerful down from their thrones and lifted up the lowly. He has filled the hungry with good things and sent the rich away empty-handed (Luke 1:51-53).

Psalm: 49

Psalm Prayer
O Giver of Life, neither wealth nor status can rescue us. We cannot affect the outcome of our lives. We can only rest in you, who blesses us so that we might bless others. Give us a heart that longs not for wealth but for you and your upside down kingdom alone. Amen.

Daily Scripture Readings

Sunday	A.	Genesis 18:1-15;
		Psalm 116:1-2, 12-19;
		Romans 5:1-8;
		Matthew 9:35–10:8
	B.	1 Samuel 15:34–16:13; Psalm 20;
		2 Corinthians 5:6-10, 14-17;
		Mark 4:26-34
	C.	1 Kings 21:1-10, 15-21;
		Psalm 5:1-8; Galatians 2:15-21;
		Luke 7:36-8:3
Monday		Deuteronomy 24:10-22
Tuesday		Isaiah 29:13-24
Wednesday		Psalm 10
Thursday		Matthew 19:16-22
Friday		Mark 10:23-31
Saturday		1 Corinthians 11:17-34*a*

Silence

Daily Readings for Reflection

Reflection: Silent or Written

Prayers: For the World, for Others, for Myself

Offering of Self to God
Loving God, we want to reflect your love to the world around us, caring especially for the widows, orphans, and immigrants we meet from day to day. Amen.

Blessing
May we go and be hospitable to the least of our brothers and sisters this day. Amen.

Readings for Reflection

⋙ Because of Jesus I have this beautiful picture of God that makes me long to be with God, to be more Godlike in all that I am and do. But if I, in my human selfishness, sinfulness, and mixed motives love my grandchildren, want to be with them, see them thrive and grow—how much more does God love me, desire to be with me, and see me thrive and grow as one of his children?
—Norman Shawchuck

⋙ Now out from such a holy Center come the commissions of life. Our fellowship with God issues in world-concern. We cannot keep the love of God to ourselves. It spills over. It quickens us. It makes us see the world's needs anew. We love people and we grieve to see them blind when they might be seeing, asleep with all the world's comforts when they ought to be awake and living sacrificially, accepting the world's goods as their right when they really hold them only in temporary trust. It is because from this holy Center we relove people, relove our neighbors as ourselves, that we are bestirred to be means of their awakening. The deepest need of men is not food and clothing and shelter, important as they are. It is God. We have mistaken the nature of poverty, and thought it was economic poverty. No, it is poverty of soul, deprivation of God's recreating, loving peace. Peer into poverty and see if we are really getting down to the deepest needs, in our economic salvation schemes. But they lie farther along the road, secondary steps toward world reconstruction. The primary step is a holy life, transformed and radiant in the glory of God.

Do we want to help people because we feel sorry for them, or because we genuinely love them? The world needs something deeper than pity; it needs love. (How trite that sounds, how real it is!) But in our love of people are we to be excitedly hurried, sweeping all men and tasks into our loving concern? No, that is God's function. But He, working within us, portions out His vast concern into bundles, and lays on each of us our portion.

—Thomas Kelly, *A Testament of Devotion*

ᴥ Doing justice means actively living it out. I am reminded of a wise little quote I bumped into (on a tea box!) that says: "People can be divided into three groups: those who make things happen, those who watch things happen, and those who wonder what happened." Well, the biblical prophets call us to be people who make things happen. "Make it your aim to do what is right, not what is evil," Amos says, "so that you may live. Then the LORD God Almighty really will be with you, as you claim he is. Hate what is evil, love what is right, and see that justice prevails in the courts. Perhaps the LORD will be merciful to the people of this nation who are still left alive" (Amos 5:14-15, TEV). The prophet insists on a radical change of attitude and behavior if we would avoid judgment. New patterns of life are called for, both individually and corporately, if we are to do justice and not merely champion it with our lips.

—Marjorie J. Thompson, "To Do Justice," *Weavings*

❧ The longing to be real, to be loved, to be free is so strong and authentic, so impossible to satisfy with the objects of our more everyday and superficial desires, that we are driven to seek its fulfillment beyond the everyday. If we don't know where to seek that fulfillment or if we find the demands of the quest too alarming, we tend to fall back on our little pleasures and diversions, trying to plug the desperate void with them. Indeed, our consumer society energetically organizes these means of avoiding the quest for God, offering us a false quest that is sustained with enormous force and skill by the engines of economy, media, and government. It requires an equal force and determination to uphold the gospel's counterclaim that we will find ourselves only by emptying ourselves, that our real thirst is for the one thing that no economy or culture can produce. Those who have discovered that they are thirsty for God have a responsibility to hold up that thirst and the quest to fulfill it before a world that has deluded itself into thinking that it only wants a better brand of soda.

—David Rensberger, "Thirsty for God," *Weavings*

❧ "Do not be conformed to this world, but be transformed by the renewing of your minds" [Rom. 12:2]. These quiet words have the potential to turn the world upside down.

—David Rensberger, "Not Conformed, But Transformed," *Weavings*

❧ As we increasingly abide in Jesus Christ, live in that heart, see through those eyes, we begin to notice a strange paradox. We the sheep begin to take on the nature of the Shepherd! Every metaphor and parable has its limits, and this story in John 10 puts us in the role of sheep. Sheep are not notable for their charm or intelligence. They are singularly clueless. They wander off and get lost. They eat poisonous weeds. They fall into ravines. They graze at the same spot until they strip it of all grass and pollute the ground. (Actually, this *does* sound like a lot of us humans!) At best sheep are neither exciting nor creative. Is this really the way God sees us? Does God want us to be, at best, submissive sheep?

Not at all. Jesus told many other stories that reveal humans as complex and potentially creative sons and daughters of God. We are not just to be obedient animals for all eternity. This story centers on the deep love, the trust, the bond, and the discerning recognition of the characteristics of the shepherd. This particular story does not emphasize the tremendous paradoxical truth that we the sheep *change*. In our shepherding role to others—as parent, teacher, caregiver, counselor, listening friend—we begin to guide as we have been guided. Our faces and voices will change. The way we listen and respond will change, not through imitation but spontaneously through deep love. "When he is revealed, we will be like him, for we will see him as he is" (1 John 3:2).

—Flora Slosson Wuellner, *Enter by the Gate*

The Season after Pentecost/Ordinary Time
Sunday between June 19 and June 25
(If after Trinity Sunday; otherwise turn to next Sunday.)

34. Time of Trial

Affirmation
The LORD is for me—I won't be afraid. What can anyone do to me? (Ps. 118:6).

Psalm: 37

Psalm Prayer
Dear Lord, it is often difficult to embrace your love when we face moments of trial. Transform our hearts so that we can trust you and do good no matter the circumstances. When it appears that wrongdoers are prospering, remind us that you are a God of justice. Instead of desiring wrath, help us desire to grow more deeply in you. Rescue us, for we take refuge in you. Amen.

Daily Scripture Readings

Sunday	A.	Genesis 21:8-21; Psalm 86:1-10, 16-17; Romans 6:1-11; Matthew 10:24-39
	B.	1 Samuel 17:1, 4-11, 32-49; Psalm 9:9-20; 2 Corinthians 6:1-13; Mark 4:35-41
	C.	1 Kings 19:1-4, 8-15; Psalms 42–43; Galatians 3:23-29; Luke 8:26-39
Monday		Exodus 17:1-7
Tuesday		Esther 8
Wednesday		Psalm 18
Thursday		Daniel 1
Friday		Mark 13:3-13
Saturday		1 Peter 1:12-19

Silence

Daily Readings for Reflection

Reflection: Silent or Written

Prayers: For the World, for Others, for Myself

Offering of Self to God
O God, in our times of trouble, remind us that you are near so that we can be near to others in their times of trial. Amen.

Blessing
The LORD bless you and keep you. The LORD make his face shine on you and be gracious to you. The LORD lift up his face to you and grant you peace (Num. 6:24-26). Amen.

Readings for Reflection

❧ His closest companions, those he trusted the most, could not keep awake with him for one hour. His hour of agony was lonely and hard. The cross loomed large and the resurrection was still only a promise. The darkness of the night was superseded only by the darkness of the promise for tomorrow. This is where Jesus found himself in the garden of Gethsemane, praying his heart out to God the Father who he knew loved him but permitted him to be in this lonely valley of decision making without light or support. It appeared that all his systems of support had failed. It seemed that nothing worked and everything had failed.

Some would call the experience the dark night of the soul. Others would call it betrayal in the worst possible way. And those who have gone before tell us that if we live long enough, most of us will know what it is like to have our comfortable and trusted support systems evaporate like a morning fog. When they do, we are often left with empty hands, aching hearts, and troubled minds. Is it the end when all our systems fail? Or is it the mark of a new beginning? When we are the ones with empty hands, troubled hearts, and confused minds, it is hard to think of new beginnings. When the reality of brokenness and darkness is so pervasive, clinging to hope and light can be nearly impossible.

Yet if our feeble faith can reach out to the living God and remember a little of the two thousand years of Christian experience, we discover much that remains strong and sure even after all our systems have failed. Perhaps this is the time when, with anxious hearts and empty hands, we are ready to receive the presence and the power of the One who raised Jesus from the dead. The One who earlier had inspired Mary to say, "Here am I, the servant of the Lord; let it be with me according to your word" (Luke 1:38). The same One who brought Jesus from the tomb and called Lazarus to life seeks to bring new hope and life to us even when that seems an impossible feat, even for God.

—Rueben P. Job

&. I can well understand why Christian spirituality is often described as a journey rather than a destination. The spiritual life is characterized by movement and discovery, challenge and change, adversity and joy, uncertainty and fulfillment. It is also marked in a special way by companionship, first with the One we seek to follow and second with those who also seek to follow Jesus Christ.

The Bible is filled with images of spiritual life as journey. Perhaps the most remarkable illustration of spiritual journey in the Bible is the story of the Exodus. For forty years the Hebrew people struggled to move from Egyptian bondage to the freedom of the Promised Land. Some trials were met with obedience, others with dismal failures of faith, yet God's constant faithfulness kept them safe through the wilderness sojourn. At times our certainties about life seem seriously undermined, if not completely shattered. At other times, through conscious effort or quite apart from it, we move from disorientation to a new constellation of meaning and wholeness. Life is not a stationary experience. New insights and developments continually challenge our understanding of life and our experience of God. Yet if we see the spiritual life as a journey, these cycles of change will not alarm us or turn us aside from our primary goal—to know and love God.

—Rueben P. Job and Marjorie J. Thompson, *Companions in Christ*

❧ Will I be remembered? Will I be remembered even if my mind dies before my body? Yes, I will be remembered. Verna, our daughters, our family, and God will remember me. To be remembered is to be alive!

Yet, I pray for healing. I want more than to be remembered. I want to be healed. And I pray that healing may come before insanity. Certainly I would choose death over insanity and mental incapacitation. So I pray each day, "O God, heal me and hasten the day when a cure is found for Alzheimer's. Heal me or permit me to die before I am incapacitated. Or before I become too great a burden to Verna. Dear God, care for Verna in this time of trial and beyond. Care for my family and hold them each close to yourself and to one another." This is my prayer.

—Norman Shawchuck

❧ Faith sets hope at work, hope sets patience at work. Faith says to hope, Look for what is promised; hope says to faith, So I do, and will wait for it too.

Faith looks through the word of God in Christ; hope looks through faith, beyond the world, to glory.

Thus faith saves, and thus hope saves. Faith saves by laying hold of God by Christ; hope saves by prevailing with the soul to suffer all troubles, afflictions, and adversities that it meets with betwixt this and the world to come, for the sake thereof.

Hope has a thick skin, and will endure many a blow; it will put on patience as a vestment, it will wade through a sea of blood, it will endure all things if it be of the right kind, for the joy that is set before it. Hence patience is called "patience of hope," because it is hope that makes the soul exercise patience and long-suffering under the cross, until the time comes to enjoy the crown.

Learn of Abraham not to faint, stumble, or doubt, at the sight of your own weakness; for if you do, hope will stay below, and creak in the wheels as it goes, because it will want the oil of faith.

—John Bunyan, *Selections from the Writings of John Bunyan*

❧ What is prayer? A sincere, sensible, affectionate pouring out of the soul to God through Christ, in the strength and assistance of the Spirit, for such things as God hath promised. The best prayers have often more groans than words.

—John Bunyan, *Selections from the Writings of John Bunyan*

❧ God's advocacy consists of God's saving actions: past, present, and promised. Such advocacy takes form when God bestows courage and boldness on us to speak and live by the faith we claim and in which we are claimed by holy presence and gracious favor. Such advocacy takes shape when God helps those whose need for aid surpasses our capabilities. Contrary to one popular opinion, God does help those who cannot help themselves. Such advocacy takes hold as God upholds us when and where we might otherwise flounder and give in to fear. God's presence and favor, whether mediated through Spirit or sacrament, community or scripture, neighbor or stranger, acts to save us. We need not live afraid.

—John Indermark, *Do Not Live Afraid*

35. Suffering

Affirmation

Sing, heavens! Rejoice, earth! Break out, mountains, with a song. The LORD has comforted his people, and taken pity on those who suffer (Isa. 49:13).

Psalm: 138

Psalm Prayer

God, our steadfast helper, you are truly great. In your constant care for us you bend close to hear the whispered cries of our heart and the anguished shouts of oppressed people everywhere. Strengthen your church to be a refuge for the poor and needy, and empower your people to join you in the work of delivering all creation from its ancient groaning. Amen.

Daily Scripture Readings

Sunday	A.	Genesis 22:1-14; Psalm 13; Romans 6:12-23; Matthew 10:40-42
	B.	2 Samuel 1:1, 17-27; Psalm 130; 2 Corinthians 8:7-15; Mark 5:21-43
	C.	2 Kings 2:1-2, 6-14; Psalm 77:1-2, 11-20; Galatians 5:1, 13-25; Luke 9:51-62
Monday		Genesis 3:1-13
Tuesday		2 Samuel 22:1-20
Wednesday		Job 3:1-10
Thursday		Isaiah 58:1-12
Friday		Mark 15:1-37
Saturday		1 Peter 5:1-11

Silence

Daily Readings for Reflection

Reflection: Silent or Written

Prayers: For the World, for Others, for Myself

Offering of Self to God
Compassionate God, in the outstretched arms of your crucified Son, you have embraced the world in which no creature is a stranger to suffering. By your grace, let our pain be the medium of our solidarity with all who stumble beneath the weight of adversity. And may the pain you know through your solidarity with us be for us a source of courage to follow you on the way that leads to life. Amen.

Blessing
As we pass through the menacing valley of suffering, may the Lord who accompanies us make our steps firm and our trust secure so that God's saving power may be more fully known throughout the earth. Amen.

Readings for Reflection

ᣥ God is good and works continually for good in the world, especially in and for and through those who love God. However, the goodness of God's purposes in the world is not accomplished without suffering. We see this truth most clearly in the life of Jesus Christ. Jesus himself promises his followers that they too will suffer in this world if they choose to be his disciples. Yet the greater promise is joy, the incomparable joy of a life lived not for our own sake or from our own center, but for God and centered in Christ. Life in Christ is life abundant!

—Rueben P. Job and Marjorie J. Thompson, *Companions in Christ*

᠉ We need not wonder about the cost of discipleship. We need only look upon Jesus on the cross. There we see the awful cost of the ministry that is offered in the life, nature, and spirit of Jesus.

The cost is awful indeed. But if our work introduces men and women to Jesus and to God's love, this cost must be accepted. In our own self-emptying, those who gaze upon us may see Jesus. In our conviction, people may be convinced to look upon the cross of Jesus and say, "Truly this is the Son of God."

We have heard it said, "We can never wear the crown until we bear the cross," but for those who willingly enter into the sufferings of Jesus, the cross is their crown, and they wear it with dignity and submission.
—Norman Shawchuck

᠉ Most of us have experienced grief and loss. Perhaps we have known a sudden and traumatic death of one near us. Perhaps we have watched as a loved one slipped away from us, passing out of our control and beyond every medical intervention. We have clung to hopes. We have had regrets. We have grieved.

The first words spoken by Martha to Jesus upon his arrival express complaint, even blame: "Lord, if you had been here, my brother would not have died." Mary later echoes the same sentiment when she greets Jesus. Their words, in one sense, confess faith. Jesus could have changed things. Perhaps we have felt the same way at times for another or for ourselves: Jesus could have healed. . . . Jesus could have intervened between. . . . Jesus could have opened the heart of. . . . If only he had come in time! Could he not have done these things?

Grace abounds in Jesus' response to the sisters. He does not reproach them for their grief-filled lament. Rather Jesus receives their words the way we imagine God received the grievances of the psalmist who asked, "How long, O Lord?" or who lamented that tears were Israel's food and drink. Coming to Martha and Mary

in their loss, Jesus not only accepts their profound grief but joins them in it.
—John Indermark, *The Way of Grace*

⋙ [O]ur suffering in this life may be unspeakable; we may feel ourselves to be completely isolated and alone, but in truth God is with us. Not . . . assuaging or canceling the pain, but inhabiting it—and thereby transforming it.
—Deborah Smith Douglas, "Enclosed in Darkness," *Weavings*

⋙ Many today wander in a soul-withering desert brought on by the suffering of job loss, setback, or an abiding concern for the struggling economy, war, and ecological destruction. The pain goes deep. We can pretend to get on with our lives but inner discontent shows itself in fear and anxiety. The insecurity we feel serves as a wake-up call to a new vision, one that releases us from unnecessary worry and dread. We can choose to embrace the desert and its fertile darkness for the truth it can teach us or flee.

The question is: are we willing to stay put long enough, to wait in the darkness, and to trust that the waiting will be fruitful? Do we believe that inner balance and even spiritual renewal can be found at a time of desolation and seeming loss of hope? Are we willing to listen to the voice of truth that releases us from cultural expectations and prejudiced ways of seeing so that we can discover a new vision?
—Wayne E. Simsic, "For Darkness Is as Light," *Weavings*

⋙ "Suffering doesn't ennoble people," my professor said, leaning over the podium, removing her glasses, as she always did when she was making a particularly urgent point. "It may ennoble some people," she went on, "but it makes others petty or self-indulgent or cruel.

Virtue is not an inevitable by-product of suffering." Her words have stayed with me these many years, not only because they were startling in their edgy realism but also because she spoke with authority. She was a survivor of two concentration camps and a childhood marked with a yellow star in the Viennese ghetto. She had seen people suffer, some with very little grace. She had suffered.

[My professor] taught me not to be glibly optimistic about the hope that suffering produces wisdom. It does, however, seem characteristic of those who are wise that they are receptive to the hard, costly lessons suffering offers. But that receptivity may come only in retrospect, years after the pain has abated, only upon reflection.

Reflection itself is work. It requires not only willingness to "go there"—back into the darkness of a difficult time, back into feelings one would rather leave buried—but also the humility to recognize the ordinariness of one's own suffering. Suffering doesn't make us heroic any more than it makes us virtuous. Nancy Mairs, who has written remarkable, wise, witty essays about her own experience with multiple sclerosis, ends one with her own response to the "Why me?" question that comes up so readily in the midst of pain: "Why not me?" Things happen to people, she points out. When it is our turn to suffer, we are indeed summoned to some theological reflection on the human condition, but it may be that it is best to start in humble recognition of the fact that we weren't singled out for abuse. It's just our turn.

—Marilyn Chandler McEntyre, "What You Get for the Price," *Weavings*

⁓ What does it look like to live in a world bereft of any apparent justice? In the face of the suffering resulting from such imbalances, we find ourselves tempted to voice Job's self-loathing or self-justification, both of which lead to fear, bitterness, and resentment. Love knows another way. In its "art," love opens us to showing mercy—first to ourselves, as [Etty] Hillesum reminds us in *An Interrupted Life*, and then toward others—man to woman; neighbor to stranger; friend to enemy. "Love your neighbor *as you love yourself*," which is to say, "God is God."

How are we to live in the face of escalating violence that too often seems to be void of any sturdy sense of justice? How are we to be those "preparing the new age" in our lives, and in public and political terms in this epoch of our history? Here, the path advocated by Job's counselors—that of justifying one's own actions, or vilifying others—only perpetuates the spiral of violence. The path opening to us the "kingdom of God" opens to us the "origins of change." It is the mystical path by which we find ourselves "preparing the new age," not as a call of duty but rather as discovering that "the most essential and the deepest in [us] hearken[s] unto the most essential and the deepest in the other." Even to the point of loving our enemy, the most demanding "coincidence of opposites." This is the true art of loving, as Hillesum reminds us in a manner that echoes Jesus' teaching, the invitation to live into the ultimate depths of reality. A "passion that we feel," as the poet Wallace Stevens reminds us, a hearkening of the depths we know in ourselves and the depths we find in others.
—Mark S. Burrows, "A Passion That We Feel," *Weavings*

❧ When the grace of God comes to people, they can do all things, but when it leaves them, they become poor and weak, as if abandoned to affliction. Yet in this condition they should not become dejected or despair. On the contrary, they should calmly await the will of God and bear whatever befalls them in praise of Jesus Christ, for after winter comes summer, after night, the day, and after the storm, a great calm.
—Thomas à Kempis, *A Pattern of Life*

36. Perseverance

Affirmation

Therefore, since we are surrounded by so great a cloud of witnesses, let us also lay aside every weight and the sin that clings so closely, and let us run with perseverance the race that is set before us, looking to Jesus the pioneer and perfecter of our faith, who for the sake of the joy that was set before him endured the cross, disregarding its shame, and has taken his seat at the right hand of the throne of God (Heb. 12:1-2, NRSV).

Psalm: 71

Psalm Prayer

Wondrous God, your saving help is the rock on which our hope is built and our shelter in times of trial. May the memory of your faithfulness sustain our faithfulness to you. And let us never tire of praising you, no matter how difficult our circumstances may be. Amen.

Daily Scripture Readings

Sunday	A.	Genesis 24:34-38, 42-49, 58-67; Psalm 45:10-17; Romans 7:15-25; Matthew 11:16-19, 25-30
	B.	2 Samuel 5:1-5, 9-10; Psalm 48; 2 Corinthians 12:2-10; Mark 6:1-13
	C.	2 Kings 5:1-14; Psalm 30; Galatians 6:1-16; Luke 10:1-11, 16-20
Monday		Ezekiel 36:22-36
Tuesday		Proverbs 7:1-3
Wednesday		Luke 21:5-19
Thursday		Acts 5:12-42
Friday		2 Corinthians 6:1-10
Saturday		Philippians 3:1-12

Silence

Daily Readings for Reflection

Reflection: Silent or Written

Prayers: For the World, for Others, for Myself

Offering of Self to God
Dearly beloved Lord, you know our frailties as well as our strengths. Our largeness of heart can shrink to the size of the next distraction and our power to will one thing can drain away before the insistent claims of many things. Therefore I give you my strengths, that they may be made more resilient. And I offer you my weaknesses, that they may become strengths. In the name of our Lord Jesus Christ, who remained steadfast to the end. Amen.

Blessing
Let us stand firm in the grace of God, which waters the soil of our lives so that we can bring forth the fruits of persevering love in due season. Amen.

Readings for Reflection

᠅ We are destined to be conformed to the image of Christ, who is himself "the image of the invisible God" (Col. 1:15); the divine image in which we were originally created is restored to us in Jesus Christ. But this process of being reshaped according to God's intended pattern takes time. It is the work of the Holy Spirit and is called sanctification in Christian theology. After turning our hearts back to God and receiving the justification that comes through faith in Christ, then begins the work of bringing our whole character in line with that of Christ. We begin to mature in knowledge, wisdom, and love. Our growth in the Spirit is marked by movements up and down, forward and backward, and sometimes even in circles! For human beings, the spiritual life is no straight line of unimpeded progress. It is, however, by God's unwavering goodness, always undergirded by grace. This is what gives us the hope and courage to persevere. Persevering on the journey is illustrated quite simply by the response of a monk once made to a curious person's question, "What do you do up there in that monastery anyway?" The monk replied, "We take a few steps, then we fall down. Then we get up, take another step, and fall down again. And then we get up. . . ." As someone has observed, "It is not falling in the water that drowns us, but staying there."

—Rueben P. Job and Marjorie J. Thompson, *Companions in Christ*

⧫ O, Lord, how I long for the discipline which can make me spiritually strong. Strip me of everything that hinders, and set me to running the race with my eyes fixed on Jesus, my example and my prize. Amen.

The weight of the scriptures is on the side of the idea that the Lord faithfully comes to those who come to him and expectantly wait for him. Just as I am to be a channel from God to people, so I must also be a channel, a conduit from people to God. I am a conductor, and a bridge, not a depository.

If I am to fulfill this ministry for you, then direct me and enable me to do it. All that I am and all that I have you gave to me. I now give it back to you and invite you to dispose of it according to your own good pleasure.

—Norman Shawchuck

⧫ When I was in high school, I spent several months working with a child who had been brain damaged at birth. Volunteers in teams of two would place the boy face down on a table. We would stand on each side of the child, grasp his arms and legs firmly, and begin exercising his limbs in alternating rhythms that resembled the swimmer's crawl stroke: left arm and leg forward and back, then right arm and leg back and forth for the prescribed time. The conviction underlying the work was that rhythmic movement of the child's members would create new nerve pathways in his brain. The goal was to strengthen basic patterns of motor coordination so that the boy's movements could be freer and more intentional.

The deep rhythms of the Christian life are like the patterning exercises used in that boy's physical therapy. These rhythms, which are reflected in the seasons and liturgies of our common Christian heritage, stimulate new spiritual sensitivities in us. Their purpose is to reinforce healthy patterns of discipleship so that our witness to the mystery of Christ among us might be unimpaired. And the conviction behind this understanding is that these deep rhythms mirror the rhythms of God's own life revealed in Jesus Christ and imparted to us through our baptismal union with him. Such rhythms therefore trace a pattern of new life with God and one another measured by the stature of the fullness of Christ (Eph. 4:13).

—John S. Mogabgab, "Editor's Introduction," *Weavings* (September/October 1987)

&. The source of perseverance, like the Christian undertaking itself, is not of human origin. Our capacity to sustain a deep and enduring commitment to Gospel living is as uncertain as Peter's fidelity on the morning the cock crowed. Like Peter, we may be earnest in our desire to be faithful, and like him, we may not have an accurate measure of ourselves. Graciously, the Holy One understands that what God needs from us God must supply. What God supplies is a plan for the healing of the nations and a promise to be with us always, a plan and promise that span time as a rainbow spans horizons. To persevere means to cling to this plan and promise in realistic expectation that what a faithful and just God intends cannot be overthrown by human

schemes. Perseverance is, to borrow a phrase from Howard Thurman, "the distilled result of confidence."
—John S. Mogabgab, "Editor's Introduction," *Weavings* (July/August 2005)

❧ As we pass through times of feeling adrift, not knowing where we are going or what we are meant to do, we can learn from the rich biblical examples of those who literally floated at sea and had no idea what they were to do.

Noah bobbed about on an oceanic flood, clueless as to when his ordeal would end (Gen. 7–8). All he could do was wait on God's timing. Eventually, over the long and landless days, waiting turned to watching. *Let's send out a dove,* he thought and the dove was gone. *Ah. It's coming back! But what is this? It carries nothing. It has found nowhere to land.* Days passed. More waiting. *Let's send it out again.* A long watch until evening. Then finally, *Ah, here it comes with a leaf in its beak!* Noah watched. Amid the waiting, hope and a sense of future possibility emerged.

Paul and a half-starved shipload of travelers dodged shoals one stormy night off the coast of Malta (Acts 27). All they could do was wait in fear and uncertainty. Wait for the next ugly rock to slice out of the darkness. Wait for the nearly inevitable crunch and splintering of boards. Wait and, it turned out, do one other thing. At Paul's urging, they broke bread and gave thanks to God. It was a crazy, wild act. Wilder than the wind, crazier than the pitching of the boat. Their spirits lightened. They made it through the night. Dawn finally glowed crimson in the east. The ship itself shattered on a reef, yet all on board safely reached land, waiting and adrift no more.

At times we drift in our lives. Amid the uncertainty and suspense of not knowing, or the sheer tedium of things remaining the same, we can learn to keep our eyes wide open, scanning the horizon of our experience. Like Noah we may have to do this for a long time until at last some green sprig signals, "There's land ahead." Signs may beckon through something as ordinary as a phone call, as intimate as the touch of a child's hand, or as subtle as an inner urge whispering, "This is where you need to go!" Like Paul and his near-sinking boatload, we would be wise to feast ourselves again and again on signs of promise and hope even as we are tossed about on the sea of not knowing.

—Stephen V. Doughty and Marjorie J. Thompson, *The Way of Discernment*

❧ The test of our belief is always in our practice. There are a great many of us who profess a belief in God and His supreme revelation of Himself in Jesus Christ. At any rate, we should be quite firm in our refusal to deny it. Then we go on as if nothing had happened. Yet if this great thing is true it will be the most ordinary common sense that we should perpetually come back to Him to check our thoughts, all our desires, and all our plans.

What we cannot expect to happen is that our characters are going to change through our holding an opinion which we keep somewhere in a pigeon-hole of the mind merely to be brought out on demand. . . .

Our characters are shaped by our companions and by the objects to which we give most of our thoughts and with which we fill our imaginations. We cannot always be thinking even about Christ, but we can refuse to dwell on any thoughts which are out of tune with Him. We can quite deliberately turn our minds towards Him at any time when those thoughts come in.

You will find it is not possible for a vivid memory of Jesus Christ and an unclean thought or a mean and treacherous desire to be in your mind at the same time. It cannot happen. What we have to drill ourselves in is quite constantly to bring our minds, thoughts, desires, hopes, plans, and ambitions back to the touch-stone: will they stand without discord in His presence?

—William Temple, *Selections from the Writings of William Temple* a· Jesus reaches out to people in love and acceptance and healing. Ours is to receive or not receive, and in the receiving comes the transformation. The grace of healing calls forth deeper awareness and more complete healing of ourselves and our world.

Spirituality is a process that involves owning our life experience and opening to new depth of relationship with God. That process becomes the wellspring that transforms our personal lives and relationships. Spirituality also demands interface with the world in which we live. Conscious depth of relationship with God can facilitate physical, mental, emotional, and spiritual development and encourage living into the social environmental implications of that development. In that unfolding journey, we are called to a constant remolding of our lives, our visions, and our world. "As clay is in the potter's hand, so you are in mine" (Jer. 18:6, JB).
—Eleanor McKenzie DelBene, "As Clay in the Potter's Hands," *Weavings*

a· Perhaps the church is too much at home in the world. We talk much about meeting people on their own ground, about understanding the spirit of our age, about keeping abreast of the times. Within certain very narrow limits there is truth in these phrases; but there is not in all of them put together, and in all kindred pleas and policies, one atom of the truth that saves the world. There are some who would have the church sit at the feet of the successful businessperson. They rise in our councils, these baptized worldlings, and talk as if the things we really need could be picked up in the head office of a smart and hustling firm. They say we do not speak the language of the people and are not sufficiently in touch with all the swift, subtle changes in the world's shifting and complex life. And such criticism is wrong, as all shallow things are wrong. It is not this world we need to know better; it is the other world. It is not the language of the street we need to master; it is the language of the kingdom where He reigns whose voice has the music and throb of many waters (Ezek. 43:2). We need to move with surer step and keener vision and warmer response amid eternal things.

—Percy C. Ainsworth, "The Pilgrim Church," *Weavings*

❧ God's people are always, and ever, standing on the banks of the River Jordan. We are always, and ever, on the threshold of the coming of the kingdom, the coming of the governance of God. We are not there yet. We are on the way. It is a journey, not a destination. And therefore, we are ever living with discontinuity— leaving continuity, leaving security, behind in order to embrace what lies ahead. We, of course, give thanks for what has been. We did not arrive at the banks of the Jordan without a history, without leaders, without tradition. We value these and give thanks for them. We tell stories and celebrate what has been. It is how we prepare ourselves to face the future with hope and with joyful anticipation.

With thanks for what has been and with faith in what, by the grace of God, is yet to be, we step off into the Jordan River. It's deep and wide, but milk and honey's on the other side.

—K. C. Ptomey Jr., "The Waters of Discontinuity," *Weavings*

The Season after Pentecost/Ordinary Time
Sunday between July 10 and July 16

37. Loneliness

Affirmation
The LORD is close to the brokenhearted; he saves those
whose spirits are crushed (Ps. 34:18).

Psalm: 102

Psalm Prayer
Holy God, sometimes we feel like we are all alone.
However, we know that even when our friends forsake
us, you remain near. Hear our call for help. Restore our
broken relationships. Give all your children a sense of
your peace. We will be bold to trust you this day and
give thanks for the steadfast love you have shown to
every generation. Amen.

Daily Scripture Readings

Sunday	A.	Genesis 25:19-34;
		Psalm 119:105-112;
		Romans 8:1-11;
		Matthew 13:1-9, 18-23
	B.	2 Samuel 6:1-5, 12-19; Psalm 24;
		Ephesians 1:3-14; Mark 6:14-29
	C.	Amos 7:7-17; Psalm 82;
		Colossians 1:1-14; Luke 10:25-37
Monday		Genesis 18:22-33
Tuesday		1 Kings 19:1-18
Wednesday		Psalm 27:7-14
Thursday		Mark 14:32-50
Friday		Acts 2:22-36
Saturday		Romans 11:1-6

Silence

Daily Readings for Reflection

Reflection: Silent or Written

Prayers: For the World, for Others, for Myself

Offering of Self to God
O Lord, we want to embrace your presence in our lives while being present to the people around us. Amen.

Blessing
May we feel the nearness of the Lord this day. Amen.

Readings for Reflection

❧ Jesus lived his life in community. From his childhood with Mary and Joseph to his calling and traveling with the disciples to his declaration that he and the Father were one, Jesus lived in community. A community of faith nurtured him, supported him, and informed him ("Who do the crowds say that I am?" [Luke 9:18]). It is unthinkable that we would try to live a faithful life without the gifts offered in a faithful community of Jesus. Jesus was known for valuing solitude since he retired to rest and pray, but living in community also marked his life.

Jesus makes a dramatic and revolutionary promise when he says, "Where two or three are gathered in my name, I am there among them" (Matt. 18:20). This is a welcome promise to those who may wonder if God is present in their lives or their affairs. This is a hopeful promise for those who sometimes feel alone and forsaken. This is an enormous assurance for those who face the unknown and need companionship and community.

We can be sure that Jesus keeps his promise and that when we gather in his name, he will be with us. We are often blessed by being in community. We receive encouragement, guidance, comfort, and hope by participating in a community. These gifts of community are available to us all, and we receive them more readily when we remember that Jesus meets us there.

—Rueben P. Job

❧ What a difference in hope and presence an hour or two in prayer can make. Yesterday and today, God is near. After yesterday's morning prayer I felt new hope. Nothing has changed; yet I have changed. It is again like an awakening. Is this a season of slumber and then awakening of God or a season of my own neglect and return? Again, O Lord, I pray, let me stay always in this desire for you, this beautiful awareness of your presence. And I pray, as though the Spirit leads, deep within. O Lord Jesus, when I have no place other to go, I naturally pray, turn to you. For when I have played out my little string, and all seems lost, I naturally hope in you.

It is in this discovery about myself that tells me more than anything else, that God is, and that He is at work in the unseeable, unknowable depths of my being. I hope, believe, and pray without seeing or feeling. This cannot be of myself, for it is contrary to all natural inclination that when I see the less I should hope the more, that when I experience less demonstration that I should believe more, that when I hear less I am nevertheless driven to pray more.

It is true, God calls and comes to me in darkness, and remains hidden and shrouded, but always there is that within me that hopes, Lord, let this be the day of your appearing! How could one bear such burdens without God? How empty and desperate must be the lives of those who have not heard of God, sensed his call, and come to know him as a God who is faithful and loving. He has promised to guard my coming and my going. It is enough, and I am content to await his full appearance.

—Norman Shawchuck

❧ "My strength left me, and my complexion grew deathly pale, and I retained no strength" (Dan. 10:8). Buckles on the edge of the gurney gouged my side as the ambulance lurched into motion. A routine diagnostic procedure earlier in the day had resulted in a hemorrhage, and now I was being rushed back to the hospital I had left less than an hour before. The emergency room medical team skillfully stabilized my vital signs before attending to a seriously injured person next door.

In that twilight reality of dim lights, intravenous tubes, and silent monitors, my mind drifted to other settings of human isolation: the lethal injection table in an execution chamber, the stretcher in a preoperative holding area, the outpatient clinic of the wounded veteran, the unkempt room of the neglected child, the unheated apartment of the elderly poor, the cramped social and economic niches to which people are often consigned. Unlike the prophet Daniel, my loss of strength did not come from the shock of beholding a powerful heavenly being in human form. Rather, it confirmed and further clarified a vision of the God who assumed human form to be with us in the lonely places of life.

"Turn to me, and be gracious to me, for I am lonely and afflicted" (Ps. 25:16). . . . Lying on my trauma room gurney, I realized afresh that in Jesus we see how familiar God is with lonely places; indeed, how much God is drawn to them. The lonely vulnerability of the manger anticipates the lonely suffering of the cross. The shepherd who goes to lonely barrens in search of one lost sheep (Luke 15:1-7) portrays the God who goes to Calvary's forsakenness in search of lost humanity. The rabbi who left disciples behind and prayed in a deserted place (Mark 1:35) anticipates the Spirit who enters lonely places of the heart to pray our prayer when we cannot (Rom. 8:26-27).

—John S. Mogabgab, "Editor's Introduction," *Weavings* (November/December 2008)

❧ [S]o much in the Christian faith is paradoxical: three-in-one, fully-human-fully-divine, new life from death. And here it is: another paradox. Solitude as loneliness and solitude as grace. One speaks of sorrow; the other is often cast as gift. The latter concept is rich and has been hallowed and fleshed out for us in the lives of early Christian saints and exemplars. Through them, solitude is known to be gift and opportunity, a richly textured medium through which authentic intimacy with God and humankind might be fashioned. Yet at the same time, being alone is also experienced as a fearful reality. Our culture views solitude as a severe punishment, a confinement, reserved for the most grievous offenders against human codes of conduct. We tend to shun the solitary places populated by those left abandoned on the margins of human community: places where outcasts, misfits, the forgotten, the unloved and unlovable are hidden. Yet despite our shunning, the lonely sort of solitude is still all around us in the emotionally and spiritually troubled. For these, solitude is a desperate and desolate place. An alienated and isolated place in which hearts wither and hope is abandoned. It is such a paradox.

—Wendy M. Wright, "Thoughts on Solitude," *Weavings*

❧ Solitude as grace and solitude as loneliness. As with all paradox, we find no easy resolution. It would be glib to suggest that the involuntary solitude of the troubled or the marginalized can easily be transformed into the grace of chosen solitude. We can pray that the gift of community comes to those whose loneliness leads to desolation. We can become alert to the possibility that there are those who need our companionship or those whose efforts to form intentional community might be applauded and supported by us, no matter how different they may be. We can work to alleviate the loneliness of those close to us. We can offer hospitality to the marginalized, even if it is merely by acknowledging that each person deserves to be treated with dignity and has a story to tell. We can cultivate attentiveness to the still stirring of divine life in even the most arid of environments.

And we might also learn that, in a strange way, each of us walks a solitary path; that no two persons live out the same destiny; no one lives another's life. The spiritual journey is lonely in the sense that no one else can journey for us. Accompanied, nurtured, surrounded, met, hopefully, yes, but we are all solitaries nonetheless. Such is the profound paradox: that there are lonely places in the human heart and in the community of hearts, places where we fear to tread and yet which invite us. Sometimes we are chosen to be apart in solitude to traverse the inner deserts as contemplatives. Sometimes our inner deserts are too barren to survive, and we are compelled to reach out to others for support. Sometimes we are called to venture into the lonely places on the margins of social respectability and meet those whose solitude has yielded to despair. Sometimes we are left to struggle with the paradox. But always, solitude is before us, around us, inside us, repelling and beckoning, offering both loneliness and grace.

—Wendy M. Wright, "Thoughts on Solitude," *Weavings*

❧ Feelings of loneliness do not disappear because we pay attention to them but through an ever-deepening encounter with Christ, we come to experience our belovedness as the counterpoint to our loneliness.

—Elizabeth J. Canham, "Solo Journey," *Weavings*

❧ Those who follow Christ become family—they share the oneness of divine love. This is the primary belonging of all God's people. Only when we know in heart as well as mind that we are beloved children in the family of God can we look at our lives—whether we are married or single—and see our loneliness for what it truly is. Our hearts are restless and lonely until we leave behind the attempt to find satisfaction

in anything other than the Source of our being made visible in Christ through the Spirit.
—Elizabeth J. Canham, "Solo Journey," *Weavings*

❧ Contemporary life provides precious little space for discernment, given the overriding burden of time. We hurry from one task to another, expressing thoughts and emotions on the fly but rarely sitting down to discern what they may be saying to us. Even accomplished multitaskers know moments of loneliness. In a quiet, predawn moment or while daydreaming between gulps of coffee at a traffic light, an ache may surface. We yearn to share the ordinary ups and downs of our lives with someone, the unspoken prayers we don't feel comfortable uttering at a church meeting and experiences like the moment when we realized God had healed our heart after years of grieving a loss.
—Stephanie Ford, *Kindred Souls*

38. Fear Not

Affirmation
Lord, you go before in all that we do; therefore, we will not be afraid.

Psalm: 3

Psalm Prayer
Almighty God, you know the difficulties we face each day. Remind us that you are very near to us, that indeed you are a shield around us. We do not fear our adversaries because salvation comes from you. Amen.

Daily Scripture Readings

Sunday	A.	Genesis 28:10-19;
		Psalm 139:1-12, 23-24;
		Romans 8:12-25;
		Matthew 13:24-30, 36-43
	B.	2 Samuel 7:1-14; Psalm 89:20-37;
		Ephesians 2:11-22;
		Mark 6:30-34, 53-56
	C.	Amos 8:1-12; Psalm 52;
		Colossians 1:15-28;
		Luke 10:38-42
Monday		2 Kings 6:8-23
Tuesday		Isaiah 12:1-6
Wednesday		Psalm 56
Thursday		Matthew 14:22-33
Friday		Hebrews 13:1-6
Saturday		1 John 4:13-21

Silence

Daily Readings for Reflection

Reflection: Silent or Written

Prayers: For the World, for Others, for Myself

Offering of Self to God
We want to be bold to trust you, O God, and to bear witness to the calm of your kingdom. Amen.

Blessing
May we have eyes to see that, with God, there is no need to fear. Amen.

Readings for Reflection

☙ I didn't want it to happen, but it did. Before I knew it, anxiety found its way into my restless heart and robbed me of the peace promised to all who place their trust in God. Ah, so that is the reason for my anxious heart: I forgot to trust in God!

Many demands upon our time and many opportunities waiting to be explored often fill our lives too full with activities and distractions. When this happens it is not surprising that we grow anxious and lose our sense of peace and tranquility. Today remember that God and God alone is able to care for all that exists; we can trust our smallest and largest concern to the wisdom and love of God. Peace, hope, calm, and joy are the fruits of placing our confidence in God. May these gifts be yours in abundance.
—Rueben P. Job

☙ Jesus himself reminds us that we have to do with a covenant-making God. His last meal with the disciples was declared to be the new covenant. The covenant theme begins in Genesis with Adam and continues through Abraham and then Moses and David and finally comes to fulfillment in Jesus. Jesus was the utter trustworthiness and fidelity, and the unconditional love of God incarnate.

In looking at Jesus we begin to understand the love and fidelity of this covenant-making God. It is this God with whom we have to do in our spiritual life. "God is faithful; by him you were called into the fellowship of his Son, Jesus Christ our Lord" (1 Cor. 1:9).

This covenant-making and covenant-keeping God promises to be with us, to relate to us as beloved children, to companion us in this life and the life to come. No chaos or catastrophe can overcome this mighty God, and no power can snatch us from the presence and care of this covenant-making God.

God is faithful. God can be trusted. God is able to provide. God keeps promises. God is tender and compassionate as well as mighty and just. God invites all to come home and live all of life in intimate relationship with God. God is love. This is the picture that Jesus gives us of God.

—Rueben P. Job, *Spiritual Life in the Congregation*

❧ Wisdom begins when we learn for ourselves that God is not safe, cannot be approached without fear and trembling. But it is only when we become convinced that God is also good and loving that we can truly begin to grow as Christians. Awe, reverent fear, forms the foundation for a formative rather than deformative relationship with God. It enables us to entrust ourselves fully to God.

—Keith Beasley-Topliffe, "The Beginning of Wisdom,"
  Weavings

❧ What is true of nature and human nature is also true of the Divine. It is time to reappropriate the importance of holy fear before the God who is the source of the process of creation.

But doesn't "perfect love cast out fear"? The fear that Saint John says is cast out by God's love "has to do with punishment" (1 John 4:18). Unless we can shed our fear of a vindictive God lurking to strike out through calamity or adversity, we may not be able to stand in holy fear before the One from whom all the mighty powers of creation flow. Absorbing the reality that nothing can separate us from the compassionate love manifested in Christ (Rom. 8:39), we can face the blessings and dangers of creation with full consciousness, ready to tread with fear but fundamentally unafraid.

We can face fully that as gifted and as powerful as we may be, we are still small, fragile creatures who walk in the midst of titanic powers that rightly invoke breathtaking awe. It is not that the power of the storm, the intensity of the sunlight, or the passionate nature of love are out to harm us; it is that they are powerful in their working and we must tread carefully in their presence. Only as we learn how to comport ourselves respectfully can we drink deeply of their goodness.

Surely the same is true of the God who sources it all. The Love that knocks at the door of our heart is also the One who spins this world into its teeming, boisterous life.

—Robert Corin Morris, "Holy Fear and the Wildness of God," *Weavings*

✎ Jesus' agonizing encounters with fear and abandonment in the garden and on the cross give hope to the rest of us, for ultimately Abba did not abandon him. Peter learned the importance of a prayerful retreat in those days of waiting in the Upper Room before Pentecost. And each experience of imprisonment for Peter surely must have called him to a more prayerful union with the crucified and risen Jesus.

In our own time, we have the testimony of countless heroes of faith for whom a prayerful, intimate relationship with Abba, Jesus, and the Spirit carried them through raging storms. In their prison journals, Dietrich Bonhoeffer, Etty Hillesum, Phil Berrigan, and John Dear speak convincingly of the power of prayer and love to overcome the power of fear. Gandhi courageously walked alone as a disarming presence of love into the incredible violence between Hindus and Muslims in the villages of India in 1946–47 because he was convinced that Jesus walked with him. Certainly the lives of Ita Ford, Maura Clark, Jean Donovan, and Dorothy Kazel—the four religious women assassinated in El Salvador in 1980 because they dared to live in solidarity with the oppressed Salvadoran people—confirm the power of prayer and love to overcome fear and domination. Placing ourselves in the presence of Abba, Jesus, and the Spirit of love allows us to confidently embark each day on the journey from fear to love.

—James McGinnis, "Go Out into the Deep," *Weavings*

  ❧ When Jesus asked Peter and the other disciples to row to the other side of the lake a second time, this time without him, they found their limits tested again. As Matthew describes this scene, "The boat, battered by the waves, was far from the land, for the wind was against them " (Matt. 14:24). They had to learn that they could survive such danger and that Jesus would always be with them. Then Jesus tested Peter even further and asked him to walk across the water to him. Impetuous Peter accepted the challenge. But "when he noticed the strong wind, he became frightened, and beginning to sink, he cried out, 'Lord, save me!' Jesus immediately reached out his hand and caught him, saying to him, 'You of little faith, why did you doubt?'" (Matt. 14:30-31).

Similarly, Jesus tests our limits and invites us to go out into the deep, far from the secure shores of large savings accounts, comfortable routines, familiar places and situations. There have been many times when I felt overwhelmed by work and family responsibilities. There have been times when I felt depressed, wanting to escape to the comfort of home or to the security of familiar tasks. I was afraid of what lay ahead. Every year we wonder where the money will come from to sustain our ministry. But in every one of these situations, Jesus has been there beckoning me, beckoning us, beyond the security of shallow water to go with him into the deep.

Jesus is there for us, just as we were there for our young children when they were first learning to swim. "Come on, you can do it," we said, "See, I'm right here. Just swim to me." How much more can we count on Jesus being there for us. If it does get stormy, we can cry out for help in confidence. Jesus sleeps no more. No matter how long the storm, Jesus is always at the helm. He can calm our frightened, turbulent spirits so we can ride out the storm together. What confidence we can have going into each day, each challenge of life. Jesus will never let us drown. But we have to ask for the help we need, crying out as loudly and persistently as the situation warrants.

—James McGinnis, "Go Out into the Deep," *Weavings*

❧ Catherine of Siena (1347–80) . . . warns against giving in to slavish fear of critics, enemies, and demons. Such fear is characteristic of those who hope only in themselves, not in God. They must always be careful not to offend those who are more powerful. Holy fear, on the other hand, is freeing. Those who have it "are not afraid of the devils' delusions; because of the supernatural light of grace and the light of Holy Scripture, they recognize them for what they are and they suffer neither darkness nor spiritual distress from them." Holy fear, God's gracious gift, sets people free to love both God and neighbor.

Spiritual growth, then, is in part a growth from fear of the world to fear of God and then from simple fear to the reverent fear that is awe.

—Keith Beasley-Topliffe, "The Beginning of Wisdom," *Weavings*

❧ Many fear the darkness they encounter during desert times because they assume it will be negative, an experience of disintegration or even punishment. Though at first the darkness may unsettle us because it removes our comfort zone and prompts us to trust the unseen, it has the potential to become a balm for an ailing soul. It may introduce us to an inner freedom, a release from the narrow view of self that weighs down the soul. A desert landscape that at first seemed barren and stark has the potential to intensify vision and reveal hidden color and spectacular form.

When the teachings of St. John of the Cross concerning the dark path of the soul were found by a group of Carmelite nuns to be too harsh, he referred them to his poems and told them that in the metaphors they would find his original inspiration. For John, darkness is poetry: it does not bear down on the soul but rather buoys it with love, namely "the living flame of love." It is this love that lures us toward an infinite horizon where God can get our attention. In the deep stillness of a dark night a hush comes over the soul and the Spirit has room to work.

—Wayne E. Simsic, "For Darkness Is as Light," *Weavings*

❧ The words of Matthew 28:1, 8 might be taken as a study in fear. They take us back to the world's first Eastertide. The Resurrection morning was the Judgment Day of fear. It did not banish the word forever from our lips and the fact from our lives. It called the thousand fears of life to give account of themselves. Some it slew just where they stood. They were the children of darkness and of weakness and of shame, and they had no right to live. Some it cleansed and uplifted, and made them the friends and helpers of all lowly and faithful souls. Most wondrous of all, a new and holy fear came forth into the world—a true and steadfast fear of life.

Let us look at these things for a while. In the light of the sepulcher, the arch fear of the human heart—the fear of death—was called by its name and stigmatized as the crowning delusion of these mortal years. In that same light we have learned to see life more vast and solemn and significant than ever before we had dreamed it to be. . . .

So, my friends, let us pass this day into the holy fear and healing joy of the Resurrection morning. Let us fear as becomes those who have been delivered from the false emphasis of death and given to feel the true emphasis of life, for this is that fear of the Lord that is clean and endures forever. And let us rejoice as we remember for our great and endless comfort that he whom death could not hold waits to call us by our name, as he named the woman of Magdala in the garden, to talk with us as he talked with two who walked into the country till our hearts glow, as did theirs, with the warm message of his lips. To cheer us as he cheered the disciples coming ashore after a night of vain toil. To plead with us as he pleaded with the brokenhearted son of Jonas. And to stand in our midst whenever we come together in some common act of worship and hour of communion, as he stood among the disciples on that first Easter even, saying in tones calmer than silence, "Peace be unto you."

—Percy C. Ainsworth, "Fear and Joy," *Weavings*

39. Forgiveness

Affirmation
Compassion and deep forgiveness belong to my Lord, our God (Dan. 9:9).

Psalm: 32

Psalm Prayer
You are loving, merciful, and forgiving, O God. You pardon our wrongdoing and cover our transgressions. May we forgive and pardon others as you have forgiven and pardoned us, so that we, as a forgiven and reconciled people, glad and upright in heart, may rejoice in you, O Lord, this day and always. Amen.

Daily Scripture Readings

Sunday	A.	Genesis 29:15-28; Psalm 128; Romans 8:26-39; Matthew 13:31-33, 44-52
	B.	2 Samuel 11:1-15; Psalm 14; Ephesians 3:14-21; John 6:1-21
	C.	Hosea 1:2-10; Psalm 85; Colossians 2:6-15; Luke 11:1-13
Monday		Genesis 45:1-15
Tuesday		Exodus 10:12-20
Wednesday		Matthew 18:21-35
Thursday		John 8:1-11
Friday		Colossians 3:12-17
Saturday		1 Timothy 1:12-17

Silence

Daily Readings for Reflection

Reflection: Silent or Written

Prayers: For the World, for Others, for Myself

Offering of Self to God
Holy God, from this day forward may we forgive others as we ourselves have been forgiven. Amen.

Blessing
As a forgiven and reconciled people, may we go forth with the strength and confidence to endure all that life throws our way, forgiving others as we have been forgiven, rejoicing always in God's steadfast love. Amen.

Readings for Reflection

᠍᠊᠍ There are some things that only God can do. We look at the rise of violence around the globe or the rising tide of population and hunger and know that some of these problems are so deep-seated that without God's help they will not be resolved. Then we look into our own hearts and know that sin—our failure to do what we want to do and our doing what we know we do not want to do—can only be remedied with God's help. We are not the first to discover these truths.

When Jesus had dinner at Simon's house (Luke 7:36-50), a woman identified as a known sinner came and washed the feet of Jesus with her tears, drying his feet with her hair. The rest of the dinner crowd was astonished and outraged. Why did this righteous man not recognize who this woman was? And if he did recognize who she was, why did he not rebuke her? Jesus pointed out that her love was greater and demonstrated love more beautifully than that of the host. Jesus then declared in the hearing of all that the woman was forgiven. She was cleansed and sent on her way with Jesus' blessing.

The dinner guests were still astounded. They knew that only God could forgive sins, and they were not yet able to believe that this carpenter's son was also son of God. Jesus said that the woman was saved by her faith, but the rest of the guests missed out on the divine gift of forgiveness and the blessing of peace Jesus was offering.

The good news Christians tell one another and the world is that only God can wipe away the failures, errors, and missed opportunities that sometimes plague us. We cannot wipe away or forgive our sins or those of another. But God can, and therein lies our hope, joy, and peace—a message we proclaim to all.
—Rueben P. Job

☙ "The Lord says I am going to call my shepherds to account." This too strikes to the heart of my condition—God will surely call me to account. No foolishness, no escape! Should not, then, I live out my life and ministry in preparation for that singular moment when I am called to give account: Am I so living and working?

Is God's flock being gathered and fed through my life and ministry? Are the strays brought back, the inactive made active again? Are the lost and unchurched found, the wounded in spirit being healed and cared for? Do I view my ministry in this light every day?

My God, chief shepherd and judge—forgive me, save me; help me to be faithful in my walk and in my work.
—Norman Shawchuck

☙ Forgiveness is a mystery. It belongs to the realm of freedom rather than the realm of necessity; it is scented with the spices of grace rather than the sweat of legalism; it delights and humbles with the impact of wholly unexpected bounty; gentler than a tender embrace, it is tougher than the bands of retribution that strap us tightly to our pain.
—John S. Mogabgab, "Editor's Introduction," *Weavings* (March/April 1992)

☙ Forgiving does not mean denying our hurt. What on the surface appears to be a forgiving attitude may

merely reveal that we have succeeded in suppressing our pain. If we bury our hurt or pretend it isn't real, we experience no sense of being wronged that would require our forgiveness. Forgiveness is a possibility only when we acknowledge the negative impact of a person's actions or attitudes on our lives. This holds true whether or not harm was intended by the offender. Until we are honest about our actual feelings, forgiveness has no meaning.
—Marjorie J. Thompson, "Moving Toward Forgiveness," *Weavings*

  Why are you forever trailing your heart along the earth? Lift up your heart; reach forward; love your enemies. If you cannot love them in their violence, love them at least when they ask pardon.
—Augustine, *Hungering for God*

  Let us all, brothers, give heed to what the Lord says: "Love your enemies, and do good to them that hate you." For our Lord Jesus, whose footsteps we ought to follow, called His betrayer friend, and offered Himself willingly to His crucifiers. Therefore all those who unjustly inflict upon us tribulations and anguishes, shames and injuries, sorrows and torments, martyrdom and death are our friends whom we ought to love much, because we gain eternal life by that which they make us suffer.
—Francis of Assisi, *Selections from the Writings of St. Francis of Assisi*

  When we recognize our need for God's care, both personally and in our relationships, we may be more prepared to give up our illusion of control. Our deep-seated belief that we ought to be in a position to judge and punish the faults of others is part of our "control agenda" in life. It is a painful but inevitable part of spiritual maturation to discover that vengeance upon the perpetrators of evil is not our responsibility. "'Vengeance is mine,' . . . says the Lord" (Rom. 12:19,

RSV). Only God has the wisdom to know what consequences are needed in any person's life to heal and restore human sanity and wholeness. As Christians, we trust that God's ways of dealing with sin are more merciful than our own inclinations are likely to be.

As we recognize more deeply our dependence on God, we will also come in touch more profoundly with our shortcomings. We may become aware of the beam in our own eye that has prevented us from seeing clearly how small the speck is in our sister's or brother's eye. Discovering the depth of our sin has a way of putting the faults of others in perspective. It is shocking to some when Mother Teresa of Calcutta claims she engages in her ministry of love because she knows there is a Hitler inside her. The great saints are not shocked by any form of degradation in the human heart; they know its potential deep within themselves.

This capacity to identify with human sin to its outer reaches characterizes the humility and lack of judgmentalism present in so many holy ones through the centuries. Mercy for others grows from sorrowful knowledge of the human heart we share. The ability to acknowledge fully one's own sin is thus a powerful path to forgiveness of others.

—Marjorie J. Thompson, "Moving Toward Forgiveness," *Weavings*

❧ I cannot believe that a person who comes so close to Mercy itself, where he realizes what he is and the great deal God has pardoned him of, would fail to pardon his offender immediately, in complete ease, and with a readiness to remain on very good terms with him. Such a person is mindful he saw signs of great love; and he rejoices that an opportunity is offered whereby he can show the Lord some love. Since Jesus knows this well, He says resolutely to His holy Father that "we pardon our debtors."

—Teresa of Avila, *The Soul's Passion for God*

․ What will you do? You have enemies, for who can live on this earth without them? For your own sake, love them. In no way can your enemies so hurt you by their violence as you hurt yourself if you do not love them. They may injure your estate, or flocks, or house, or your servants, or your child, or your spouse, or at most, if they are given enough power, your body. But can they injure your soul, as you can yourself? Reach forward, dearly beloved, I beg you, to this perfection. Have I given you this power? The only one who has given it is the one to whom you say, *"Your will be done, on earth as it is in heaven."* Do not let it seem impossible to you. I know, I have known by experience, that there are Christians who do love their enemies. If it seems impossible to you, you will not do it. Believe then first that it can be done, and pray that the will of God may be done in you. For what good can your neighbors' ill will do you? If they had no ill will, they would not even be your enemies. Wish them well then, that they may end their ill will, and they will be your enemies no longer. For it is not their human nature that is at enmity with you, but their sin. Are they therefore your enemies because they have souls and bodies? In this they are like you. You have a soul and so do they. You have a body and so do they. They are of the same substance as you are. Both of you were made out of the same earth and given life by the same Lord. In all this they are just like you. Acknowledge them, then, as brothers and sisters.
—Augustine, *Hungering for God*

․ But still you are saying, "Who can do, who has ever done this [loved their enemies]? May God bring it to effect in your hearts! I know as well as you that there are but few who do it. Those who do are great and spiritual individuals. Are all the faithful in the church who approach the altar and take the Body and Blood of Christ—are they all such? And yet they all say, *"Forgive our debts, as we also have forgiven our debtors."* What if God should answer them, "Why do you ask me to do what I have promised, when you do not what I have commanded? What have I promised? 'To forgive your debts.' What have I commanded? 'That you also forgive your debtors.' How can you do this if you do not love your enemies?" What then must we do, brothers and sisters? Is the flock of Christ reduced to such a scanty number? If only those who love their enemies ought to say, *"Forgive us our debts as we also have forgiven our debtors,"* I do not know what to do or what to say. Must I say to you, "If you do not love your enemies, do not pray"? I dare not say so! Pray rather that you may love them. Then must I say to you, "If you do not love your enemies, do not say in the Lord's Prayer, *'Forgive us our debts, as we also have forgiven our debtors'*"? Suppose that I were to say, "Do not use these words." If you do not, your debts are not forgiven. And if you do use them and do not act on them, they are not forgiven. In order therefore that they may be forgiven, you must both use the prayer and act on it.

—Augustine, *Hungering for God*

❧ Reconciliation is the promise that lies at the heart of forgiveness; it is the full flower of the seed of forgiveness, even when that seed is hidden from sight. The gift of forgiveness will always feel incomplete if it does not bear fruit in reconciliation. This, I am convinced, holds as true in God's forgiveness of us as it does in our forgiveness of one another. Reconciliation means full restoration of a whole relationship, and as such requires conscious mutuality. No reconciliation can take place unless the offender recognizes the offense, desires to be forgiven, and is willing to receive forgiveness. Thus, the role of acknowledgment and confession of sin belongs to the dynamic of forgiveness in relation to reconciliation, not to forgiveness alone.

—Marjorie J. Thompson, "Moving Toward Forgiveness," *Weavings*

40. Pray for One Another

Affirmation
God, listen to my cry; pay attention to my prayer!
(Ps. 61:1).

Psalm: 143

Psalm Prayer
We confess, O Lord, that we become so distracted by
the busyness of life that we often fail to pray as we
should. Quiet and center our minds today that we may
focus our attention wholly on you. Hear our prayers, O
God, those we offer for ourselves and for others. Amen.

Daily Scripture Readings

Sunday	A.	Genesis 32:22-31; Psalm 17:1-7, 15; Romans 9:1-5; Matthew 14:13-21
	B.	2 Samuel 11:26-12:13; Psalm 51:1-12; Ephesians 4:1-16; John 6:24-35
	C.	Hosea 11:1-11; Psalm 107:1-9, 43; Colossians 3:1-11; Luke 12:13-21
Monday		Nehemiah 1:1-11
Tuesday		Matthew 5:43-48, 6:5-15
Wednesday		Luke 11:5-13
Thursday		Luke 22:31-34
Friday		Colossians 1:3-14
Saturday		James 5:13-20

Silence

Daily Readings for Reflection

Reflection: Silent or Written

Prayers: For the World, for Others, for Myself

Offering of Self to God
Let us be glad in the Lord for the Lord is near, and always lift up our requests to God in prayers and petitions. Amen.

Blessing
May the peace of God that exceeds all understanding keep our hearts and minds safe in Christ Jesus. Amen.

Readings for Reflection

❧ A loving, living relationship with God is impossible without prayer. We cannot know the mind and heart of Christ, receive God's direction, hear God's voice, or respond to God's call without this means of grace. We may enter God's kingdom without the benefit of some of the means of grace but not without prayer. Prayer is so important that Jesus left even the needy crowd to pray (Mark 6:31). His entire life and ministry were set in the context of prayer. Those who choose to follow him can do no better than to take up his example.
—Rueben P. Job and Marjorie J. Thompson, *Companions in Christ*

❧ I am particularly struck with the fact that Christ's prayer was not in the least for himself. If prayer has meaning only for oneself, it will not be heard. If it voices the aspirations of humanity, it will be heard. There was not the slightest trace of selfishness in Christ's prayer: "If for the redemption of humankind, it is necessary that I should be killed, I am willing to go to my death." This attitude is the acme of the life of faith. To pray in this spirit is the highest type of religious consciousness. When in poverty, distress, or any sort of trouble we pray in this spirit, we gain the victory.
—Toyohiko Kagawa, *Living Out Christ's Love*

❧ For there is nothing that makes us love a person so much as praying for him or her. When you can once do this sincerely for anyone, you have fitted your soul for the performance of everything that is kind and civil toward that person. This will fill your heart with a generosity and tenderness that will give you a better and sweeter behavior than anything that is called fine breeding and good manners.

—William Law, *Total Devotion to God*

❧ Alas, how few there be in the world whose heart and mouth in prayer shall go together. Dost thou, when you askest for the Spirit, or faith, or love to God, to holiness, to saints, to the word, and the like, ask for them with love to them, desire of them, hungering after them? Oh, this is a mighty thing; and yet prayer is no more before God than as it is seasoned with these blessed qualifications.

Wherefore it is said, that while men are praying, God is searching the heart to see what is the meaning of the Spirit, or whether there be the Spirit and his meaning in all that the mouth hath uttered, either by words, sighs, or groans, because it is by him and through his help only that any make prayers according to the will of God (Rom. 8:26, 27).

Before you enter into prayer, ask thy soul these questions: To what end, O my soul, art thou retired into this place? Art thou not come to discourse the Lord in prayer? Is he present, will he hear thee? Is he merciful, will he help thee? Is thy business slight, is it not concerning the welfare of thy soul? What words wilt thou use to move him to compassion?

—John Bunyan, *Selections from the Writings of John Bunyan*

❧ Upright Christians pray without ceasing; though they pray not always with their mouths, yet their hearts pray continually, sleeping and waking; for the sigh of a true Christian is a prayer. As the Psalm saith:

"Because of the deep sighing of the poor, I will up, saith the Lord," &c. In like manner a true Christian always carries the cross, though he feel it not always.

The Lord's prayer binds the people together, and knits them one to another, so that one prays for another, and together one with another; and it is so strong and powerful that it even drives away the fear of death.

Prayer preserves the church, and hitherto has done the best for the church; therefore we must continually pray. Hence, Christ says: "Ask, and ye shall have; seek, and ye shall find; knock, and it shall be opened unto you."

First when we are in trouble, he will have us to pray; for God often as it were, hides himself, and will not hear; yea, will not suffer himself to be found. Then we must seek him; that is, we must continue in prayer. When we seek him, he often locks himself up, as it were, in a private chamber; if we intend to come in unto him, then we must knock, and when we have knocked once or twice, then he begins a little to hear. At last, when we make much knocking, then he opens, and says: What will ye have? Lord, say we, we would have this or that; then, say he, Take it unto you. In such sort must we persist in praying, and waken God up.
—Martin Luther, *Table-Talk*

ɤ It was . . . holy intercession that raised Christians to such a state of mutual love, as far exceeded all that had been praised and admired in human friendship. And when the same spirit of intercession is again in the world, when Christianity has the same power over the hearts of people that it then had, this holy friendship will be again in fashion, and Christians will be again the wonder of the world, for that exceeding love which they bear to one another.

For a frequent intercession with God, earnestly beseeching Him to forgive the sins of all mankind, to bless them with His providence, enlighten them with

His Spirit, and bring them to everlasting happiness, is the divinest exercise that the heart of man can be engaged in.

Be daily, therefore, on your knees, in a solemn deliberate performance of this devotion, praying for others in such forms, with such length, importunity, and earnestness, as you use for yourself; and you will find all little, ill-natured passions die away, your heart grow great and generous, delighting in the common happiness of others, as you used only to delight in your own.

For he that daily prays to God, that all men may be happy in Heaven, takes the likeliest way to make him wish for, and delight in their happiness on earth. And it is hardly possible for you to beseech and entreat God to make any one happy in the highest enjoyments of his glory to all eternity, and yet be troubled to see him enjoy the much smaller gifts of God in his short and low state of human life. For how strange and unnatural would it be, to pray to God to grant health and longer life to a sick man, and at the same time to envy him the poor pleasure of agreeable medicines!

Yet this would be no more strange or unnatural than to pray to God that your neighbour may enjoy the highest degrees of His mercy and favour, and yet at the same time envy him the little credit and figure he hath amongst his fellow creatures.

When therefore you have once habituated your heart to a serious performance of this holy intercession, you have done a great deal to render it incapable of spite and envy, and to make it naturally delight in the happiness of all mankind.

This is the natural effect of a general intercession for all mankind. But the greatest benefits of it are then received, when it descends to such particular instances as our state and condition in life more particularly require of us.

—William Law, *A Serious Call to a Devout and Holy Life*

❧ Growth in spiritual personality means growth in charity. And charity—energetic love of God, and of all men in God—operating in the world of prayer, is the live wire along which the power of God, indwelling our finite spirits, can and does act on other souls and other things; rescuing, healing, giving support and light. That, of course, is real intercession; which is gravely misunderstood by us, if we think of it mainly in terms of asking God to grant particular needs and desires. Such secret intercessory prayer ought to penetrate and accompany all our active work, if it is really to be turned to the purposes of God. It is the supreme expression of the spiritual life on earth: moving from God to man, through us, because we have ceased to be self-centered units, but are woven into the great fabric of praying souls, the "mystical body" through which the work of Christ goes on being done.

Those who deal much with souls soon come to know something about the strange spiritual currents which are at work under the surface of life, and the extent in which charity can work on supernatural levels for supernatural ends. But if you are to do that, the one thing that matters is that you should care supremely about it; care in fact, so much that you do not mind how much you suffer for it. We cannot help anyone until we do care, for it is only by love that spirit penetrates spirit.

—Evelyn Underhill, *Selections from the Writings of Evelyn Underhill*

41. Contemplative Life

Affirmation

The Lord is good to those who hope in him, to the person who seeks him. It's good to wait in silence for the Lord's deliverance (Lam. 3:25-26).

Psalm: 25

Psalm Prayer

Holy God, grant us peace in this noisy world, that all our attention may be directed toward you. May your ways be made known to us through the calming of our hearts and quieting of our minds, in the name of your Son, Jesus Christ. Amen.

Daily Scripture Readings

Sunday	A.	Genesis 37:1-4, 12-28;
		Psalm 105:1-6, 16-22, 45;
		Romans 10:5-15;
		Matthew 14:22-33
	B.	2 Samuel 18:5-9, 15, 31-33;
		Psalm 130; Ephesians 4:25–5:2;
		John 6:35, 41-51
	C.	Isaiah 1:1, 10-20;
		Psalm 50:1-8, 22-23;
		Hebrews 11:1-3, 8-16;
		Luke 12:32-40
Monday		Leviticus 23:1-3
Tuesday		Psalm 62:1-2, 5-8
Wednesday		Psalm 48:9-11
Thursday		Matthew 26:36-44
Friday		Acts 10:9-33
Saturday		Ephesians 1:15-19

Silence

Daily Readings for Reflection

Reflections: Silent or Written

Prayers: For the World, for Others, for Myself

Offering of Self to God
May we find our strength in quietness and trust, O God, and discover the peace found only in you (Isa. 30:15). Amen.

Blessing
We put our hope in the LORD. He is our help and our shield. Our heart rejoices in God because we trust his holy name. LORD, let your faithful love surround us, because we wait for you (Ps. 33:20-22). The grace of the Lord Jesus Christ be with us, now and forever. Amen.

Readings for Reflection

✺ Deep in our hearts we know that many things cannot be hurried without endangering the results for which we wait. Friendship, character, personal transformation, pregnancy, ripened fruit, and sprouting seeds all take time. Each has its own schedule. While we may encourage a peach to ripen, it still requires a certain number of days on the tree and in the sun. Trying to hasten the process can lead to less than desirable results.
—Rueben P. Job

✺ Richard Baxter, the seventeenth-century English divine, once described the chief end of contemplation as "acquaintance and fellowship with God" (*The Saints' Everlasting Rest*). The homely simplicity of Baxter's definition points to the essential dimensions of contemplative life. It is, in the first place, a life of deepening acquaintance with God, a life of removing the layers of misunderstanding that obscure our relationship with the Holy One. As we strip away the fear, mistrust, anger, or pain that encases our heart, we come to see that our desire for God is in fact an echo of God's far more encompassing and passionate desire for us. Contemplative awareness confirms that God is closer than we think, that there is no path to God that is not first God's path to us. Contemplative life explores these paths; it is wholly dedicated to the one thing necessary; it is a life consumed with and by God, and therefore a life committed to ever more unguarded exposure to the love that is at once the source, transformation, and joy of human existence.

—John S. Mogabgab, "Editor's Introduction," *Weavings*
   (July/August 1992)

    Contemplation is the ever-fresh world of the spiritual heart. Noncontemplation is the ever-constricted world of the head, sense, and feelings separated from that heart. The spiritual heart is the true center of our being. It is the placeless place where divine Spirit and human spirit live together. When the great historical spiritual elders of the church advocated keeping the mind in the heart, I believe they were speaking of the need to keep our thoughts, feelings, bodies, actions, wills, and sense of identity connected with our spiritual heart day by day, moment by moment. Our sanity and authentic discernment, love, and delight depend on this connectedness.

—Tilden H. Edwards Jr., "Living the Day from the
   Heart," *Weavings*

    When the Israelites were wandering in the desert, they were hungry and thirsty and complained constantly that God must have abandoned them, lured them into the desert so they could die there. Despite all of their grumbling, God reached out to them in mercy to meet their needs. God gave them manna and quails to eat. And God told Moses to strike a rock. When he did so, water poured forth, living water (which is to say, flowing water rather than the dead water of a pool). When we feel lost and thirsty, we find that God has already reached out to us in mercy, just as God did for those people long ago. God has given us Jesus, the source of the living water that bubbles up inside us so that we need never thirst; Jesus, who was wounded for our salvation. If I meditate on the story and identify myself with the grumbling children of Israel, there can be no question about how to identify the rock. The rock is Christ.

—Keith Beasley-Topliffe, "And the Rock Was Christ," *Weavings*

᠕ If contemplative prayer differs significantly from other forms of prayer cultivated throughout Christendom, past and present—petition, methodical meditation, praise, lament—its distinctiveness is that in contemplation we allow ourselves to be acted upon rather than act as agents. When we ask God for things, when we seek to intercede for others, when we lift our voices in hymnic worship, when we consider the words of scripture, we tend to be about bringing our own intentions, images, and perceptions into the presence of God. I don't mean this to be in any way a negative comment. We know and love God precisely though our capacities to conceptualize and perceive. We praise and grow intimate with the Divine Lover revealed to us through the Word and through the Word made flesh. That is the magnificent and startling insight of our Christian faith—that God is with us, God is revealed among us.

But contemplation is a form of prayer that leads us through and, ultimately, beyond our present concepts and images. The contemplative life, as a consciously walked path, is a process of letting go of the familiar ways we have known and experienced God. As a spiritual reality it is intertwined with the psychological experience of growth and moral development. As we mature, we encounter ideas and events that profoundly challenge the sense we have made of human life. Sometimes the encounter is shattering, so much so that we feel, or may actually be, utterly adrift. When this happens, we employ various strategies to create a psychic field of equilibrium—retreat to previously known categories, deny or reject our experience, adopt a callous cynicism, fade into apathy, create separate psychic spaces for varied kinds of knowing (we are particularly good at having a freestanding psychic box for "religion" that doesn't seem to touch other "business," "politics," or "relationship" boxes)—or we just might be changed and have our new experience modify, enlarge, or enrich our previous ways of knowing.

Our experiences and perceptions of God and of reality grounded in God undergo similar transformations. The contemplative life is that radical and risky opening of self to be changed by and, in some way, *into* God's own self. It is a *formative* life; it changes us and our perceptions. It causes us to see beyond our present seeing. Thus it is a life of continual dying, of being stripped over and over again of the comfortable and familiar, a life of letting go and allowing a reality beyond our own to shape us. From another perspective, it is a life of emerging spaciousness, of being made wide and broad and empty enough to hold the vast and magnificent and excruciating paradoxes of created life in the crucible of love.

—Wendy M. Wright, "Contemplation in Time of War,"
  Weavings

❧ There is an indifferent, or even negative, attitude toward silence which sees in it a disparagement of God's revelation in the Word. This is the view which misinterprets silence as a ceremonial gesture, as a mystical desire to get beyond the Word. This is to miss the essential relationship of silence to the Word. Silence is the simple stillness of the individual under the Word of God. We are silent before hearing the Word because our thoughts are already directed to the Word, as a child is quiet when he enters his father's room. We are silent after hearing the Word because the Word is still speaking and dwelling within us. We are silent at the beginning of the day because God should have the first word, and we are silent before going to sleep because the last word also belongs to God. We keep silence solely for the sake of the Word, and therefore not in order to show disregard for the Word but rather to honor and receive it.

Silence is nothing else but waiting for God's Word and coming from God's Word with a blessing. But everybody already knows that this is something that needs to be practiced and learned, in these days when talkativeness prevails. Real silence, real stillness, really holding one's tongue comes only as the sober consequence of spiritual stillness.

—Dietrich Bonhoeffer, *Selections from the Writings of Dietrich Bonhoeffer*

ᐳ We need also times of silent waiting, alone, when the busy intellect is not leaping from problem to problem, and from puzzle to puzzle. If we learn the secret of carrying a living silence in the center of our being we can listen on the run. The listening silence can become intertwined with all our inward prayers. A few moments of relaxed silence, alone, every day, are desperately important. When distracting noises come, don't fight against them, do not elbow them out, but accept them and weave them by prayer into the silence. Does the wind rattle the window? Then pray, "So let the wind of the Spirit shake the Christian church into life," and absorb it into the silent listening. Does a child cry in the street outside? Then pray, "So cries my infant soul, which does not know the breadth of Thy heart," and absorb it into the silent listening of prayer.

—Thomas Kelly, *The Sanctuary of the Soul*

ᐳ When the heart is fixed on God, it can easily accustom itself to suspend the natural movements of ardent feeling, and to wait for the favorable moment when the voice within may speak. This is the continual sacrifice of self and the life of faith. This death of self is a blessed life; for the grace that brings peace succeeds to the passions that produce trouble. Endeavor to acquire a habit of looking to this light within you; then all your life will gradually become a prayer.

—Francois Fenelon, *Selections from the Writings of Francois Fenelon*

  All that Christians do, even in eating and sleeping, is prayer when done in simplicity, according to the order of God, without either adding to or diminishing from it by their own choice.

—John Wesley, *A Longing for Holiness*

The Season after Pentecost/Ordinary Time
Sunday between August 14 and August 20

42. Discernment

Affirmation
An understanding mind gains knowledge; the ear of
the wise seeks knowledge (Prov. 18:15).

Psalm: 139

Psalm Prayer
O God, the source of all understanding, wisdom, and
knowledge, instill within us discerning hearts and
minds that we may come to know your plan for our
lives. May we trust in your will and walk boldly and
with confidence the path you have set before us, this
day and always. Amen.

Daily Scripture Readings

Sunday	A.	Genesis 45:1-15; Psalm 133; Romans 11:1-2, 29-32; Matthew 15:21-28
	B.	1 Kings 2:10-12; 3:3-14; Psalm 111; Ephesians 5:15-20; John 6:51-58
	C.	Isaiah 5:1-7; Psalm 80:1-2, 8-19; Hebrews 11:29–12:2; Luke 12:49-56
Monday		1 Kings 3:10-14
Tuesday		Daniel 2:17-23
Wednesday		Mark 10:17-22
Thursday		John 8:12-20
Friday		Ephesians 4:7-16
Saturday		Philippians 1:3-11

Silence

Daily Readings for Reflection

Reflections: Silent or Written

Prayers: For the World, for Others, for Myself

Offering of Self to God
You, LORD, are my portion, my cup; you control my destiny. . . . I will bless the LORD who advises me; even at night I am instructed in the depths of my mind (Ps. 16:5, 7). Amen.

Blessing
May the Lord of peace, insight, and discernment, the God in whom "all the treasures of wisdom and knowledge are hidden" (Col. 2:3), be with us throughout this day and always. Amen.

Readings for Reflection

❧ According to the final verses of the Gospel of Matthew, Jesus met the disciples to give them direction and the promise of his presence. The Bible is filled with stories of people who received direction from God. Through the centuries, faithful disciples have discovered some essential qualities for the life and stance that permit us to receive God's direction.

Practicing a preference for God and God's will is the place to begin. That means putting God ahead of all else in our list of priorities. This is not only the way to receive direction but also the way to a joyful and faithful walk with God every day. Preference for God profoundly affects our lives. We not only receive direction but find our lives transformed as we learn to turn to God and seek to walk with God.

This kind of companionship with God leads to a life of trust and confidence in God that permits us to receive and respond to God's whisper of direction. Do you want to live increasingly in God's presence, receive God's direction, and walk in God's presence? Begin practicing a preference for God and you will discover a growing capacity to receive and respond to God's direction of your life.

—Rueben P. Job

&. Discernment for the Christian community begins with the individual Christian. Do I want to know God's will more than anything else? This question is the entryway into discernment. And it can be answered with affirmation only by those who love God and have learned to trust God. If we have any higher priority in our search for God's guidance, we will not be able to trust our discernment. I must spend enough time in prayer and faithful listening to the voice of God to be brought to that moment of trust and surrender when I can give up my preconceived ideas and become open to God's idea. My first concern is not my desired result. My first concern is always God and the fidelity of our relationship, and then the result of my discernment efforts will come quite naturally. We know that God is completely faithful, and we must be alert, prayerful, open, and ready to respond in obedience if we are to be led toward greater faithfulness on our part.

—Rueben P. Job, *A Guide to Spiritual Discernment*

&. Can Christians know God's will? Can the Church know God's will? Can our congregation know God's will? Nearly two thousand years of experience shout a resounding yes! But it will not be easy to know God's will because such knowledge begins with us. We first must offer our lives to God in all of the completeness we can bring and then listen in all the ways we know for the voice of the One who alone can transform our lives, our congregations, our denomination, the entire Body of Christ, and even the world. As we listen, hear, and respond, we will discover transformation occurring within and around us and perhaps, even to our surprise, we will begin to see clearly God's will. May it be so!

—Rueben P. Job, *A Guide to Spiritual Discernment*

◆ Discernment calls to us in our own deep yearnings. It beckons as a pathway we can take in response to these yearnings. . . . [D]iscernment comes to us as a gift, pure and simple.

Seeing discernment as a gift puts all our efforts in perspective. Yes, we follow certain counsels of wisdom as we seek to discern. We engage in specific processes, take particular steps. From one angle of vision, we rightly see discernment as a pathway or method. Yet that method cannot guarantee that, with sufficient personal effort, we will arrive at clarity. It is not even a pathway we take accompanied by God so that we may, with a bit of help, attain a sharper vision. We take the pathway simply and solely to prepare ourselves to receive the gift of discernment however and wherever it comes.
—Stephen V. Doughty and Marjorie J. Thompson, *The Way of Discernment*

◆ The monk Thomas Merton once asked an earnest student a question that he immediately answered himself: "How does an apple ripen? It just sits in the sun." The student, James Finley, thought long about that image and years later wrote, "A small green apple cannot ripen in one night by tightening all its muscles, squinting its eyes and tightening its jaw in order to find itself the next morning miraculously large, red, ripe and juicy." The apple just sits in the sun. It is naturally positioned to receive the daily nourishment it needs to ripen. This is similar to how we mature in the fullness of God's life, except that we are not naturally positioned like the apple. We must place ourselves where we can receive the light of God, and this is the purpose of spiritual disciplines. Through them we position ourselves to receive the sunlight of God's grace.
—Stephen V. Doughty and Marjorie J. Thompson, *The Way of Discernment*

◆ Early on in my pastoral education, a supervisor warned me, "When you go back to that local congregation, somebody is going to say to you, 'Preacher, this [program, agenda, business venture—you fill in the blank] is gold. This is genuine.' Not everything people in the church offer or promote will be gold. Use your nose. Some of it will stink like garbage." Herod beseeched the magi to search for the king. As I play out this scene in my mind's eye, I envision Herod's adding, "Great will be your reward."

Maybe the magi believe Herod until they hear the Herodian chortle, "Yes, great will be your reward. That's gold!" When the magi sniff the air, they realize that Herod's gold stinks. Perhaps their study and devotion lead them to this conclusion. Perhaps their openness to God's leading awakens them to Herod's evil.

—George Hovaness Donigian, "All that Glitters May Not Be Gold," *The Upper Room Disciplines 1999*

❧ Knowing God is a gift of the Spirit, which God gives to those who open themselves to the teaching of the Spirit. God's Spirit comprehends and relays those things that are beyond human knowing, beyond sight and hearing, to those who love God.

The Spirit's teaching enables us to discern our God-given gifts. In the meeting of our gifts and the world's need, we discover our Christian vocation. The Spirit's teachings speak to our hearts of things spiritual.

Having the mind of Christ enables us to use our senses and our minds in disciplined and faithful ways; we are open to discern God's justice and God's compassion. Having the mind of Christ means thinking, loving, and caring beyond the boundaries of human time and understanding.

Discerning goes beyond using our minds to figure things out. It goes beyond what our senses convey to us. Discerning is opening our hearts and minds to God's Spirit so that we may understand the gifts that God bestows on us.

—Linda J. Vogel, "Called to Live and Teach God's Commands," *The Upper Room Disciplines 1999*

❧ Even as discernment beckons through our inmost desires, it stretches out as a path before us and invites us to enter. The word *discernment* itself implies the existence of a pathway toward greater clarity in our times of wondering. It comes from the Latin *discernere*, meaning "to separate," "to distinguish." The word *discernment* denotes an activity or process. It suggests that when we yearn to find what is right and fitting, there will be a means to do so. On the most elemental level, to discern is to sort and sift through the possibilities when we face a variety of choices. It is to distinguish and separate the alternatives. The very word *discernment* thus suggests a helpful means of going forward.

From deep within ourselves we sense a desire to engage in right actions, to make wise choices, to live in a fruitful manner. Then from beyond ourselves we begin to hear, "Look, there is a way you can follow that leads toward greater understanding. There are steps you can take that will open you to the clarity you seek." We stand before the forest of our own wonderings. Then bit by bit, we become aware of a path through the forest.

Many of us have caught hints of this path in simple practices we learned during our earliest years or picked up from persons wiser than ourselves. We make a decision but then say, "I really need the perspective of a trusted friend," or "I am going to take time to consider where my decision might lead in the long run." When we engage in such practices, we do so with the sense that there is at least a partial path through our wondering.

—Stephen V. Doughty and Marjorie J. Thompson, *The Way of Discernment*

The Season after Pentecost/Ordinary Time
Sunday between August 21 and August 27

43. Wisdom

Affirmation
Happy are those who find wisdom and those who gain understanding. Her profit is better than silver, and her gain better than gold (Prov. 3:13-14).

Psalm: 111

Psalm Prayer
True wisdom is found only in you, O Lord. Grant us the wisdom to know what it is you would have us do, to follow and serve you, today and forever. Amen.

Daily Scripture Readings

Sunday	A.	Exodus 1:8-2:10; Psalm 124; Romans 12:1-8; Matthew 16:13-20
	B.	1 Kings 8:1, 6, 10-11, 22-30, 41-43; Psalm 84; Ephesians 6:10-20; John 6:56-69
	C.	Jeremiah 1:4-10; Psalm 71:1-6; Hebrews 12:18-29; Luke 13:10-17
Monday		2 Chronicles 1:7-13
Tuesday		Job 28:12-28
Wednesday		Proverbs 2:1-15, 20-22
Thursday		Matthew 18:1-5
Friday		1 Corinthians 2:6-16
Saturday		James 1:19-27

Silence

Daily Readings for Reflection

Reflection: Silent or Written

Prayers: For the World, for Others, for Myself

Offering of Self to God
I will bless the LORD who advises me; even at night I am instructed in the depths of my mind. I always put the LORD in front of me; I will not stumble because he is on my right side (Ps. 16:7-8). Amen.

Blessing
May our prayer be this: that our love might become richer with knowledge and insight. May the God of peace be with us all. Amen.

Readings for Reflection

❧ What does the voice of God sound like? The voice from heaven reported in Matthew 17:1-8 suggests that when we listen to Jesus, we hear the voice of God. The voice the disciples heard was understandable, and it directed them to listen to Jesus, the beloved son. It is not that difficult to read the words of Jesus. To listen to and obey those words is more demanding.

As Christians we share the good news that God can be heard, understood, and obeyed. We have scriptures, nature, history, and the stories of our lives that speak God's truth. Further we have the capacity to "hear" God's voice deep within our own souls. Through the centuries, faithful listeners have discovered ways to sharpen their listening skills. Practices and disciplines increase our desire and capacity to be faithful to what we hear and know to be the voice of God. John Wesley called these practices "means of grace," that is, practices that mediate God's love, will, presence, and power in very special ways.

A complete list of the means of grace likely includes all things. A God for whom all things are possible may use any and all things to address us. And yet it seems most often the voice and message of God are heard and the presence and power of God are felt when people quietly, fervently, and faithfully pray, worship, witness, and serve humankind. Do you want to hear

God speak to you? Polish up your practices of prayer, worship, witness, and service, and you will be amazed at what you hear.
—Rueben P. Job

❧ Years ago I was consulting with a congregation about their future. In a large gathering, to which all members had been invited, the question was raised, "What would you most like your congregation to do for you?"

Much to everyone's surprise, the answer from one person was, "Teach me to pray." This older adult said she had been baptized at the altar of the church, confirmed there, married there, saw her own children baptized and confirmed there, and held her husband's memorial service there. Yet, in all of those experiences and in all of those years, no one had ever taught her how to pray.

Of course, we could say that she could have been learning to pray on her own, and I am sure she did. But the point was well made. We often fail to give Christians adequate tools to cultivate their relationship with God or to live as faithful disciples. The inheritance that belongs to every Christian is frequently left unclaimed. So many of us live a poverty-stricken spiritual life.

Regular classes on prayer that teach a variety of methods and provide a variety of experiences of prayer are a vital part of any ministry that desires to feed the hungry hearts of members, visitors, and friends. Many have not been taught the most elementary lessons of Bible study or of prayer. Learning to listen for the voice of God in all of life is a discipline infrequently employed. And learning to discriminate among all the voices clamoring for our attention is a forgotten gift. Consequently, the rich spiritual gifts that God is eager to give often go unrecognized and unclaimed.
—Rueben P. Job, *Spiritual Life in the Congregation*

᭥ Autumn is making its way across the prairie, and with it God's silent and unseen artists turn the entire landscape into a magnificent work of art. The colors of the trees, the little touches added by the farmers—green and golden fields, hay bales put in just the right places. Cattle—red, brown, black, white; the little wild turkeys and their ever-watchful mothers just outside my window; indeed, never has there been an artist like God.

Thank you Creator God for the artistic changes of the seasons, for the beauty of your fascinating and ever changing creation! Come dear autumn, bathe our senses with your beauty and lay living nature gently to sleep in the arms of winter. There all may rest to be restored in the blazing beauty of spring!
—Norman Shawchuck

᭥ [W]isdom is not limited to the ivory towers of a privileged few but is revealed in all walks of life for any who live in righteousness, justice, equity, and prudence. Wisdom comes into the heart of all who embrace God's way (Prov. 2:9-11).
—Elizabeth J. Canham, "Where Shall Wisdom Be Found?" *Weavings*

᭥ Holy wisdom, then, embraces and enables our knowledge, judgment, insight, even as it draws us beyond them. We are given words when we have nothing to say. We are kept silent when we ache to run off at the mouth. We reach out when we would otherwise pull back, cut off, turn away. Our own wisdom is rooted in God's gift of wisdom to us. The soil it grows in is our daily lives, including our relationships with God, ourselves, and others. Only by trusting what little we know, by pushing the edges of our own wisdom, will wisdom grow.

Trusting our own wisdom requires both rigorous self-examination and radical self-acceptance. Self-examination keeps us honest about feelings, motives, and desires. Honesty about self and life is a foundation stone of wisdom. Through self-acceptance, we allow ourselves—both in our strengths and weaknesses—to be embraced as God's beloved. Radical, or rooted, self-acceptance reveals both the transcendence and immanence of God. We sense God's transcendence as our struggles to live wisely draw us beyond our small selves toward the true selves God desires us to be. Likewise, radical self-acceptance confronts us with God's immanence by asking us if we really trust that God is present *in* us and can work in and through us. In trusting our own wisdom, we embrace the Source of all wisdom that is present and active within, even as we acknowledge the greater wisdom beyond the boundaries of our being. This wisdom, present both in us and beyond us, is dynamic, relational, responsive. It is crucial for our own well-being and the well-being of our world.

—Jean M. Blomquist, "Fried Dirt and Frayed Faith," *Weavings*

❧ Truth sees God, and wisdom beholds God, and from these two comes the third, and that is a marvelous delight in God, which is love. Where truth and wisdom are, truly there is love, coming from both of them. All are of God's making. For God is endless sovereign truth, endless sovereign wisdom, endless sovereign uncreated love. The human soul is a creature in which God has created the same properties. More and more it does what it was made for: it sees God and beholds God and loves God. So God rejoices in the creature and the creature in God, endlessly marveling. In this marveling we see our God, our Lord, our Maker, so high, great, and good in comparison to us creatures that we scarcely seem anything at all to ourselves. But the brightness and clearness of truth and wisdom make us see and know that we are made for love. And in this love God protects us forever.

—Julian of Norwich, *Encounter with God's Love*

❧ In the scriptures, the way of wisdom is not an easy way, but it is life-giving. In the magnificent opening chapter of John's Gospel, Jesus is the Word through whom all things come into being. Jesus comes to his own people with the good news of new life and a new relationship with God for all who receive him but, sadly, many turn away. The same was true in the Old Testament where Wisdom (the feminine image of God) offered her riches to people though many turned away. "Wisdom cries out in the street; in the squares she raises her voice. At the busiest corner she cries out; at the entrance of the city gates she speaks . . ." (Prov. 1:20-21). As this first chapter in Proverbs unfolds we meet the scoffers, those who do not fear God but choose waywardness. Chapter two reveals the blessings of wisdom for those who search for her like silver and hidden treasures (2:4) and promises that she will take up residence in their hearts. A number of biblical scholars have noted that in the first chapter of the Johannine portrait of Jesus, the author blends the images of Word and Wisdom: Jesus is the Word made flesh, but Jesus is also like Wisdom and just as people turned away from Wisdom offered in the Hebrew scriptures, so too many of Jesus' listeners turn away from the way of life he offers. But those who believe in him, who truly hear God's Word, receive the authority to become children of God and to follow the Wisdom-Word Christ out of darkness onto a path of light and life. In Jesus, the Word became flesh and lived among us (John 1:14) and as his life unfolds he clearly speaks and teaches with the voice of God's wisdom.

—Elizabeth J. Canham, "Where Shall Wisdom Be Found?" *Weavings*

❧ Ultimately, the Word of God offers life-changing wisdom for us all. As I search for God in the written and spoken word, I encounter the Word who came among us and shares the joys and struggles of being fully human. I also find wisdom nudging me to "mine" more deeply into the dark places of my own life and of the suffering human community beyond me so that "gems" of God's wisdom might be brought to light in these difficult times. It is from these same depths, the depths from which Jesus overcame darkness and brought forth light and life, that God continues to call us all to search for wisdom that can be found.

—Elizabeth J. Canham, "Where Shall Wisdom Be Found?" *Weavings*

ﮠ "Wisdom" in scripture isn't abstract philosophy, but practical, down-to-earth know-how to pursue the good in the midst of challenge, temptation, and difficulty. The price of wisdom, in the biblical sense, is the willingness to learn: "Get wisdom, and whatever else you get, get insight," say the biblical wise ones (Prov. 4:7*b*). The price of such learning sometimes involves unlearning—having our illusions exploded.

—Robert Corin Morris, "Disillusionment, Deliverance, and Delight," *Weavings*

44. Mind Your Call

Affirmation
I know the plans I have in mind for you, declares the
Lord; they are plans for peace, not disaster, to give you
a future filled with hope (Jer. 29:11).

Psalm: 29

Psalm Prayer
Gracious, merciful, and loving God, whose voice calls
to us from over the waters like thunder, may we be
ever mindful and attentive to your call so we might
know what it is you would have us do. Be with us
as we faithfully accept our calling without hesitation
or fear, and enter into it with persistence, trust, and
strength. Amen.

Daily Scripture Readings

Sunday	A.	Exodus 3:1-15;
		Psalm 105:1-6, 23-26, 45;
		Romans 12:9-21;
		Matthew 16:21-28
	B.	Song of Solomon 2:8-13;
		Psalm 45:1-2, 6-9; James 1:17-27;
		Mark 7:1-8, 14-15, 21-23
	C.	Jeremiah 2:4-13;
		Psalm 81:1, 10-16;
		Hebrews 13:1-8, 15-16;
		Luke 14:1, 7-14
Monday		Exodus 3:7-12
Tuesday		1 Samuel 3:11-21
Wednesday		Jonah 1:1-3; 3
Thursday		Matthew 4:18-22
Friday		Luke 8:4-15
Saturday		Acts 10:1-8

Silence

Daily Readings for Reflection

Reflection: Silent and Written

Prayers: For the World, for Others, for Myself

Offering of Self to God
Teach me your way, LORD, so that I can walk in your truth. Make my heart focused only on honoring your name. I give thanks to you, my Lord, my God, with all my heart, and I will glorify your name forever (Ps. 86:11-12). Amen.

Blessing
May the eyes of our hearts "have enough light to see what is the hope of God's call, what is the richness of God's glorious inheritance among believers, and what is the overwhelming greatness of God's power that is working among us believers" (Eph. 1:18-19). Amen.

Readings for Reflection

࿎ God draws each one of us to the heart of life in a time and manner uniquely suited to our own nature and circumstance. Your journey and mine cannot be the same, even if we are identical twins! Yet our many journeys share remarkable commonalities, points where we find comfort in human identification and common ground. The signs of God's grace at work in us are often strikingly similar: perhaps a sense of being overwhelmed by prayer answered beyond our best hopes; the experience of anguish over prayer not answered the way we had hoped, yet in retrospect answered in an unexpected and perhaps deeper way; the intuition that God has called us to a task we felt was beyond our gifts or capacity, yet through faith and

perseverance, we discovered it to be a genuine call for which God equipped us.
—Rueben P. Job and Marjorie J. Thompson, *Companions in Christ*

≈ There is as much guidance in the way that closes behind us as there is in the way that opens ahead of us. The opening way reveals our potentials while the closing way reveals our limitations—and the two are the flip sides of the same coin, the coin called my true and created self. In the spiritual life, self-knowledge is the coin of the realm, and we can learn much about the whole coin from studying either side. . . .

The truth is that every time a door closes behind us, the rest of the world opens up in front of us. All we need to do is stop pounding on the door that is closed, turn around, and see the largeness of life that now lies open to our soul.

If we are to live our lives fully and well, we must learn to embrace the opposites, to live in a creative tension between our limits and our potentials. We must honor our limitations in ways that do not distort our nature—and trust and use our gifts in ways that fulfill the potentials God gave us. We must take the "no" of the way that closes and find the guidance it has to offer—and take the "yes" of the way that opens and respond with the "yes" of our lives.
—Parker J. Palmer, "On Minding Your Call," *Weavings*

≈ My God, in these quiet moments I caught a glimpse of your vision for me. Inspire me, my God, to carry into the everydayness of my life all to which I aspire at such a moment as this. May my faith have feet and hands, a voice and a heart, that it may minister to others—that the gospel I profess may be seen in my life.

I go this hour to encounter the routine of the duty with a new vision. Equip me for my common tasks, that I may this day apply myself to them with fidelity and devotion. And not for myself alone do I pray:

Bless homemakers, mothers, and servants, who minister in the home and who maintain sacred sanctuaries to which tired persons return at the end of the day.

Bless doctors and nurses. May their work reflect God's love and pity on those who leave this earth today.

Bless the teachers, the school administrators, and those who labor to keep school buildings clean and pleasant for those who study and learn there.

Bless coal miners and all who toil in grime and darkness, that we may enjoy clean and pleasant lives.

May your blessing rest upon all men and women who minister to others. May each one come to know the joy of partnership with you.

I give this prayer to you who inflames my soul with vision and desire, that I may be a faithful laborer in the fields you have assigned to my stewardship. Help me to be a good and faithful steward.

—Norman Shawchuck

&. There is no "typical" call. Other persons, no doubt more open-minded and willing than I, seem to experience their call in a gentler process, involving a gradual clarifying. Others make step-by-step choices, learning from their experience, heeding the counsel of mentors and friends, sorting and discerning. Commitment then becomes a kind of distilling process guided over a period of time by the Holy Spirit. The focus too of the call can differ. I name "the desire for God" as the grounding of my own call; others might name their calls in terms of a life of service, community, or the poor. A call might be such that it requires all one's life energies and a life commitment, or it might be, at a different level, a temporary call to service in a particular situation that lies as a burden on one's heart. Its temporary quality does not make it any less a call. For most, the call has a particular container—a marriage, a church community, a mission site. At the deepest level, the call *frees* us. It enables us to see what really matters, to focus our love, to dedicate ourselves to something/ Someone larger than ourselves, and so to enter consciously into that continual stream of losing and finding ourselves that is the mystery of life. God uses a variety of ways to get through to us, tailoring the call to the condition of the recipient. No matter how the call comes, whether explosively or gently, the response has to be worked out in daily fidelity, in ordinary life. Keeping the focus in the midst of the seductive values of the culture becomes our life task.

—Elaine M. Prevallet, SL, "Minding the Call," *Weavings*

❧ When we say Yes or No to calls for service on the basis of heady decisions, we have to give reasons, to ourselves and to others. But when we say Yes or No to calls, on the basis of inner guidance and whispered promptings of encouragement from the Center of our life, or on the basis of a lack of any inward "rising" of that Life to encourage us in the call, we have no reason to give, except one—the will of God as we discern it. Then we have begun to live in guidance. And I find He never guides us into an intolerable scramble of panting feverishness. The Cosmic Patience becomes, in part, our patience, for after all God is at work in the world. It is not we alone who are at work in the world, frantically finishing a work to be offered to God.

Life from the Center is a life of unhurried peace and power. It is simple. It is serene. It is amazing. It is triumphant. It is radiant. It takes no time, but it occupies all our time. And it makes our life programs new and overcoming. We need not get frantic. He is at the helm. And when our little day is done we lie down quietly in peace, for all is well.

—Thomas Kelly, *A Testament of Devotion*

❧ Endeavor to be inclined always:
   not to the easiest, but to the most difficult;

not to the most delightful, but to the most
   distasteful;
not to the most gratifying, but to the less pleasant;
not to what means rest for you, but to hard work;
not to the most, but to the least;
not to the highest and most precious, but to the
   lowest and most despised;
not to wanting something, but to wanting nothing.
—John of the Cross, *Loving God through the Darkness*

≈ St. Paul did not want to be an apostle to the Gentiles.
. . . He wanted to be a clever and appreciated young
Jewish scholar, and kicked against the pricks. St.
Ambrose and St. Augustine did not want to be over-
worked and worried bishops. Nothing was farther from
their intention. St. Cuthbert wanted the solitude and
freedom of his hermitage on the Farne; but he did not
often get there. St. Francis Xavier's preference was for
an ordered life close to his beloved master, St. Ignatius.
At a few hours' notice he was sent out to be the Apostle
of the Indies and never returned to Europe again. Henry
Martyn, the fragile and exquisite scholar, was compelled to sacrifice the intellectual life to which he was
so perfectly fitted for the missionary life to which he felt
he was decisively called. In all these, a power beyond
themselves decided the direction of life. Yet in all, we
recognize not frustration, but the highest of all types of
achievement. Things like this—and they are constantly
happening—gradually convince us that the overruling
reality of life is the Will and Choice of a Spirit acting not
in a mechanical but in a living and personal way; and
that the spiritual life of man does not consist in mere
individual betterment, or assiduous attention to his
own soul, but in a free and unconditional response to
that Spirit's pressure and call, whatever the cost may be.
—Evelyn Underhill, *Selections from the Writings of
   Evelyn Underhill*

❧ Once having the vision, the second step to holy obedience is this: Begin where you are. Obey *now*. Use what little obedience you are capable of, even if it be like a grain of mustard seed. Begin where you are. Live this present moment, this present hour as you now sit in your seats, in utter, utter submission and openness toward Him. Listen outwardly to these words, but within, behind the scenes, in the deeper levels of your lives where you are all alone with God the Loving Eternal One, keep up a silent prayer, "Open Thou my life. Guide my thoughts where I dare not let them go. But Thou darest. Thy will be done."
—Thomas Kelly, *The Sanctuary of the Soul*

The Season after Pentecost/Ordinary Time
Sunday between September 4 and September 10

45. Practicing the Presence of God

Affirmation
I am about to come and dwell among you, says the
LORD. Many nations will be joined to the LORD on that
day. They will become my people, and I will dwell
among you so you will know that the LORD of heavenly
forces sent me to you. . . . Be silent, everyone, in the
LORD's presence, because he has moved from his holy
habitation! (Zech. 2:10*b*-11, 13)

Psalm: 132

Psalm Prayer
May we be forever mindful today, O God, that you are
in your dwelling place. Give us full knowledge and
awareness of your saving presence, a presence that surrounds us at all times and reveals itself in love, compassion, and truth. Make yourself known to us today so
we may dwell in you and you in us. Amen.

Daily Scripture Readings

Sunday	A.	Exodus 12:1-14; Psalm 149; Romans 13:8-14; Matthew 18:15-20
	B.	Proverbs 22:1-2, 8-9, 22-23; Psalm 125; James 2:1-10, 14-17; Mark 7:24-37
	C.	Jeremiah 18:1-11; Psalm 139:1-6, 13-18; Philemon 1-21; Luke 14:25-33
Monday		Exodus 33:7-23
Tuesday		Isaiah 63:7-14
Wednesday		Joel 2:18-27
Thursday		Matthew 1:18-25
Friday		Luke 24:13-35
Saturday		Revelation 21:1-7

Silence

Daily Readings for Reflection

Reflection: Silent and Written

Prayers: For the World, for Others, for Myself

Offering of Self to God
Teach us, O Lord, the way of life. In your presence is total celebration. Beautiful things are always in your right hand. Amen.

Blessing
May we have more and more grace and peace through the knowledge of God and Jesus our Lord (2 Pet. 1:2). Amen.

Readings for Reflection

❧ All of us want faithful leaders, and we reject the notion that leaders don't make a difference to the organizations, movements, and groups influencing our lives. We have seen dramatic evidence of the importance of faithful leaders. While we desire faithful leaders, we sometimes make it hard to choose them and even more difficult to keep them. Was the early church better at this than we are? Could the methods used and the qualities sought in those times instruct us in choosing leaders today?

It seems clear that a primary method in the early church was a deliberate search for the will of God. From the choice of David and Gideon to Matthias and Stephen, the method was centered in God and depended upon God. Choosing faithful leaders meant starting with God, continuing with God, concluding with God. Of course, other things were important, but the primary requirement was to know God's choice.
—Rueben P. Job

▪ My God, every fiber of my being vibrates at the touch of your grace—whereby I am given the privilege of being your child. My joy at your overwhelming gestures of love and the high privilege you extend to me of entering into your life invades my being with an acute sense of your ever-nearness. In response to this, my Lord, I offer praises to you.

Yet, my Lord, I am often cold toward you. I forget to love you for long periods of time—and this to my own harm and regret. Forgive me, Lord! Ever-loving God, set my life aflame with love for you only. O my God, I long to reflect your image throughout the world so that others might observe your doing in me and themselves be convinced that you love them also.
—Norman Shawchuck

▪ This morning Jesus touches my heart. He is with me and within me. I love him. I ponder death and the afterlife these days. This life has a sense of value and destiny because it is finite. But there comes an end, and things left undone are left forever unfinished.

But life thereafter seems without end and no final destiny. What then gives it value or motivation? Today there is always another day to do what is left undone. But what of the life to come, what will God replace with this sense of destiny? Will we slip into laziness and sloth? Perhaps this is one reason the scripture urges us to work diligently, to be productive, to establish habits that we will need in the life to come, lest we inherit an eternity of blessed boredom!
(Written shortly after his father's death)
—Norman Shawchuck

▪ Recent rummaging through my home library unearthed a book I had all but forgotten. Its unexpected appearance provided an opportunity to experience again the wonder held within its pages. *Magic Eye II* contains computer-generated illustrations that appear, on first glance, to be nothing more than interesting patterns of color and line. However, when you relax your eyes and gaze through the image rather than at it, an extraordinary transformation occurs. What was a two-dimensional design on the surface of the page changes into a complex three-dimensional graphic. You find yourself drawn through the plane of the page into a marvelous world of spinning planets, dancing ballerinas, and mysterious sea creatures. The authors suggest that learning to see what lies beneath the surface takes practice and may be easier in a quiet, meditative environment.

Daily life careens across the surface of a vast reality whose ancient depths hold unseen beauty and truth. We live and move and have our very being only because of this reality, and yet remain largely unaware of its presence. To become increasingly aware, to plunge through the surface film of life into the immeasurable riches of God's life with us, is the great invitation Jesus gave the disciples of John. When they met Jesus and asked him where he dwelt, Jesus responded, "Come and see" (John 1:35-39). He issues the same invitation to us. Come apart to a quiet place with me and begin to learn the art of deep vision.

Deep vision reveals the unique three-dimensionality of people and things against the backdrop of God's presence. As we cultivate appreciation for this "holy angularity" in all creation, we will find ourselves constantly surprised by new facets of God's love. We may even find ourselves echoing the astonished words of Jacob: "How awesome is this place! This is none other than the house of God, and this is the gate of heaven" (Gen. 28:17).

—John S. Mogabgab, "Editor's Introduction," *Weavings* (January/February 2003)

❧ For when Scripture enjoins us to lay aside private regard to ourselves, it not only divests our minds of an excessive longing for wealth or power or human favor, but eradicates all ambition and thirst for worldly glory, and other more secret pests. The Christian ought, indeed, to be so trained and disposed as to consider that during his whole life he has to do with God. For this reason, as he will bring all things to the disposal and estimate of God, so he will religiously direct his whole mind to Him. For he who has learned to look to God in everything he does, is at the same time diverted from all vain thoughts.

—John Calvin, *Selections from the Writings of John Calvin*

❧ It is an amazing discovery, at first, to find that a creative power and Life is at work in the world. God is no longer the object of a belief; He is a Reality, who has continued, within us, His real Presence in the world. God is aggressive. He is an intruder, a lofty lowly conqueror on whom we had counted too little, because we had counted on ourselves. Too long have we supposed that we must carry the banner of religion, that it was *our* concern. But religion is not our concern; it is God's concern. Our task is to call people to "be still, and know that I am God," to hearken to that of God within them, to invite, to unclasp the clenched fists of self-resolution, to be pliant in His firm guidance, sensitive to the inflections of the inner voice.

—Thomas Kelly, *The Sanctuary of the Soul*

❧ The more you seek for God, the nearer He will be to you; every step that you take toward Him will bring you peace and consolation.

—Francois Fenelon, *Selections from the Writings of Francois Fenelon*

❧ You will do well so to regulate your time that you may have every day a little leisure for reading, meditation, and prayer, to review your defects, to study your duties, and to hold communion with God. You will be happy when a true love to Him shall make this duty easy. When we love God, we do not ask what we shall say to Him. We have no difficulty in conversing with a friend. Our hearts are ever open to Him. We do not think what we shall say to Him, but we say it without reflection. We cannot be reserved. Even when we have nothing to say to Him, we are satisfied with being with Him. Oh, how much better are we sustained by love than by fear! Fear enslaves, constrains, and troubles us; but love persuades, consoles, animates us; possesses our whole soul, and makes us desire goodness for its own sake.

—Francois Fenelon, *Selections from the Writings of Francois Fenelon*

❧ A simple lay monk, Brother Lawrence, made famous the phrase, "practicing the presence of God." He was speaking of a conscious awareness of God in the midst of washing dishes, preparing meals, and having conversations in the community that was his "family." Evelyn Underhill writes of "practical mysticism" in much the same vein, referring to the art of seeing Reality in common, daily realities. Family life is an arena in which most of us have natural occasion to "practice" God's presence—to learn the discipline of keeping our eyes open to the divine Reality shining through our most ordinary moments.

Do you believe that God is present in the smile of a child, in the tears of a parent's grief over a suffering adolescent, in the sudden breakthrough of understanding between quarreling spouses? Eternal truths can be learned by observing the most common elements of life: nursing an infant may be a window onto God's nurturing care for each of us; bandaging a cut can help us know the healing desire of God; playing games may speak of the divine playfulness that knows our need for recreation; tending a garden may teach us the dynamics of growth. Families learn that they are sacred communities when they begin to name and claim the many forms of God's grace in their daily life.

—Marjorie J. Thompson, *Family the Forming Center*

46. Attentiveness

Affirmation
Taste and see how good the LORD is! The one who takes refuge in him is truly happy! (Ps. 34:8).

Psalm: 66

Psalm Prayer
Truly, O Lord, you are the God of faithful love whose awesome deeds have brought us through desert wastes and darkening valleys. May the memory of your great acts on our behalf alert the eyes and ears of our heart to signs of your presence in the thick of daily life. Like the wise virgins awaiting the arrival of the bridegroom, may we greet you with joy and the honor due your name. Amen.

Daily Scripture Readings

Sunday	A.	Exodus 14:19-31; Psalm 114; Romans 14:1-12; Matthew 18:21-35
	B.	Proverbs 1:20-33; Psalm 19; James 3:1-12; Mark 8:27-38
	C.	Jeremiah 4:11-12, 22-28; Psalm 14; 1 Timothy 1:12-17; Luke 15:1-10
Monday		Isaiah 48:12-19
Tuesday		Jeremiah 6:16-19
Wednesday		Ezekiel 11:17-20
Thursday		Mark 4:21-25
Friday		Hebrews 10:23-25
Saturday		2 Peter 1:10-19

Silence

Daily Readings for Reflection

Reflection: Silent or Written

Prayers: For the World, for Others, for Myself

Offering of Self to God
God of immeasurable creativity, you remind us to remain attentive to the new things you are doing to gather us into one, loving, peaceful human community. Even though we are prone to become drowsy in the heavy atmosphere of habit that blankets our days, we commend ourselves to your refreshing grace, that it might awaken us to serve you with renewed attentiveness and energy. Amen.

Blessing
Rejoice, for the Lord is nearby. May the Holy Spirit awaken our capacity to perceive what God is doing in our midst. Amen.

Readings for Reflection

❧ Being a disciple was becoming stressful. The pace clearly had quickened during this three-year course in discipleship. The crowds had grown larger and demanded more. The lessons to be learned often seemed over the heads of the disciples. Jesus talked more and more about his own death and what was to follow. Frankly the disciples did not understand it, and the more confused they became, the more frustrated they became. We can appreciate that phenomenon. It happens to us. When we are under a heavy load for a long period of time, we often become frustrated, impatient, and sometimes not very nice to be around. We even begin to compare ourselves to others and begin to think that we deserve a little bigger slice of the reward pie than even our closest friend.

That kind of reaction to stress may explain why the disciples began arguing about who was to be regarded as the greatest among those who followed Jesus. Jesus shattered their hopes of achieving special status or special reward (Luke 22:26).

The world's system of reward has nothing to do with the disciple's system of reward. A disciple of Jesus Christ is called first to be servant of all, and the leader is to take the lowliest position of service. This system turns the world's concept of leadership upside down. The first disciples found it hard to understand and even more difficult to live by such a value system. But Jesus seems to say there is no other way. Disciples serve.
—Rueben P. Job

ॐ When we stand ready to suffer for our faith, we are standing where Jesus stood—and where he stands even now. He stands with one foot in heaven and the other upon the earth, his hands and side scarred by nails and spear. He stands at the very heart of human history, human suffering, human death, anguish, and tragedy.

But he stands there like a rock! He stands there having endured everything—every human suffering in thought and body. And he says to us, "This is where you must stand, not in a dreamland of faith that deceives you into thinking you can float into heaven on a billowy cloud. No, if ever you are to enter heaven, you will do so at the cost of serving God at the vortex of human suffering and tragedy, and your only earthly reward will be that people curse you for it."

In offering this to you, Jesus is merely suggesting what he already has endured. Saint Paul points to this truth when he suggests that we "run with perseverance the race that is set before us, looking to Jesus the pioneer and perfecter of our faith, who for the sake of the joy that was set before him endured the cross, disregarding its shame, and has taken his seat at the right hand of the throne of God" (Heb. 12:1-2).

So it is! If we follow Jesus closely enough, we may experience all that he endured. Do you remember the poignant question he put to his disciples, "Are you prepared to drink of the cup from which I shall drink?" "Yes," the giddy disciples responded. And so they did.

This must be our answer also. Then when suffering and sacrifice are required of us, we must respond like Isaiah. "Whom shall I send?" inquired the Lord, "Here!" called Isaiah, "Here I am, send me." Like a sheep among wolves. Like the Son of God among broken humanity, send me, O Lord, send me!

—Norman Shawchuck

↜ God's grace precedes, follows, surrounds, and sustains us. It is a constant and completely consistent gift. We cannot stop, alter, or change it. We are eternally cradled in God's abundant and life-giving grace.

While the initiative and the invitation to companionship are entirely God's, response lies with us. God gives us grace to respond to the awakening call of the Holy Spirit, but we can choose to turn away and refuse the invitation. Or we can choose, by the Spirit's help, to walk in faithfulness and harmony with God. By doing so we claim our true and full inheritance as children of God. Choosing to open ourselves to grace means receiving life's greatest gift and walking the path of spiritual abundance.

—Rueben P. Job and Marjorie J. Thompson, *Companions in Christ*

↜ It's not enough to read about prayer or study the lives of the saints or have theological conversation about spiritual practices. We learn to pray by praying. Prayer is both an act and an attitude. We pray in response to the reality of the Triune God by paying attention or by being attentive. God is always present and attentive to us, always pursuing, blessing, and loving us. God is always reaching out to offer grace and goodness to us. God is inexhaustible and unrelenting in pure presence.

Prayer is then our attentiveness to God. It enables us to live in this presence and to engage in actions that keep us responsive and attentive. We often speak of prayer as conversation, communication, or communion with God, and this is true. But for me, the word *prayer* describes what Brother Lawrence called "the practice of the presence of God."

—Daniel Vestal, *Being the Presence of Christ*

❧ Whenever we come near to the beautiful in life, we are judged by it. We are put on trial concerning our soul's purity and work and acquitted or condemned according as we are found able or unable to understand and appreciate. We never know what day may be a judgment day for the soul. We never know when we shall be called to give account of our stewardship of life's hidden things. God has so many ways of trying us, that it may stand revealed what manner of people we are. And one of those ways is by the vision of beauty. Very simply, very suddenly, amid the dust and monotony of the workaday world, the veil is drawn aside from the prosaism and seeming commonplaceness of existence, and the beautiful, pure, holy things that are always present are made manifest. And whenever that is so, the dividing line goes forth between those that see and those that see not—between those who gather the true significance of life and those who miss it.

—Percy C. Ainsworth, "The Waste of the Ointment," *Weavings*

❧ The art of attentiveness, of perceiving the self as part of a relationship, of "leaning into" that relationship with an attitude of listening, of cultivating the capacity for responsive action, of being in the present moment—this is an art that mirrors the art of prayer. At the same time, attentiveness is capable of becoming a spiritual dead end for a woman if it is not coupled with a strong sense of self-knowledge. Attentiveness can degenerate into simply living through someone else. It can lead to the parody of the person who is no person. But if attentiveness is cultivated as an art of self-giving, not of self-annihilation, it can yield blessed fruit.

—Wendy M. Wright, "In the Circle of a Mother's Arms," *Weavings*

❧ A life with God is a life in which the rhythms of silence and listening alternate with the rhythms of sharing and service. By praying with every part of who we are, we allow the grace that pours from the well of living water to trickle through all the aspects of our being, nourishing and hydrating that which was parched and dis-eased.

So begin the adventure, start the journey, follow Jesus. Allow God to transform your mind such that everything you are and everything you encounter speaks with the breath of the Spirit.

—Daniel Wolpert, *Creating a Life with God*

47. Gratitude

Affirmation
It is good to give thanks to the LORD, to sing praises to your name, Most High; to proclaim your loyal love in the morning, your faithfulness at nighttime (Ps. 92:1).

Psalm: 136

Psalm Prayer
Generous Lord, the wonders of your extravagant love display themselves in the glittering beauty of the night sky and the abundant fruitfulness of the earth. You have led us faithfully throughout our years and in Jesus you have shown us the way to fullness of life. May our gratitude know no bounds as we praise your name in word and deed. Amen.

Daily Scripture Readings

Sunday	A.	Exodus 16:2-15; Psalm 105:1-6, 37-45; Philippians 1:21-30; Matthew 20:1-16
	B.	Proverbs 31:10-31; Psalm 1; James 3:13–4:3, 7-8; Mark 9:30-37
	C.	Jeremiah 8:18-9:1; Psalm 79:1-9; 1 Timothy 2:1-7; Luke 16:1-13
Monday		1 Chronicles 16:8-26
Tuesday		Psalm 26:1-12
Wednesday		Jeremiah 33:10-17
Thursday		Matthew 15:32-39
Friday		Ephesians 5:15-21
Saturday		1 Thessalonians 5:12-24

Silence

Daily Readings for Reflection

Reflection: Silent or Written

Prayers: For the World, for Others, for Myself

Offering of Self to God
Faithful God, you remain true to us even when our
loyalty to you wavers and our hearts forget all that
you have done for our good. Receive our desire to live
in your presence with ever-growing gratitude, and by
your grace multiply our offerings even as your Son
multiplied the loaves and fish as a sign of your abundant love. Amen.

Blessing
May the boundaries of our hearts extend to a world-
embracing gratefulness for the wonders of God's love.
Amen.

Readings for Reflection

❧ Precisely because God is so gracious and generous toward us, in the face of all our waywardness, the
Christian life is especially marked by gratitude and
trust. Gratitude is the hallmark of the heart that knows
its Redeemer personally and intimately. Grasping the
true significance of God's gift overwhelms the soul
with thanksgiving. And a thankful life is naturally a
generous life, desiring ways to give something back to
God, however small the gesture may seem.
—Rueben P. Job and Marjorie J. Thompson, *Companions
in Christ*

❧ Here! At last! How I have longed for and ached for
this little piece of prairie. For here God is close to me,
or I close to Him, as nowhere else on earth. This is the
womb from whence I came from God and the womb

to whence [which] I return to be with my Creator and my loving companion.

Here I dreamed my boyhood dreams. Here I planned my youthful conquests. Here I learned the love of father and mother, learned what it means to be cared for! Here I learned to love God's creation, the animals, the birds, the limitless sky, the awesome lightning and thunder, the freshness following a springtime shower, a freshness so palpable I could taste it, feel it, smell it. This marvelous creation can wrap itself around you like a blanket of pure, refreshing, delightful and indescribable newness. God is in the prairie shower, falling down upon us and all creation, and allowing us to experience for a brief moment the paradise where all creatures and all creation enjoy one another in the continued delight of the Creator's love and care.

—Norman Shawchuck

&❧ How do we remain alert for the signs of God's entrance into our lives and the life of our time? What can keep us awake in the drowsy atmosphere of habit that cozily blankets our days? According to Paul, the answer is gratitude. To the Colossians he writes, "Devote yourselves to prayer, keeping alert in it with thanksgiving" (Col. 4:2). Paul is here pointing to the profound relation between spiritual alertness and the act of offering thanks. Gratitude gathers us into that double helix of grace descending and praise ascending that forms the basic design of life with God. Gratitude is the gesture of a heart opened to receive God, a heart acquainted with the shape of things to come, a heart alert to the tremors of a new creation in the birthing.

—John S. Mogabgab, "Editor's Introduction," *Weavings*
    (November/December 1992)

&❧ I am gradually learning that the call to gratitude asks us to say "everything is grace." When our gratitude for

the past is only partial, our hope for a new future can never be full.
—Henri J. M. Nouwen, "All Is Grace," *Weavings*

❧ The deepest understanding of having received expresses itself in gratefully giving back. Gifts given to us are gifts to be returned to the Giver. It is the one fundamental thing that is asked of us. This is where we become accountable. Our gifts are not just for us. Placed in our hands, these gifts are meant to be used and shared. Each day is a day entrusted to us—a day for response. Living in God and for God, we are asked to offer our hearts and hands in service to life. Could we then begin to sense that as we honor, we are honored; that as we love, we are loved; that as we receive, we are received? More and more able to return God's gifts to God, we become more response-able to the world in kinship and reverence.
—Gunilla Norris, "The Heart of Response-Ability," *Weavings*

❧ Both *grace* and *gratitude* have their source in the Latin word *gratia*, which can mean both favor and pleasure. Thus gratitude is not simply receiving or returning a favor (with the hint of obligation), it is also taking pleasure in some gift or relationship. From this same source, however, comes "gratuity," for a practice that seems to have begun as a free offering in gratitude for services rendered but has now become an expectation.

It is important to recognize that *gratitude* and *grace* may even go back to the ancient Sanskrit word *gurtas*, meaning religious celebration. In essence this is still what saying grace is all about, the celebration of the people, places, and things of our lives by ourselves living a life of gratitude.

For Christians the primary place where we should see such gracious living modeled is in the celebration of the Eucharist. In fact, the word *Eucharist* bespeaks a joyful celebration, rather than the severe and penitential experience many of us have at Communion. At this holy meal we remember that Jesus offered thanks over the bread and wine before passing it among his disciples, of whom one had betrayed him, one would deny him, and all would desert him. Still he offered thanks, saying grace by offering up both words and his very life. Jesus graced the dreadful evening of his betrayal with gratitude.

As we gather at the table we remember that last supper and participate as disciples who have betrayed, denied, and deserted the one who offered his life for us. We also look forward to that banquet in a time beyond time at which all those God has loved beyond our failures will gather in joyful celebration.

—Michael E. Williams, "Saying Grace," *Weavings*

48. Gentleness

Affirmation
Come to me, all you who are struggling hard and carrying heavy loads, and I will give you rest. Put on my yoke, and learn from me. I'm gentle and humble. And you will find rest for yourselves. My yoke is easy to bear, and my burden is light (Matt. 11:28-30).

Psalm: 119:73-80

Psalm Prayer
Dearest Lord, you have gently fashioned each one of us in your loving image. May we delight in your word and meditate on your precepts every day with great joy. And may those who see us see your gentle love. Amen.

Daily Scripture Readings

Sunday	A.	Exodus 17:1-7;
		Psalm 78:1-4, 12-16;
		Philippians 2:1-13;
		Matthew 21:23-32
	B.	Esther 7:1-6, 9-10; 9:20-22;
		Psalm 124; James 5:13-20;
		Mark 9:38-50
	C.	Jeremiah 32:1-3, 6-15;
		Psalm 91:1-6, 14-16;
		1 Timothy 6:6-19; Luke 16:19-31
Monday		Deuteronomy 32:1-14
Tuesday		Isaiah 11:1-9
Wednesday		John 1:29-39
Thursday		Acts 8:26-40
Friday		1 Peter 1:17-25
Saturday		Revelation 5

Silence

Daily Readings for Reflection

Reflection: Silent or Written

Prayers: For the World, for Others, for Myself

Offering of Self to God
O Lord, may we be as gentle as lambs when we interact with your good creation, remembering always that our Passover Lamb has been sacrificed. Inspire us to live according to Christ's love. Amen.

Blessing
May we go forth in peace, living in the newness brought about through Christ Jesus, newness that allows even lions and lambs to be at peace with one another. Amen.

Readings for Reflection

❧ To hear God call our name awes us. To consider facing such an experience without trembling knees is unthinkable. To stand before the One, the author of all that exists, stretches our imaginations to the breaking point. Then to have that One speak our name transforms and changes life. Jesus too heard the voice from heaven saying what he already knew. He was God's beloved. What a wonderful message! To be the beloved child of the Creator. To know one is loved like that transforms and prepares us for anything. Perhaps that is why the Gospels tell us that Jesus left the baptismal service and God's affirming voice to go into the desert to be tempted by Satan. Jesus prevailed because he remembered the voice; he remembered who he was and who was with him.

The biblical record clearly affirms the fact that God knows us and calls us by name as well. We are not strangers or aliens to God. We are each and all God's beloved. We have as our lover the Creator and Master of all that exists. The One who calls us beloved is also the one who knows us so intimately and well that even the number of hairs on our head is known.

To remember who creates us and recreates, who calls us again and again, who knows us completely, and who loves us unconditionally is to be prepared, as Jesus was, for all that is to come. We need have no fear of today or anxiety about tomorrow. We belong to God who claims us as beloved children and holds us close in the embrace of strength and love. Listen and remember today that God calls your name, and be transformed and sustained in all that awaits you.
—Rueben P. Job

꙳ It matters not whether you believe in life after death or resurrection or pie in the sky when you die. God's designs do not depend upon your assent. Rather, you can depend upon God's ability to bring to pass those things regarding which God has spoken. The awesome promises of God depend upon God and not whether you can or cannot believe God's promises.
—Norman Shawchuck

꙳ " 'What do you want?' " (John 1:38, JB). Here is the question that searches the depths of human existence, asked by the one who knows those depths as no other. The disciples of John the Baptist to whom Jesus addressed these words must have felt their enormous spiritual resonance. These were followers of the desert prophet, seekers who surely knew the sweet anguish of holy desire inflaming muscle and bone, imagination and will. Could they have been unfamiliar with desire's insistent prodding, its magnetic draw upon energy and attention? And you, surely you are not a stranger to the bold quest of desire for what alone will satisfy its ardent longing. What do you want?

A vast arc of desire stretches across human existence, a long sweep of mutual longing between Creator and creature that constitutes the innermost dynamism of history. "Where are you?" calls God to a hiding Adam and Eve (Gen. 3:9). "Where do you live?" ask John's disciples when they encounter the Son of God (John 1:38, JB). Expressed in the disciples' words are the many urgent, bewildered, painful questions concerning the whereabouts of God in a harsh world. And to those words, in their simplicity and gravity, Jesus responds with the great invitation to all spiritual seekers: "Come and see" (John 1:39).

"Come," Jesus says, calling us to step away from personal attitudes, cultural values, even religious convictions that hinder recognition of the God who is closer than we think. How God must cherish our company to number the hairs on our head (Luke 12:7) and to decipher the inarticulate groanings of our soul (Rom. 8:22-27). And if indeed God is sometimes hidden, it is not to deny our desire for God's presence but to hallow and intensify it. Freshly roused thirst for God may be precisely the way we discover the invitation to come and see.

—John S. Mogabgab, "Editor's Introduction," *Weavings* (January/February 2004)

❧ When developing a disciplined practice, one of the most valuable gifts we can give ourselves is gentleness. In everyday life, we tend to associate discipline with rigidity, rules, and consequences for misbehavior. Sometimes this kind of discipline is indeed necessary. However, we tend to downplay the equally important role of gentleness in making changes. Change requires a great deal of effort from anyone engaged in it, even if the change is positive. Change plunges a previously ordered system into temporary chaos, and chaos is stressful. Gentleness takes into account our effort and stress; treating ourselves gently is a way of offering encouragement and appreciation for the work being done.

—Sarah Parsons, *A Clearing Season*

❧ The book of Proverbs tells us that "a gentle answer turns away wrath" (15:1, NIV). Proverbs also reminds us, surprisingly, that "a gentle tongue can break a bone" (25:15, NIV). In a time when those who are called to be peacemakers need urgently to speak truth to power, and when that power includes control of so much of our public discourse, we may need to reconsider and reclaim a fuller biblical understanding of gentleness as a criterion for right and effective speech and action. I say "fuller" because gentleness, like many other popular virtues, has been sentimentalized and oversimplified to mean mild, bland, innocuous, even reticent. The person we describe as gentle seems often to be the one who does not make trouble, hurt feelings, or do much of anything with vigor and conviction.

But gentleness has more to do with vigor, conviction, and even, sometimes, with knowing how to make trouble, than we commonly think. It is as related to clarity as it is to caring, and has more to do with discernment than with deference. I think of Jesus and the rich young man—how gentle must have been the knowing look with which Jesus greeted him (see Mark 10:17-22). "And Jesus looked at him," we read, "and loved him" (NIV). And yet Jesus' next step was a radical challenge to all the young man held dear. No sermon. No blame. Not even an admonition. Just an invitation, but one so demanding it turned him away. I like to think it did not turn him away forever. As I read the story, it leaves a door wide open to reconsider and return. The young man had a lot to think over. And Jesus could afford to give him the freedom and the time to do that.

Real gentleness, in fact, comes from a place of spiritual abundance—because we who are poor are rich in Christ. We can only afford to be gentle when we are secure enough to lay aside our instincts for self-protection, defensiveness, or aggression—when we know that we have what we need.

—Marilyn Chandler McEntyre, "A Gentle Word," *Weavings*

❧ We witness divine courtesy in Jesus' encounter with the "doubting Thomas" in the twentieth chapter of John's Gospel. Thomas was adamant about needing to see for himself what the other disciples were claiming, that their Teacher had indeed risen from the dead. Thomas told his companions, "Unless I see the mark of the nails in his hands, and put my finger in the mark of the nails and my hand in his side, I will not believe" (John 20:25b). It was a bold and intimate request. Not asking only to see the signs of Jesus' death, Thomas wanted to touch, feel, and know the reality of a living Jesus and his wounds; he would not be vulnerable to an imposter. And what did Jesus see when he finally met Thomas, as he looked gently into the eyes of his forlorn follower? An anxious, grieving soul perhaps? Certainly, here was a man not easily swayed by wild rumors of his beloved mentor alive again.

Jesus honors Thomas's questioning personality. He invites Thomas, "Put your finger here and see my hands. Reach out your hand and put it in my side. Do not doubt but believe" (John 20:27). Seeing the desire of Thomas's heart, Jesus meets that longing with tender vulnerability. He opens his wounds, literally. "Reach out your hand," he invites with gentle courtesy. "Put it *in* my side." Thomas has a need he cannot surrender and Jesus respects it, caring for the trembling soul before him. This is not to say that Jesus does not also speak some stern words to Thomas; he does. Because you have seen me, you have believed, says Jesus. "Blessed are those who have not seen and yet have come to believe" (John 20:29). Jesus bids Thomas to risk a new way of faith, one that will demand Thomas to let go of his habitual need of proof, a habit that can hinder the life of the Spirit.

—Stephanie Ford, "A Dance with Gentleness," *Weavings*

The Season after Pentecost/Ordinary Time
Sunday between October 2 and October 8

49. Simplicity

Affirmation
"Allow the children to come to me," Jesus said. "Don't forbid them, because the kingdom of heaven belongs to people like these children" (Matt. 19:14).

Psalm: 116

Psalm Prayer
O God of mercy, we thank you for hearing our cry. When we have sojourned near death, you have held us firmly and protected us. We can never thank you enough for loving us, but we desire to share your love with those around us. Please instill in us simple hearts of love, thanksgiving, and praise. Amen.

Daily Scripture Readings

Sunday	A.	Exodus 20:1-4, 7-9, 12-20;
		Psalm 80:7-15;
		Philippians 3:4-14;
		Matthew 21:33-46
	B.	Job 1:1; 2:1-10; Psalm 26;
		Hebrews 1:1-4; 2:5-12;
		Mark 10:2-16
	C.	Lamentations 1:1-6; Psalm 137;
		2 Timothy 1:1-14; Luke 17:5-10
Monday		Joshua 4
Tuesday		Ecclesiastes 2:1-11
Wednesday		Psalm 19
Thursday		Luke 12:13-21
Friday		Acts 2:42-47; 4:32-35
Saturday		2 Corinthians 1:7-14

Silence

Daily Readings for Reflection

Reflection: Silent or Written

Prayers: For the World, for Others, for Myself

Offering of Self to God
God of mercy, we desire to give our lives as a simple testament of your goodness. May we always tell the story of your steadfast love, embodying your care for all of humanity. Create in us hearts like those of the children whom Jesus invited into his presence. Amen.

Blessing
May we live faithfully this day, embracing God's abundant simplicity in every aspect of life. Amen.

Readings for Reflection

❧ Everywhere in reading and in meditation I hear Christ calling me to faith in his ability and desire to give me the desires of my heart and that I will only know his concern for me as I launch out into "deep waters." I can never be sure of his ability and desire as long as I wade only in the shallows.

Help me to hear you, Lord God, correctly and clearly for I will do as you say; I will do your will regardless of how it may cut across my selfish desires and pride. My Father God, in all things give me only your will, your love, and your mercy. I will ask for nothing else. For then I will be rich enough.
—Norman Shawchuck

❧ Simplicity locates the spiritual life where it belongs—in the ordinary events of daily life.
—John S. Mogabgab, "Editor's Introduction," *Weavings* (September/October 1986)

❧ I was six years old when my family took a trip of more than one day. We traveled from North Dakota to Wyoming—my parents, two brothers, and I, along with clothes and food for many days—all packed into a 1929 Durant automobile. My parents had planned carefully for overnight stops, and daily meals were served from an old wooden apple crate. We ate lunches beside the road or in a shady village park. Breakfast and supper were shared where we spent the night at roadside cabins that preceded modern motels.

But what a glorious trip it was! Every day was filled with new surprises and sometimes with delight beyond description. The entire journey informed and transformed us as we shared new perceptions, made discoveries, and learned from our experience together.

We learned, for example, to be patient when the engine stopped and we had to wait for help. We learned that adversity could be encountered and overcome as we experienced one flat tire after another. We learned how to face the unexpected as road construction forced detours to areas we had not planned to see. We discovered the simple joy of bread, fruit, and sausage, and the incomparable refreshment of cool water shared in the journey's pause. We marveled at vast prairies and the majesty of mountains seen for the first time. Our little car shook from a violent summer thunderstorm on the plains, and we trembled at the awesome power of nature.

After more than sixty years, memories of that journey remain vivid. . . . Lessons learned in that experience continue to inform my life, especially my spiritual life.
—Rueben P. Job and Marjorie J. Thompson, *Companions in Christ*

❧ Pure holy simplicity confounds all the wisdom of this world and the wisdom of the flesh.
—Francis of Assisi, *Selections from the Writings of St. Francis of Assisi*

❧ I find that to be a Fool as to worldly Wisdom, and commit my Cause to God, not fearing to offend Men,

who take Offence at the Simplicity of Truth, is the only Way to remain unmoved at the Sentiments of others.
—John Woolman, *Selections from the Journal of John Woolman*

❧ As with all the virtues, simplicity has both an exterior and an interior dimension. A simple life can be likened to a plain cloak that is neither heavily ornamented nor lined. This plain cloak can in turn be contrasted with an antique cloak richly embroidered with decorative elements and heavily lined with furs, a cloak designed to impress with its outer display and conceal what is hidden underneath. Like an unornamented cloak, simplicity implies that one be frank, unaffected, not posturing in speech or action. In terms of lifestyle, simplicity means distinguishing between what one needs and what one wants: living simply so that others may simply live. But this little virtue also means being interiorly simple, like an unlined cloak: unguarded, straightforward, and without concealed intentions or motives. Artlessness, unself-consciousness, and transparency: these are part of simplicity. In terms of prayer, simplicity urges one not to multiply thoughts and activities, not to be constantly self-reflexive or to strive for some sort of exceptional experience, but instead to cultivate a quiet faith that trusts in the mercy and love of God.
—Wendy M. Wright, "Little Things," *Weavings*

❧ The problem we face today needs very little time for its statement. . . . Before we know it we are bowed down with burdens, crushed under committees, strained, breathless, and hurried, panting through a never-ending program of appointments. We are too busy to be good wives to our husbands, good companions of our children, good friends to our friends, and with no time at all to be friends to the friendless. But if we withdraw from public engagements and interests, in order to spend quiet hours with the family, the guilty calls of citizenship whisper disquieting claims in our ears.

Prune and trim we must, but not with ruthless haste and ready pruning knife, until we have reflected upon the tree we trim, the environment it lives in, and the sap of life which feeds it.

—Thomas Kelly, *A Testament of Devotion*

❧ Life is meant to be lived from a Center, a divine Center. . . . There is a divine Abyss within us all, a holy Infinite Center, a Heart, a Life who speaks in us and through us to the world. We have all heard this holy Whisper at times. At times we have followed the Whisper, and amazing equilibrium of life, amazing effectiveness of living set in. But too many of us have heeded the Voice only at times. Only at times have we submitted to His holy guidance. We have not counted this Holy Thing within us to be the most precious thing in the world. We have not surrendered *all else*, to attend to it alone. Let me repeat. Most of us, I fear, have not surrendered all else, in order to attend to the Holy Within.

Under the silent, watchful eye of the Holy One we all are standing, whether we know it or not. And in that Center, in that holy Abyss where the Eternal dwells at the base of our being, our programs, our gifts to Him, our offerings of duties performed are again and again revised in their values. Many of the things we are doing seem so important to us. We haven't been able to say No to them, because they seemed so important. But if we *center down*, as the old phrase goes, and live in that holy Silence which is dearer than life, and take our life program into the silent places of the heart, with complete openness, ready to do, ready to renounce according to His leading, then many of the things we are doing lose their vitality for us. I should like to testify to this, as a personal experience, graciously given. There is a re-evaluation of much that we do or try to

do, which is *done for us*, and we know what to do and what to let alone.
—Thomas Kelly, *A Testament of Devotion*

❧ *Simplicity* is not denial of the complications of modern life. These are irrelevant to the quality of simplicity we carry within. Simplicity is not so much an outward form of speech or manner as it is the driving heartbeat that sets the rhythm of a human life. Thomas Kelly defines simplicity as living from "a divine Center." Often complications become distractions from the divine presence available to us as the center of our lives. The simplicity that characterizes this divine center allows us to make choices among the many demands on our lives.
—Michael E. Williams, "Saying Grace," *Weavings*

50. Trust

Affirmation
Those who know your name trust you because you have not abandoned any who seek you, Lord (Ps. 9:10).

Psalm: 20

Psalm Prayer
Remembering your faithfulness from age to age, O Lord, let us trust that you have our best interests in mind as you respond to our cries for help in times of need. By your grace, teach us to rely more and more on your strong hand to support and guide us in the face of adversity. Amen.

Daily Scripture Readings

Sunday	A.	Exodus 32:1-14; Psalm 106:1-6, 19-23; Philippians 4:1-9; Matthew 22:1-14
	B.	Job 23:1-9, 16-17; Psalm 22:1-15; Hebrews 4:12-16; Mark 10:17-31
	C.	Jeremiah 29:1, 4-7; Psalm 66:1-12; 2 Timothy 2:8-15; Luke 17:11-19
Monday		Exodus 34:1-9
Tuesday		2 Chronicles 20:1-20
Wednesday		Psalm 84
Thursday		Jeremiah 17:7-8
Friday		John 14:1-14
Saturday		Acts 14:21-28

Silence

Daily Readings for Reflection

Reflection: Silent or Written

Prayers: For the World, for Others, for Myself

Offering of Self to God
Into your hands I commit my whole self, Lord of time
and space, for in you all things hold together according to the generous purpose that guides your love for
all that you have made. We who truly live abundantly
move and have our being in you. Amen.

Blessing
May the one in whom we have placed our trust be
our strength for good and our hope for the healing of
creation today and always. Amen.

Readings for Reflection

❧ Many theologians declare that God cannot be absent
from creation or creature without both ceasing to exist.
Trying to convince the broken and empty-hearted of
this truth is not an easy task. Why did both the author
of Psalms and Jesus feel forsaken and alone? The
answer is not easy to find, especially for those who
experience the absence of God more readily than they
experience the presence of God. Jesus was able to move
from that forsaken feeling to the confidence and trust
of a child as he placed his life and his death fully in the
care of God. And the Resurrection becomes the final
proof that God can be trusted.

Jesus' journey from that forsaken feeling to confident trust gives hope to us in our times of loneliness
and fear of being forsaken. If the theologians are right
and God never does forsake us, we can remind ourselves frequently of God's presence. Establishing a way
of life that intentionally makes us present to God is one
way of removing the feeling of God's absence. Regular
times of daily prayer and regular times of corporate
worship offer opportunities to establish a relationship
of companionship with the One who made us and
loves us.

If the theologians are wrong and God does indeed become distant and absent, our response will be the same as we call upon God to rescue us from our aloneness, confident that the One who always responds in love and wisdom will restore our sense of companionship. The biblical witness and the witness of the saints who have gone before us testify that God does not leave us alone. Even the apparent final absence of death is not a plunge into darkness but a movement into the light of ultimate companionship with God. So the words of Jesus become our own, "Father, into your hands I commend my Spirit" (Luke 23:46).

—Rueben P. Job

❧ My Lord, Jesus Christ, touch all of my being, open the secret and known chambers of my life to your self. My Lord, possess me and fill me. I give you permission to enter my life—all of it. I am not asking for a light touch, for a redecoration. I am asking for a complete reconstruction of desires, appetite, priorities, time and activity. I abandon myself willingly into your hands.

Your promises are staggering. Your word is true. How, O Lord, do we enter them? By seeking first your kingdom and your righteousness. Help me to do this, not for "things" but for entrance into your kingdom and righteousness alone. This is the great prize. In comparison, all else is dull and base. In you, O Lord, I have all things. Lead me always in your way that is blessed with variety, opportunity, and new life. I believe, help me always to believe.

—Norman Shawchuck

❧ True devotion to God means seeking the divine will in all things. Over time, life teaches us that not getting what we want in prayer may be just what we need. It is part of God's gift that we are weaned away from false notions of who God is, as well as false understandings of what God wants us to be. To imagine that God is here simply to console, affirm, heal, and love us is to deny the holiness of a God who requires righteousness, who challenges our illusions, who confronts our idolatries. When we are being "disillusioned" from false perspectives, the spiritual journey feels arduous—more like climbing a steep mountain than like driving the great plains. Indeed, at times it feels like going over the edge of a cliff on nothing but the thin rope of faith. Sometimes we are called to endure in hope when we can see nothing positive on the horizon at all.

—Rueben P. Job and Marjorie J. Thompson, *Companions in Christ*

&. The grace of God teaches us to trust God's goodness and power. Only divine love is strong enough to transform the most unlovely of us into companions of our living Lord. Grace enables our cynical, burned-out spirits to see life with new eyes—eyes fresh with wonder like a child's. We continue to see evil, sin, and pain in the world. In fact, we see these things more clearly and feel them more acutely. But we see them encompassed by God's presence, purpose, and greater power of love. When we begin to see with the eyes of faith, we can accept God's power to heal, redeem, and transform each of us personally and all of us together.

—Rueben P. Job and Marjorie J. Thompson, *Companions in Christ*

&. At times we drift in our lives. Amid the uncertainty and suspense of not knowing or the sheer tedium of things remaining the same, we can learn to keep our eyes wide open, scanning the horizon of our experience. Like Noah we may have to do this for a long time until at least some green sprig signals, "There's land ahead." Signs may beckon through something as ordinary as a phone call, as intimate as the touch of a child's hand, or as subtle as an inner urge whispering, "This is where you need to go!" Like Paul and his near-sinking boatload, we would be wise to feast ourselves

again and again on signs of promise and hope even as we are tossed about on the sea of not knowing.
—Stephen V. Doughty and Marjorie J. Thompson, *The Way of Discernment*

  Do not dwell upon remote events; this anxiety about the future is contrary to a religious state of mind. When God bestows any blessings upon you, look only to Him in the comfort that you receive, and take every day of the manna that He sends you, as the Israelites did, without making yourself any provision for the morrow.

A life of faith produces two things. First, it enables us to see God in everything. Secondly, it holds the mind in a state of readiness for whatever may be His will. We must trust to God for whatever depends upon Him, and only think of being faithful ourselves in the performance of our duties. This continual, unceasing dependence, this state of entire peace and acquiescence of the soul in whatever may happen, is the true, silent martyrdom of self. It is so slow, and gradual, and internal, that they who experience it are hardly conscious of it.

When God deprives you of any blessing, He can replace it either by other instruments or by Himself. The very stones can in His hands become the children of Abraham. Sufficient for the day is the evil thereof; the morrow will take care of itself. He who has fed you today will take care of you tomorrow.

We shall sooner see the manna fall from heaven in the desert than the children of God shall want support.
—Francois Fenelon, *Selections from the Writings of Francois Fenelon*

  After this, our Lord brought to my mind the longing that I had for him before. I saw that nothing held me back but sin, which I saw generally in all of us. I thought that if sin had never been, we would all have been clean and like our Lord as God made us. In my folly, before this time, I often wondered why, in the great foreseeing wisdom of God, the beginning of sin was not prevented. For then, I thought, all would have been well.

I should have abandoned this line of thought. Nevertheless, I mourned and worried about this without reason or discretion. But Jesus answered with this word: "Sin is necessary, but all will be well, and all will be well, and every kind of thing will be well."

—Julian of Norwich, *Encounter with God's Love*

❧ God is good and works continually for good in the world, especially in and for and through those who love God. However, the goodness of God's purposes in the world is not accomplished without suffering. We see this truth most clearly in the life of Jesus Christ. Jesus himself promises his followers that they too will suffer in this world if they choose to be his disciples. Yet the greater promise is joy, the incomparable joy of a life lived not for our own sake or from our own center, but for God and centered in Christ. Life in Christ is life abundant! It is possible to know this joy even in the midst of turmoil and suffering.

—Rueben P. Job and Marjorie J. Thompson, *Companions in Christ*

51. Humility

Affirmation
Happy are people who are humble, because they will inherit the earth (Matt. 5:5).

Psalm: 131

Psalm Prayer
How majestic are your ways, great God of life! Although we know much, we still understand so little. Yet in Jesus Christ you have offered us "all the treasures of wisdom and knowledge" (Col. 2:3). May we therefore clothe ourselves in his humility that we might receive the gifts you have placed in the treasure trove of his heart. Amen.

Daily Scripture Readings

Sunday	A.	Exodus 33:12-23; Psalm 99; 1 Thessalonians 1:1-10; Matthew 22:15-22
	B.	Job 38:1-7; Psalm 104:1-9, 24, 35; Hebrews 5:1-10; Mark 10:35-45
	C.	Jeremiah 31:27-34; Psalm 121; 2 Timothy 3:14–4:5; Luke 18:1-8
Monday		Psalm 119:65-72
Tuesday		Proverbs 15:23-33
Wednesday		Jeremiah 13:15-19
Thursday		Zephaniah 2:1-3
Friday		Luke 18:9-14
Saturday		1 Corinthians 4:1-13

Silence

Daily Readings for Reflection

Reflection: Silent or Written

Prayers: For the World, for Others, for Myself

Offering of Self to God
Holy Lord, you lift up and you lay low, you crown and you dethrone, all for the sake of your kingdom of justice and peace. Today we declare our desire to be clothed in the garments of humility so that our thoughts and actions will confirm our citizenship in your gracious realm. Amen.

Blessing
May the Lord who humbled himself to become our servant strengthen us in the holy humility that embraces all things with sympathy and patience. Amen.

Readings for Reflection

꙳ To remember that God's will shall be accomplished completely and that we are invited to be a part of the fulfillment of that will gives a new perspective to life. We lose some of our fear of the risk of seeking and doing God's will. We know that sometimes doing God's will does get us into trouble, and at other times it saves us from trouble. Most of all we know that, when we seek to know and do God's will, we have set our feet upon a pathway of companionship, joy, and fulfillment. Our journey becomes one that holds challenge, excitement, meaning, assurance, and deep peace. Our journey gets richer day by day and will never end. Our journey is made possible by the One who walks with all those who are faithful.
—Rueben P. Job, *A Guide to Spiritual Discernment*

꙳ This is me. I am nothing! I desire the love of our Lord Jesus and to be with him always. My Lord, bring me to yourself, to the very place where you are. Let me dwell there in silence, alone with you. And, if possible, let me usher others to their place with you. Use me, Lord, in my nothingness, to help others, to awaken them, to encourage them, to feed them, to walk with them along the way. Use me, my Lord, always in accord with your will—for me and for others. Amen.

—Norman Shawchuck

• "Humility is a virtue, not a neurosis." The discerning lens of his monastic solitude helped Thomas Merton distinguish between humility distorted by wayward psychodynamics and humility clarified by the spiritual dynamics of God's activity in history. Throughout the Bible, God shows a preference for insignificant people, a commitment to raise up the humble and bring low the haughty. This is the experience of Israel, the message of the prophets, and the ministry of Jesus.

In Jesus all the riches of humility are present, all its health and strength visible, its compelling invitation at work: "Take my yoke upon you, and learn from me; for I am gentle and humble in heart, and you will find rest for your souls" (Matt. 11:29). The humility of Jesus is far from resigned submission to an imposed authority. He is humble in his heart, the core of his being, and his humility is a free offering of himself to the One whom he lovingly calls "Abba." In Jesus there is no hint of humility before God as tight-jawed obedience or penitential self-abnegation. Rather it is akin to a childlike trust in dear parents whose will for us is not capricious and whose generous provision is unwavering (Matt. 18:1-4). Yielding to the benevolent purposes of God prepares us for the yoke of kind, gentle, patient service to others. Paul, who was scarcely without strength of character, learned that humble service included voluntarily putting aside his rights and privileges for the sake of the gospel and the well-being of those to whom he proclaimed it (1 Cor. 9:2-23). Paul understood that humility both constitutes and sustains the unity of Christian community (Phil. 2:1-11). As humility places us in right relationship with God and neighbor, we do indeed find soul-reviving rest.

—John S. Mogabgab, "Editor's Introduction," *Weavings* (May/June 2000)

❧ Humility sees that each person is a bearer of Christ from whom we can learn and a child of God whom we must not judge. It also acknowledges that none of us is God and no matter the depth of our spiritual practices or our holy habits we will never match the holiness of God. This is not bad news for those steeped in humility, however, for it drives us straight into God's arms of grace and mercy.

—Michael E. Williams, "Gentle and Humble of Heart," *Weavings*

❧ Humility does not consist in having a worse opinion of ourselves than we deserve or in abasing ourselves lower than we really are. But as all virtue is founded in truth, so humility is founded in a true and just sense of our weakness, misery, and sin. Those who rightly feel and live in this sense of their condition live in humility.

—William Law, *Total Devotion to God*

❧ Let every day, therefore, be a day of humility; condescend to all the weaknesses and infirmities of your fellow-creatures, cover their frailties, love their excellencies, encourage their virtues, relieve their wants, rejoice in their prosperities, compassionate their distress, receive their friendship, overlook their unkindness, forgive their malice, be a servant of servants, and condescend to do the lowest offices to the lowest of mankind.

Aspire after nothing but your own purity and perfection, and have no ambition, but to do every thing in so reasonable and religious a manner, that you may be glad that God is everywhere present, and sees and observes all your actions. The greatest trial of humanity is an humble behaviour towards your equals in age, estate, and condition of life. Therefore be careful of all the motions of your heart towards these people. Let all your behaviour towards them be governed by unfeigned love. Have no desire to put any of your equals below you, nor any anger at those that would put themselves above you. If they are proud, they are ill of a very bad distemper; let them, therefore, have your tender pity; and perhaps your meekness may prove an occasion of their cure. But if your humility should do them no good, it will, however, be the greatest good that you can do to yourself.

—William Law, *A Serious Call to a Devout and Holy Life*

ᢤ There is no love of God without patience, and no patience without lowliness and sweetness of spirit.

Humility and patience are the surest proof of the increase of love.

Humility alone unites patience with love; without which it is impossible to draw profit from suffering, or indeed, to avoid complaint, especially when we think we have no occasion for what people make us suffer.

True humility is a kind of self-annihilation, and this is the center of all virtues.

Souls returned to God ought to be attentive to everything that is said to them, on the head of salvation, with a desire to profit thereby.

Of the sins that God has pardoned, let nothing remain but a deeper humility in the heart, and a stricter regulation in our words, in our actions, and in our sufferings.

—John Wesley, *Selections from the Journal of John Wesley*

ᢤ Our Lord says in the Gospel, "Love your enemies." One who truly loves his enemy does not bear malice for any injury that he has received from him. Because he loves God, he grieves for the sin on the other's soul and shows his love by his actions.

Many people always blame an enemy or a neighbor whenever they themselves do wrong or suffer some hurt. This is not just, for everyone has his enemy in his own power, that is, his own body, by which he sins. Blessed is the servant who keeps such an enemy constantly under his control and wisely guards against him. For so long as he does this, no other enemy, visible or invisible, can harm him.

A servant of God may recognize whether he has the Spirit of God in this way: if when God performs any good through him his natural feelings are not puffed up—for the flesh is always the enemy of all good—and if he always remembers his own unworthiness and regards himself as the least of all.

A servant of God cannot know the extent of his patience and humility as long as all goes well with him. But when a time comes that those who should treat him well do the opposite, then he shows the true extent of his patience and humility and no more.
—Francis of Assisi, *Riches of Simplicity*

❧ The meekness of Moses surfaces again and again in those who know who, and Whose, they are. Jesus himself was Lamb of God whose prophetic roar was that of a Lion of Judah! He, like all God's down-to-earth servants—the "meek and lowly in heart" (Matt 11:29, KJV)—did not pretend to be someone he was not. He let go of deception that is so much a part of our ordinary social life—that ego-drama where we put our best foot forward and carefully cover our tails. When we humbly accept our own reality as it comes, we are better able to see the world as it actually happens around us. We can then see more clearly what's called for here and now regardless of what's in it for us. This can be a terrifying quality to those weaving the web of ego and status.

The greatest devotee of humility in the Western church, Francis of Assisi, nevertheless spoke plainly

and boldly to the Pope. While showing Francis the treasures of the Vatican, the pontiff, occupant of Peter's
chair, said, "The Apostle once said to a cripple, 'Silver
and gold have I none' and now look at all Peter's suc-
cessor has: not only treasures, but power and prestige
in the world." Francis is said to have responded with
perfect Mosaic meekness. "But, Holy Father," he said,
"can you say, as Peter did to the cripple, "In the name
of Jesus Christ, arise and walk?'" Like all God's terrifying meek, Francis was content with the Christ-life
of gratitude, love, and service, rather than following
Caesar's siren call to a life of power, status, and money.
—Robert Corin Morris, "Meek as Moses," *Weavings*

❧ Jesus, Paul thought, has modeled humility for us.
Humility is the product of love, God's love. As the
fourteenth-century classic *The Cloud of Unknowing*
interpreted it, humility means to have a proper self-
estimate. There are two dimensions to that: We are
aware of our humanity, our finiteness, and our sinfulness. We look at ourselves in light of God's overwhelming love manifested in the cross of Jesus Christ. These
leave us no grounds for boasting.
—E. Glenn Hinson, "Having the Mind of Christ,"
Weavings

❧ I find it quite impossible to imagine myself ever
having such influence upon my older brother that he
would send his wife off to a nunnery in order to join
me in the monastic quest. There was something in the
humility of Bernard of Fontaines that opened a space
for his warring and wedded brothers not only to conceive a different level of being and communion but to
willingly pay the price to embrace it.

Jesus said, "Learn from me, for I am gentle and
humble in heart" (Matt. 11:29, NJB). The self-emptying of
the Incarnate God is the ultimate expression of humility, and the most compelling invitation to empty ourselves of all that is false. This radical human humility

is truth. It calls us into and opens the way to participation in the transcendent Truth who is our God. This is our destiny.

Only if together with our sisters and brothers around the world we can perceive that there is a realm of being beyond all our differences where we can enjoy a mutually supportive, beneficial, and fruitful unity, will we move ahead in solidarity. Only then will we be able to create a peaceful world, a place for the human family to blossom as it comes to know its own goodness and beauty. Only then will we find our true fulfillment and deepest joy.

—M. Basil Pennington, ocso, "Bernard's Challenge," *Weavings*

The Season after Pentecost/Ordinary Time
Sunday between October 23 and October 29

52. Compassion

Affirmation
The LORD said, "I'll make all my goodness pass in front of you, and I'll proclaim before you the name, 'The LORD.' I will be kind to whomever I wish to be kind, and I will have compassion to whomever I wish to be compassionate" (Exod. 33:19).

Psalm: 103

Psalm Prayer
Lord, you are compassionate and merciful; you are patient, faithful, and just. Help us show compassion to others as you show compassion to us. Forgive our apathy, indifference, and self-interest toward others, and transform these attitudes into kindness, charity, and love, so that we may be one with you and one with each other. Amen.

Daily Scripture Readings

Sunday	A.	Deuteronomy 34:1-12; Psalm 90:1-6, 13-17; 1 Thessalonians 2:1-8; Matthew 22:34-46
	B.	Job 42:1-6, 10-17; Psalm 34:1-8; Hebrews 7:23-28; Mark 10:46-52
	C.	Joel 2:23-32; Psalm 65; 2 Timothy 4:6-8, 16-18; Luke 18:9-14
Monday		Genesis 9:8-17
Tuesday		Exodus 2:1-10
Wednesday		Matthew 20:29-34
Thursday		John 4:7-26
Friday		Ephesians 4:25-5:2
Saturday		1 Peter 1:3-12

Silence

Daily Readings for Reflection

Reflection: Silent or Written

Prayers: For the World, for Others, for Myself

Offering of Self to God
Each day we are given the opportunity to show compassion to others, Lord. May we always be both merciful and compassionate unto others as you have been merciful and compassionate unto us. Amen.

Blessing
May the peace of Christ reign in our hearts today and always. Amen.

Readings for Reflection

❧ We need not wonder about the cost of ministry. We need only look upon the cross with Jesus suspended there, and there we see the enormous cost of the ministry that is offered in the life and death of Jesus.

The cost is great, but in the work of introducing men and women to Jesus and offering God's love to them, the cost must be accepted. For it is our own self-emptying and compassion for others that permits them to see Jesus. And seeing Jesus they will also desire God's love. It is in our living a way of love and compassion that others may be convinced to look at the cross of Jesus and also say, "Truly this is the Son of God."
—Norman Shawchuck

❧ The word most commonly used in the Synoptic Gospels to portray the compassion of Jesus recalls the ancient imagery of the womb of God (Isa. 49:15). It was from this deep inward place that Jesus brought

forth healing and new life (Matt. 14:14; Mark 1:41; Luke 7:13). Compassion expresses the inmost truth of God's nature; it is the fertile suffering of love that births a new creation.
—John S. Mogabgab, "Introduction," *Weavings* (November/December 1990)

꙳ God steps forth as loving arms, as the patient, longing heart of a mother aching to gather her children in and hold them, to speak wordlessly with the tender pressure of hand and breast of their beauty, dignity, and belovedness.

I begin to know the compassion of God. Greater and more generous than our knowing, our own evaluations, our own tidy and fearful categorizations, it pursues and overtakes us like a fretful mother or a concerned father. It follows us and finds us wherever we are.
—Wendy M. Wright, "Hints, Signs, and Showings," *Weavings*

꙳ We are each a thread woven into a vast web of the universe, linked and connected so that our lives are irrevocably bound up with one another.
—Sue Monk Kidd, "Birthing Compassion," *Weavings*

꙳ In caring, Jesus is our model and leader. Each day Jesus retreated from the demands of serving others to be prayerfully with his God. Then he was better able to come down from his mountain retreat to minister more fully to those needing and pleading for his love. He turned away no one, but he also didn't try to do it all by himself. He enlisted others to extend God's caring to all, especially to "the least" of God's people. Today he invites each of us anew to be his ministers of caring in our own time and place. In the words of Sr. Helen Prejean, how will we be "the face of Christ" for others?
—James McGinnis, "Ordinary Caring Makes Extraordinary Perseverance Possible," *Weavings*

❧ To weep with the suffering does not mean, however, that we have a good cry and get on with other things. It is more that we have a good cry and we are never the same.
—Jan Johnson, "Weeping with God as a Spiritual Discipline," *Weavings*

❧ Surely, in the end, after all our righteous judgments on what is wrong with ourselves, each other, and with the world; after we experience injustice intractably resistant to our most devoted efforts, leaving us with our thirst unquenched, our mouths dry and our throats sore from protest; surely in the end the gospel calls us to view the whole of creation, and each other, with the eyes of mercy, and to love it all anyway, with a mercying heart.
—Elaine M. Prevallet, SL, "Living in the Mercy," *Weavings*

❧ "Be perfect, therefore, as your heavenly Father is perfect," Jesus told his disciples (Matt. 5:48). The Hebrew word translated here as *perfect* actually translates better as *compassionate* or *merciful*. Jesus wasn't urging us to get a 4.0 grade-point average or never to make a mistake. He was urging us to love as completely as God loves—concretely, wholeheartedly, and universally. God's perfection is love, for *God is love*. As scripture puts it: "God is love, and those who abide in love abide in God, and God abides in them" (1 John 4:16). God is infinite love, compassion, and mercy.
—James McGinnis, "Mercy in Hard Times and Places," *Weavings*

53. Responsibility

Affirmation
Ask, and you will receive. Search, and you will find. Knock, and the door will be opened to you. For everyone who asks, receives. Whoever seeks, finds. And to everyone who knocks, the door is opened (Matt. 7:7-8).

Psalm: 1

Psalm Prayer
Truly happy is the person who loves you, Lord. Give us the wisdom, willingness of heart, and clarity of conscience to depend on you for all things—to ask for your help when we are in need, to seek you that we might find, to love your instruction and dwell in it day and night. Amen.

Daily Scripture Readings

Sunday	A.	Joshua 3:7-17;
		Psalm 107:1-7, 33-37;
		1 Thessalonians 2:9-13;
		Matthew 23:1-12
	B.	Ruth 1:1-18; Psalm 146;
		Hebrews 9:11-14; Mark 12:28-34
	C.	Habakkuk 1:1-4; 2:1-4;
		Psalm 119:137-144;
		2 Thessalonians 1:1-4, 11-12;
		Luke 19:1-10
Monday		Proverbs 28
Tuesday		Luke 14:25-33
Wednesday		Matthew 7:1-6
Thursday		Ephesians 4:1-6
Friday		1 Timothy 4:7b-16
Saturday		2 Peter 1:1-8

Silence

Daily Readings for Reflection

Reflection: Silent or Written

Prayers: For the World, for Others, for Myself

Offering of Self to God
All that we do, we will do from the heart for the Lord
and not for people. Amen.

Blessing
May we remain awake and stand firm in our faith, be
brave, and be strong, and do everything in love. Amen.

Readings for Reflection

᭗ Every United Methodist preacher since the time
of John Wesley has been asked a series of questions
before being admitted into full membership in an
annual conference. The first question is, "Have you
faith in Christ?" The second question is, "Are you
going on to perfection?" Seventeen more questions
follow, and every candidate is to be led in discussion
and understanding of the questions by the resident
bishop of the area.

Once during the turbulent sixties, Bishop Gerald
Kennedy was asking these historic questions of candi-
dates standing before him in the presence of the annual
conference session. When asked if he was going on
to perfection, one candidate responded, "No!" Bishop
Kennedy quickly replied, "Then where are you going?"
It was an appropriate question then, and it is an appropriate question now—not only for preachers but for
all Christians.

Where are you going? If you continue on the
course you have charted, where will it all end? So often
we discount Christ's return, forgetting that in many
ways Jesus Christ has never left. Or we begin reasoning
that since Christ has not returned yet, why think about

it? But the truth is that at the very best, our lives are short and soon we will have reached our destination, whether Jesus Christ will have returned in a cosmic unfolding or not. Are you going on toward God? If not, where are you going? It is always a good time to review and if necessary redirect your life toward God.
—Rueben P. Job

❧ O God, thank you for your patience. Help me to be whole—of one word and deed. I cannot be this on my own will or strength, so I pray for your will to be done and your strength to be given. Help me to attend to my daily disciplines; to have a clear witness of word, character and action; to always look for your coming and to live as though you had already arrived.
—Norman Shawchuck

❧ "From now on, therefore, we regard no one from a human point of view" (2 Cor. 5:16). Paul is speaking of how the landscape of human life now appears to those whose vision has been corrected by the lens of Christ's cross and resurrection. "See," urges the apostle, "everything has become new!" (2 Cor. 5:17). From all the fear, suspicion, anger, and terror that stalk the world, from all the empty hopes and overflowing sadness, all the sweet dreams and acid anguish, God has wrested a new creation. The human point of view—with its focus on looking out for ourselves, preoccupation with our own plans, fear of others' scornful judgment, anxious anticipation of the future—has become an outmoded paradigm. It is not (and never was) capable of revealing what is most real and true about life.

This reality and truth are wreathed in paradox. We glimpse them through the terrifying loneliness of the cross, the stifling isolation of the tomb, the blinding mystery of Easter morning. Yet what we glimpse is life woven together in love, all life interwoven in ways that do not smother and encumber but rather release and strengthen. Here is God's desire and design for created life, for all brothers and sisters of the mineral, plant, animal, and human nations with whom it is good and pleasant to dwell in unity (Ps. 133). Here too is the living matrix of responsibility.

"So then, whenever we have an opportunity, let us work for the good of all, and especially for those of the family of faith" (Gal. 6:10). No dimension of another's life lies beyond the scope of the Christian's concern and care. Whether the needs are material (Phil. 4:15-16), relational (Rom. 15:2), or spiritual (Rom. 14:13), Paul enjoins us to "bear one another's burdens" and so fulfill the commandment to love one another (Gal. 6:2). Although this is certainly important within the community of faith as a compelling sign of radically rewoven relationships, the scope of Christian responsibility is as encompassing as the new creation itself. New life in Christ manifests itself in responsibility for the other.

—John S. Mogabgab, "Editor's Introduction," *Weavings* (July/August 2008)

❧ There are countless ways we can make a difference in the balance of justice in this world. Our imagination and will are the only limits. We have tremendous resources at our disposal! And we have the freedom to use them, to exercise our conscience and put belief into practice. What a privilege and what a responsibility God has given us.

—Marjorie J. Thompson, "To Do Justice," *Weavings*

❧ Really serious commitment to your friendship with God requires some ways to hold yourself accountable. Because God does not shout, scream, or jump up and down to get your attention, you have to carry more of the responsibility for keeping the friendship alive. Do not imagine that you, as a religious leader, will have fewer spiritual difficulties than others because you are engaged in "God's business."

Religious professionals may run greater risks than ordinary saints. All too readily, caught up in the affairs of religion, they begin to turn it into a performance, a role, an act, and push their personal relationship with God to the side. Just as Jesus warned (Matt. 6:5-6), they become hypocrites, "play actors" who make sure everyone sees how devout they are and what they are doing. In the meantime, such leaders dry up inwardly and have nothing to offer the world that the world does not already have in abundance. As another early Christian observed, they have the *form* of religion but not its *power* (2 Tim. 3:5).

—E. Glenn Hinson, *Spiritual Preparation for Christian Leadership*

❧ The question "Who am I?" is forever wrapped in the deeper question of "Whose am I?" In answer, the Christian knows by being known, so strangely loved that only the name God will do. Christianity involves a yoke into which is branded the word *freedom*. Yet it is a costly freedom, tempered in the pain of repentance, and marinated with the courage to endure. Wrapped in Christ's warm mantle of many colors, one is able to enter gladly the prisons of others as if they were one's own. A freed slave, the Christian chooses the bondage of carrying a cross toward the radiance of an empty tomb.

The Christian is happily under orders, in the process of being disciplined so as to be able to love without taking thought, to taste deeply without needing permission, to embrace enemies without need of reward, and to abandon self into God for the sheer mystery of it all. And during those dry desert times, loving out of duty must suffice. Christians are active contemplatives who are profoundly inactive at the center. They hyphenate their living between being and doing, embracing all that both contain. They follow a Christ in whose hand is a whip for money changers, with an angry outcry at the greed of the rich and the

callousness of the powerful. . . . Yet their angry master is also the one who has a special love for the village outcasts of this world, and the one who carries so gently the lambs in his bosom.
—W. Paul Jones, *The Art of Spiritual Direction*

❧ In a life fed by the inner springs of divine love, we can go beyond the external demands of God's law to its very heart. In this realm, we do not act from anger against others; we quickly reconcile ourselves to sisters and brothers with whom we have been in conflict; we speak our truth without exaggeration or distortion; out of sheer generosity of heart, we offer more to others than they can rightly claim; we love those who hate us and pray for those who misuse us. By grace we can live by a higher law than retribution, guided by spiritual principles that transcend common notions of human justice. And in all this, our experience does not resemble victimhood but rather joyous freedom!
—Marjorie J. Thompson, *The Way of Forgiveness*

54. Stewards of Creation

Affirmation

The one who forms the mountains, creates the wind, makes known his thoughts to humankind, makes the morning darkness, and moves over the heights of the earth—the LORD, the God of heavenly forces is his name! (Amos 4:13).

Psalm: 148

Psalm Prayer

May we take the time, O God of creation, to notice the world around us, that our hearts and minds may be filled with wonder and gratitude for all that you have created. We confess, Lord, that we often fail to care for your creation in a way that is pleasing to you. Help us to show compassion for your creation, O God, not only for own sake, but also for the sake of future generations. Amen.

Daily Scripture Readings

Sunday	A.	Joshua 24:1-3, 14-25;
		Psalm 78:1-7;
		1 Thessalonians 4:13-18;
		Matthew 25:1-13
	B.	Ruth 3:1-5; 4:13-17; Psalm 127;
		Hebrews 9:24-28; Mark 12:38-44
	C.	Haggai 1:15–2:9; Psalm 98;
		2 Thessalonians 2:1-5, 13-17;
		Luke 20:27-38
Monday		Genesis 1:9-12
Tuesday		Leviticus 25:1-7
Wednesday		Job 38:1-24
Thursday		Matthew 18:10-14
Friday		Hebrews 1:10*b*-14
Saturday		Revelation 22:1-6

Silence

Daily Readings for Reflection

Reflection: Silent or Written

Prayers: For the World, for Others, for Myself

Offering of Self to God
LORD, you have done so many things! You made them all so wisely! The earth is full of your creations! Let the LORD's glory last forever! Let the LORD rejoice in all he has made! (Ps. 104:24, 31). Amen.

Blessing
May the God of all creation, the God who has created and is still creating, the God whose love and compassion know no end, have mercy upon us and grant us peace, this day and always. Amen.

Readings for Reflection

ء It came gently as I sat at a favorite childhood spot by the creek and watched the ice slowly melt, drop by drop, and heard the drops fall into the tiny stream six or eight inches below. Oh, the healing beauty of their music as the little drops joined their brothers that had thawed before them and had already joined the growing parade as it marched, ever growing, to the river below and the other rivers far away.

Mingled with this came the song of the meadowlark. Like a wild timpani a duck rushed past in full flight, just above the gentle stream. The sound of its flight and the coarseness of its happy call added a beautiful counterpart to the gentle sounds around me. The sun was preparing its bed in its western room; the breeze was gentle and cool. And, as I sat there being ministered to by nature's healing agents, I looked behind me to the prairie hill where one day long ago

in the summer of 1951 God allowed me to see a won-
derful sight and in that moment fixed his call to my life.
And I responded with an irretrievable "yes."
—Norman Shawchuck

❧ Summer afternoon light dappled the water of the
mountain stream as it relaxed in a long bend pool before
rushing over a small fall of rocks and tangled tree limbs.
In the shadows I could make out the delicate rises of
trout taking insects just below the surface film. A silence
as palpable as the warm air enveloped the secluded
setting. All at once a shadow on the far bank moved
upstream. The small river otter flowed as smoothly over
roots and tufts of grass as water over stones. Just before
disappearing among the exposed roots of a shoreline
tree, the otter turned to face me. We gazed at each other.
I remembered the words of poet Rainer Maria Rilke:
"love . . . consists in this, that two solitudes protect and
border and salute each other." Later I recalled how early
Christian writers had identified profound inner stillness as a condition of understanding the mysteries of
God hidden in creation and communicating these with
wisdom to others. Such understanding and communication are essential aspects of our stewardship as we
seek ways of interpreting God's design for creation to
a world impaired in its ability to listen.
—John S. Mogabgab, "Editor's Introduction," *Weavings*
  (September/October 2008)

❧ As the whole world is God's, so the whole world
is to act for God. As all men have the same relation
to God, as all men have all their powers and faculties
from God, so all men are obliged to act for God, with
all their powers and faculties.

As all things are God's, so all things are to be used
and regarded as the things of God. For men to abuse
things on earth, and live to themselves, is the same
rebellion against God, as for angels to abuse things in

Heaven; because God is just the same Lord of all on earth, as He is the Lord of all in Heaven.

Things may, and must differ in their use, but yet they are all to be used according to the will of God.
—William Law, *A Serious Call to a Devout and Holy Life*

❧ The prologue of John's Gospel states that all things came into being through God's creative Word and that "without him not one thing came into being" (John 1:3). In the Gospel, we learn that because God so loved this creation, that same Word became flesh in Jesus of Nazareth. And Jesus invites us to live in him and let him live in us—as deeply, integrally connected as a vine and its branches (John 15:4-5).

But since our human lives cannot be lived apart from the rest of creation that sustains us, might it be that "living in Christ" will mean living in communion with that Word that permeates the whole creation . . . and that therefore we do not find God "in heaven," but right here, in all our earthy reality? Then the whole creation must be viewed with reverence, held in sacred trust not just as God's gift to us, but as holy in its own right.
—Elaine M. Prevallet, SL, "Where Is Your God?" *Weavings*

❧ Now we have to make an unprecedented, gigantic move from viewing the rest of creation in a proprietary, dominating posture, to recognizing our need to live cooperatively—not just with other humans but with the whole of creation. We now need to develop a new sense of unity among all the members of our own species so that we all work together—regardless of our creeds or cultures or colors—to create a future for the planet.
—Elaine M. Prevallet, SL, "Where Is Your God?" *Weavings*

❧ The thirteenth-century theologian Thomas Aquinas emphasized the goodness of God and taught that creation is therefore good and unified because each part belongs to and contributes to the whole. All things, therefore, actualize the goodness of God and celebrate themselves as good creatures when they are at their best and helping all creation to flourish. We are stewards of creation, and this is manifested when we commit to the process of becoming fully who we are meant to be in the divine image and when we see ourselves as intimately one with creation. This is our destiny, and it is grace working in us that enables our own goodness in God to become increasingly visible through our care for the planet and its people. When we fall in love with the awesome Mystery of the cosmos; when we ponder minute particles and distant galaxies; when we are present to the weed, orchid, paw print, ocean, or the fly crawling up the window pane, we begin to see how interconnected we are and to sense a unity beyond our imagining. Stewardship of creation begins by seeing our place in the order of things as helpers so that God can go on saying, "It is very good!" (Gen. 1:31).

—Elizabeth J. Canham, "Wonder, Love, and Praise," *Weavings*

❧ In Christ, heaven and earth are indissolubly joined in a human life. Jesus does not come to destroy what Torah and Prophets affirm, but to deepen, enrich, and "fulfill" (Matt. 5:17). There is little in the Gospels to suggest the sharp division between the "earthly" and the "spiritual" so prized by later Christian history. Quite the contrary, Jesus is preparing those who follow him to "inherit the earth," as he says in the Beatitudes (Matt. 5:5).

These blessings must be taken all together as descriptors of the way Jesus himself lives on the earth and calls us to live, not as separate blessings for different personality types. To hunger and thirst after justice, to mourn over all that goes wrong, to make peace and endure persecution for seeking justice, to purify the heart and show mercy—all these not only cleanse our eyes to see God and enter God's gracious rule but grow us toward the "meekness" our first parents surrendered when they began to separate their use of Earth from God's purposes. They rejected the humble dignity of stewards and sought to "be as the gods." The "meek," as the Greek work *praus* suggests, are not weak but have their power under control. They know their true place in God's purposes and do not organize things around themselves but rather around what makes for the well-being of the whole.

—Robert Corin Morris, "An Altar of Earth," *Weavings*

᙮ We are part of Earth's rescue plan—God's plan to rescue Earth by rescuing it, first of all, from our destructiveness. Only by living into our destiny as Earth's stewards—arranging our economic, social, and, yes, spiritual life around our God-given role—will we become the children of God for which the whole creation, from oak trees to orangutans, "waits with eager longing" (Rom. 8:19). The creatures have been delivered into our hands (Gen. 9:2) and live in dread until we become Earth's true cultivators and custodians.

—Robert Corin Morris, "An Altar of Earth," *Weavings*

The Season after Pentecost/Ordinary Time
Sunday between November 13 and November 19

55. Justice

Affirmation
The LORD—he is our God. His justice is everywhere throughout the whole world (1 Chron. 16:14).

Psalm: 72

Psalm Prayer
Loving God, in Jesus Christ you have shown us the king whose rule brings abundance of life to all people. Grant that we may be faithful followers of his way by listening to the cries of those in need and seeking justice for all who are oppressed. Amen.

Daily Scripture Readings

Sunday	A.	Judges 4:1-7; Psalm 123; 1 Thessalonians 5:1-11; Matthew 25:14-30
	B.	1 Samuel 1:4-20; Psalm 16; Hebrews 10:11-14, 19-25; Mark 13:1-8
	C.	Isaiah 65:17-25; Psalm 98; 2 Thessalonians 3:6-13; Luke 21:5-19
Monday		Exodus 6:1-13
Tuesday		Psalm 89:1-14
Wednesday		Ezekiel 34:1-16
Thursday		Luke 11:37-44
Friday		Ephesians 4:17-24
Saturday		James 3:13-18

Silence

Daily Readings for Reflection

Reflection: Silent or Written

Prayers: For the World, for Others, for Myself

Offering of Self to God
Faithful God, you are an unfailing friend to those who live hard lives on the underside of society. Receive and fortify my desire to be your faithful friend by working for holy justice and peace wherever I am and whatever I am doing. Amen.

Blessing
May the Lord whose nature is love and whose path is justice help us to embody right relationships in all our undertakings. Amen.

Readings for Reflection

❧ God is close; his love is real; his faithfulness never changing, and he loves me, all those who are close to me, and all of his children. I love God and claim him as Lord and Savior; to him I swear hearty allegiance; for him, I give my strength, my intellect, and my life! I bind myself to God today with the cords of love and the chains of servanthood. This life is short, the demands great, and the responsibility paramount! No other way to go and no turning back, for I am bound to God forever.

I throw myself before God and cry, "Here am I, Lord, your willing and able servant. Send me; I am ready to live or die for you, to succeed or fail, to rise or fall; only show me your chosen path for me and there I will serve until you direct otherwise.

My God I pray for a renewal of passion for justice, for goodness, for peace, and for the lost who need your saving powers. Send your Holy Spirit to awaken my passion; to guide, strengthen, and sustain so I may fulfill the high and holy calling that comes from you.
—Norman Shawchuck

᠕ Let us reflect on the condition of a poor innocent man on whom the rich man lays heavy burdens, from a desire after wealth and luxuries. When this laborer looks over the cause of his heavy toil and considers that it is laid on him to support what has no foundation in pure wisdom, we may well suppose that an uneasiness arises in his mind toward one who might without any inconvenience deal more favorably with him. He considers that by his industry his fellow creature is benefited and sees that this wealthy man is not satisfied with being supported in a plain way, but to gratify a desire of conforming to wrong customs increases to an extreme the labors of those who occupy his estate. Then we may reasonably judge that he will think himself unkindly used. When he considers that the proceedings of the wealthy are agreeable to the customs of the times and sees no means of redress in this world, how will the sighing of this innocent person ascend to the throne of that great and good Being who created all and who has a constant care over his creatures! Those who toil year after year to furnish others with wealth and extravagances until they are wearied and oppressed by too much labor understand the meaning of that language, "You know the heart of an alien, for you were aliens in the land of Egypt."

Many at this day who do not know the heart of an alien indulge themselves in ways of life that occasion more labor than Infinite Goodness intends for people. And yet they feel compassion for the distresses of those who come directly under their observation. What if they were to change circumstances a while with their laborers and pass regularly through the means of knowing the heart of an alien and come to a feeling knowledge of the constraints and hardships that many poor innocent people pass through in obscure life? What if these who now fare sumptuously every day were to act the other part of the scene until seven times had over them and return again to their former states? I believe many of them would embrace a less expensive

life and would lighten the heavy burdens of some who now labor out of their sight and pass through tight places with which they are but little acquainted. To see their fellow creatures under difficulties to which they are in no degree accessory tends to awaken tenderness in the minds of all reasonable people. But consider the condition of those who are depressed in answering our demands and labor for us out of our sight while we pass our time in fullness. Consider also that much less than we demand would supply us with things really useful. What heart will not relent? How can reasonable people refrain from easing the suffering of which they themselves are the cause, when they may do so without inconvenience?
—John Woolman, *Walking Humbly with God*

❧ It is impossible to restrict the gospel of Christ to narrow limits. It redeems the sins of the past, restores the present, and stimulates development in the future. Moreover, this is not merely for the individual but for society as well. We must conceive of it as the liberation of the entire human race. The gospel is the message of a year of jubilee, of a year of rejoicing. It should mean the liberation economically, politically, socially, physiologically, and spiritually of the human race. It must mean the true emancipation of the whole humanity.
—Toyohiko Kagawa, *Living Out Christ's Love*

❧ To fears and sin that hold us back and weigh us down, we say: "No more. You are not the future. The future is God—and God has promised the gift of forgiveness." We are emboldened to face what we have done with the grace of what God has done and promises to do. Those confessions provide rehearsals for more public confessions of those truths by individuals and communities of faith. God would also embolden us to speak such truth with courage to those who would play on our fears and rely on our silenced timidity and

say—"No more. You are not the future. This will not stand. We trust in God's holy presence and gracious favor." And having said that, we then live that truth.
—John Indermark, *Do Not Live Afraid*

❧ Like our other forms of prayer, praying with our material lives can and will cause upheaval. Just as our minds can revolt against us in silent prayer, so too will our social circles rebel when we begin to question how we are living or what are our material priorities.
—Daniel Wolpert, *Creating a Life with God*

❧ In our society, questions concerning vocation seem natural. We live in a culture that greatly values self-fulfillment. I believe that living in alignment with God's purposes for us is the surest path to such satisfaction. But discovering our call and exercising our gifts are not of first importance in the Christian life. They cannot be, because most Christians have not had the freedom or power to make many choices about the circumstances of their lives. The slaves, the women, and the working poor who comprised so much of the early church had little say in their vocational choices. The primary call of God to us, then, must be audible in all stages, conditions, and seasons of life. This call is profoundly simple, yet, as T. S. Eliot wrote in *Four Quartets*, answering it costs "not less than everything." Moreover, the successful discovery of our gifts and particular calling depends upon our acceptance of this primal summons from God.
—Gerrit Scott Dawson, *Companions in Christ*

❧ What would grace unshackled from its exile in categories of rescue look like? I think it would look like mercy running wild across the planet, from Darfur to Sri Lanka. I think it would look like rivers of forgiveness connecting Palestine and Israel, the United States and Iran, South and North Korea, and all the places of discord and distrust. I think it would look like deep and abiding concern for the heron flying above my pond this morning, or the red-eared turtle in its ancient wisdom connecting us to mud and insects, water and lily pads. Grace would look like Mom and Dad weeping over the casket of their beloved son and little girls setting off balloons for the mother they lost.

Grace would look like the people who wrap their arms around the hurting to hold the experience of being alive in solidarity. We would return from the exile of disbelief, relentless self-criticism, and mindless attacks on other creatures, including the human creature. We would laugh and weep in grace united with the center of our being, the still point where God breathes the breath of life into us, and we know in this journey on this planet that we have each other, the earth that supports us, and the abiding love of the Eternal Spirit of all that lives.

—Mary L. Fraser, "Grace," *Weavings*

Reign of Christ Sunday

We began the church year with our focus on the birth of Jesus, and we end the church year with our focus on Christ as the Sovereign Servant, who rules like no other. Rulers are often seen gathering great armies and weapons in order to impose their rule. In the kingdom of God, where this Sovereign Servant rules, love, mercy, justice, and grace are the instruments of governance.

The rulers of this world often seek to govern through fear and intimidation. The Sovereign Servant governs with love, trust, and example. The rulers of this world seek to intimidate, dominate, and control. The Sovereign Servant seeks to encourage, inspire, strengthen, and set free. The kingdom of God that Jesus proclaims and rules is not at all like the kingdoms of this world. Their foundation, structure, and leaders can never be considered equal to those of God's kingdom, although sometimes we make the mistake of thinking we can give equal loyalty to both. The Christian may indeed be a citizen of two worlds. But Christians never forget where their true homeland is and who is their Sovereign leader.

Today we remind one another that the world as it is now will not survive because all things will become new in Jesus, the Sovereign Servant who rules with love and mercy. This new world will be a reflection of the One who rules it. Love, peace, justice, and plenty will replace hatred, violence, oppression, greed, war, and intolerance as the fully redeemed faithful respond with joyful and generous hearts to every need before it can injure or harm any of God's beloved children. Sin and sadness, pain and suffering will be no more and every child of God will be recognized as an honored member of God's great family with full inheritance of all the triune God's abundance.

On this day, we celebrate the rule of Christ in our lives, in our congregations, and over the powers that seek to destroy us and all that we love. Today, as we pray for the coming of God's kingdom on earth as it is in heaven, we once again pledge our lives and fortunes to the kingdom of God forming in our midst. This day is a joyous celebration of a year of reliving the mighty acts of God. It is also a day of transition to Advent and the great expectation of a Savior who will come to heal, deliver, and save this wounded and broken world. We end the year with hallelujahs filling our hearts. Next week we begin a new year with wonderment, excitement, and anticipation as we prepare once again to explore the mystery, beauty, salvation, and fulfillment found in our mighty Creator, the God of love.

56. End Times

Affirmation
All who take refuge in the LORD are truly happy! (Ps. 2:11*b*).

Psalm: 11

Psalm Prayer
Vigilant God, your sight is sharper than the eagle's and more penetrating than the rays of the sun. Search our hearts with compassion and test our deeds with forbearance, that when the end comes we will be able to stand upright in your presence and praise you face to face in the beauty of your holy temple. Amen.

Daily Scripture Readings

Sunday	A.	Ezekiel 34:11-16, 20-24; Psalm 100; Ephesians 1:15-23; Matthew 25:31-46
	B.	2 Samuel 23:1-7; Psalm 132:1-12; Revelation 1:4-8; John 18:33-37
	C.	Jeremiah 23:1-6; Luke 1:68-79; Colossians 1:11-20; Luke 23:33-43
Monday		Genesis 6:13-22
Tuesday		Psalm 39:1-5
Wednesday		Matthew 24:1-21
Thursday		Matthew 24:22-42
Friday		Revelation 7:9-17
Saturday		1 Peter 4:7-11

Silence

Daily Readings for Reflection

Reflection: Silent or Written

Prayers: For the World, for Others, for Myself

Offering of Self to God
In the end, when all else has passed away, there will remain only love, the love that overflows your heart, O God, and animates the distant reaches of space and time. I seek fuller immersion in that great river, trusting that the small endings of daily life are true access points through which I can participate ever more fully in the fulfillment of your design for all that is. Amen.

Blessing
Now the salvation and power and kingdom of our God, and the authority of his Christ have come (Rev. 12:10). By the grace of our kindhearted God, may we be numbered among those who dwell in the house of the Lord all their days. Amen.

Readings for Reflection

ॐ We began the seasons of the church year with anticipation, and we end the seasons of the church year declaring a certainty. In Advent we waited for the needed and longed-for definitive and ultimate self-disclosure of God in the birth of Jesus of Nazareth. On Reign of Christ Sunday we celebrate the fulfillment of the biblical revelation of God in Christ.

Once again the church has listened to, reflected upon, rehearsed in worship, and tried to live in daily experience the redemption story. We come away from this last Sunday of the church year soaked to the core in the revelation story. We come away from this last Sunday of the church year soaked to the core in the revelation of God in Christ. For us, as for those first disciples, there can be no turning back. Here in the light of Christ's triumphant presence we find our voice and declare once again, Jesus Christ is Lord of all and shall reign as Lord in my life. So committed, we are ready to face every eventuality of life because we now

know the One in whom our life is found, redeemed, and kept secure. Our radical trust is in the One who is completely trustworthy (2 Tim. 1:12). Life in Christ is good and complete.
—Rueben P. Job

❧ Hope has always been a dominant quality in the life of the Christian community. From the time of the resurrection of Jesus until today, individual Christians and the Christian community have been full of hope. In the face of fierce opposition and persecution, followers of Jesus never lost hope. Even when failure interrupted their journey, hope was the undercurrent that swept them to repentance, forgiveness, and companionship with the living Lord once more.

The source of this resolute hope was never found in the surroundings or how things were going for the Church. Rather, hope was found in God and the assurance that God was at work in the Church and in the world. The disciples felt a calm confidence that God's work and will would ultimately be completed and fulfilled. And they were assured that every Christian was invited into a partnership with God that moved toward the fulfillment of God's grand design for all creation. Such assurance is fertile ground in which the seeds of hope can flourish and bear the fruit of faithful living.
—Rueben P. Job, *A Guide to Spiritual Discernment*

❧ I am in the middle of it again. God has chosen me for a never-before-done project. My prayer has been answered that God would give me a work so difficult, or so unappealing that no one else wants it, but that it is of great importance to God. Blessed Holy Spirit, draw nearer as I need you now as never before.

The promise is sure that no matter how dangerous the course, no matter the difficulties in this changing world, even though the mountains all slip into the sea, by your grace the faithful will always find their true home with you. So with hope and confidence I set my course to follow you, knowing that all is well and my home with you secure.

—Norman Shawchuck

✌ We need to open our eyes and ears. In a culture so fixed on the superficial, the negative, the sensational, and the tawdry, we need to be a people who look for the movements of God's grace and stand ready to follow where those movements lead. The question is so straightforward: "Where have we seen the reign of Christ since we last met?"

—Stephen V. Doughty and Marjorie J. Thompson, *The Way of Discernment*

✌ The fact that Jesus Christ died is more important than the fact that I shall die, and the fact that Jesus Christ rose from the dead is the sole ground of my hope that I, too, shall be raised on the Last Day.

—Dietrich Bonhoeffer, *Selections from the Writings of Dietrich Bonhoeffer*

✌ What form the "glorification" of human beings and Earth may take is something we know only in amazing events like the Transfiguration, where a mortal human body shines with the light of the Divine itself, or the Resurrection, where that which is mortal puts on immortality (1 Cor. 15:54). Whatever the ultimate meaning of the symbols, a glorified and renewed world, in which the kings of the earth bring all their treasures in tribute to a City that has descended *from* heaven *to Earth*, is presented as the end-game of God's plan for us.

And who will inherit this world where humanity and nature, nation and nation are reconciled? As we have seen, Jesus makes it very clear: the "meek"—those who have submitted their human powers to the discipline of God's love. The growing crisis of Earth's life makes it abundantly clear that he was not a starry-eyed idealist but a prophet of the utmost practicality. And more than a prophet: for he is the Way back to the humble humanity that is our true destiny, and Earth's best hope.

—Robert Corin Morris, "An Altar of Earth," *Weavings*

❧ We are more than a curious accident, more than a chance occurrence in time and space. This intricate world, so full of beauty and terror by turns, is on a journey. Up from dust and nothingness toward order, toward mind and spirit, it makes its way, guided by the hand of God. It is going somewhere. For us who follow Jesus and call ourselves by his name, it is a journey toward the kingdom of God. We have no language adequate to express what it means, but there are times when we can hear the distant trumpets and catch a fleeting glimpse of the towers of the eternal city. That is why biblical writers speak of gates of pearl and streets of gold, using the richest language at their disposal. That is why Christianity faces east, toward the dawn. Our faith makes us people of the morning. That is why the spiritual says, "There's a great day comin' by and by." We are leaning into the future in expectation.

—Ronald S. James, "Communion and the Coming Kingdom," *Weavings*

A Personal Retreat Day

Introduction

Why should we take regular days apart for personal retreat? Douglas Steere, the twentieth-century Quaker spiritual writer, suggests one answer. Citing a Japanese translation of Hosea 2:14 ("I will entice you into the desert and there I will speak to you in the depth of your heart"), he comments, "The verse links solitariness with prayer in an almost inimitable way. For until I have been lured into the desert, until I have been brought in solitude to the very ground of my being, where I am beyond the grip of my surface self with all of its plans and distractions, I am not able to hear the divine whisper."* In our busy lives and distracted culture, it can be difficult indeed to discern God's presence and to heed God's voice. Therefore we need to be intentional about finding or creating environments that support our desire for a deepening relationship with God. When we commit ourselves to days set aside for God, we join the psalmist in affirming: "For God alone my soul waits in silence; from him comes my salvation" (Psalm 62:1, NRSV).

Days devoted to personal retreat could be said to have a threefold purpose: Listening to God, loving God, and resting in God. Each posture enriches the others and leads us farther along the path that leads to fullness of life. The schedule for the day suggested here has been designed to support this multilayered purpose.

Preparation

Thoughtful preparation for our day of retreat is already a confirmation of our desire to enter an environment uncluttered by typical daily preoccupations. Here is

---

* Douglas V. Steere, *Together in Solitude* (New York: Crossroad, 1982), 92.

a list of possible items to take with us into our quiet day. Remember that this is a time for exploring "being" rather than "doing," so be selective and take only what you need for the purpose of your retreat.

- Comfortable clothing and footwear, with extra apparel for layering
- Insect repellent, sun screen, or other supplies to make time out-of-doors more pleasant
- Clock or watch with gentle alarm to mark the various parts of the day
- Food and beverages; depending on availability of refrigeration and cooking facilities
- Candle with matches, icon, or other object symbolizing the presence of God
- Bible
- Prayer book or another source for prayer during the day
- Journal or notebook (physical or digital)
- Favorite writing instrument
- Other spiritual reading material (novels, poems)
- Music and device on which to listen to it
- Art or craft materials

The Day Alone with God

8:45—Arrive

Where should we take our retreat day? It is important to select a location free of distractions and interruptions. While our home is a possible choice, it usually is not the ideal place for retreat because we will likely find ourselves surrounded by familiar unfinished tasks, happy or unhappy memories, and potentially disrupting phone calls, deliveries, or visitors. If home is the best option, then we should make every effort to insure that disturbances can be kept to a minimum. One immediate benefit of choosing a location away from home is the physical and psychological experience of leaving behind the ordinary contexts of our life in order to be more fully present to God. Our place apart should be comfortable and quiet, with adequate light and surroundings suitable for walking or other outdoor activities. If we anticipate that napping may be a part of our day, then we need to be sure that the retreat setting has a good bed. Whether we spend the day in a retreat center, camp, church building, or home of a friend, we want a place that offers hospitality to a hungry heart and helps us, as Douglas Steere would say, to be present where we are.*

9:00—Becoming Present Where You Are

• *Settling in, quieting yourself, preparing for the day*
Once we arrive at the retreat setting, we need to be there. Our soul, with its many concerns and preoccupations, needs to catch up with our body. Simple rituals can help us quietly settle into the space and prepare our environment for the day ahead. If we are at a retreat center or similar facility, we may want to familiarize ourselves with the buildings and grounds, identifying spots we might return to later in the day. Unpacking our bag and carefully placing our Bible, prayer book, journal, and writing instrument on a table or desk in our room can create a sense of expectancy. Putting away a simple lunch can remind us of God's provision. Lighting a candle (if safe to do) can symbolize the presence of the Holy Spirit, who desires to lead us to greater truth (John 16:13).

• *Rhythms of the day*
The deepest formational rhythms of the day are listening to God, loving God, and resting in God. These correspond to the movements of *lectio divina*, a pattern of prayer associated with the Benedictine

---

* Douglas V. Steere, *Together in Solitude*, 158–77.

monastic tradition. These movements are *lectio* (reading), *meditatio* (meditation/listening), *oratio* (prayer/loving), and *contemplatio* (contemplation/resting).

9:30—**Morning Prayer** *(lectio* and *oratio)*

The first prayer of the day may follow a formal pattern such as that found in this *Guide*, or it can be a free-form time of becoming present to the God who is always present to us. Choose a way of prayer that is familiar and comfortable or new and inviting. Whatever the shape of our morning prayer time, let it be centered on the Bible. This is the worshipful beginning of a day spent in solitude and silence with God's word.

Several ways of dwelling with God's word in scripture commend themselves. We might choose to read the Bible consecutively by beginning at some point and following the text to another point (for example, the Book of Proverbs or an entire Gospel). We might decide to allow a lectionary to determine our reading (the Sunday and Weekday readings in this *Guide*, for example). Or we could approach the Bible topically, searching out texts that address forgiveness or trust. Other possibilities include reading a psalm, a Gospel story or portion of an Epistle, the Lord's Prayer, or the Beatitudes. Our experience with biblical texts can be enriched by pairing them with other sources such as spiritual classics, novels, poetry, and music.

Attending to words, phrases, or images from scripture that especially draw our attention may then lead us to shape a prayerful response to what we have heard. We can express our love for God in prayers of praise, petition, thanksgiving, intercession, or simple silence. Lancelot Andrewes (1555–1626), a Cambridge University scholar and Anglican Bishop, suggests that over time these expressions of love can form the content of our own personal prayer book.

10:00—Journaling, Walking Meditation *(meditatio)*

• *Making God's word your home*
Meditation on our chosen text is the process of actively receiving the rich spiritual nutrients it contains. For some, writing in a physical or digital journal facilitates a deeper listening in which connections surface between God's word and our life circumstances. For others, the physical movement of walking meditation promotes alert attentiveness to signs of God's presence illumined by the scripture text. However we choose to enter more deeply into the Bible, our hope is to receive a life-giving word by making our home in God's word.

11:00—Rest *(contemplatio)*

• *Playing in the garden of God's word*
Contemplation is not the esoteric province of some spiritual elite. Rather, it is the birthright of every Christian. We have received the Holy Spirit in our baptism and therefore have been drawn by the Spirit into the intimacy of God's triune life. Contemplation is the growing awareness and enjoyment of life *with* God but also life *in* God. Contemplative experience confirms Paul's assertion that in God "we live and move and have our being" (Acts 17:28, NRSV).

Contemplation invites us to set aside the more active postures of reading, meditating, and expressing our love in order to enter a time of resting in God's presence. Contemplative resting may take the form of play (for example, arts, crafts, music either performed or composed, gentle body movement such as tai chi), or sleep (recalling the wisdom of Song of Songs 5:2: "I was sleeping, but my heart was awake"). Contemplative experience in its many forms is characterized by deep contentment in simply being with God. This is the wholly relaxed contentment of the weaned child on her mother's breast, who desires nothing more than to be in that place of complete acceptance and love (Psalm 131). It is said that cats purr when they are happy and when they are concentrating intensely. Contemplation is when we are purring spiritually.

11:30—**Midday Prayer** *(lectio* and *oratio)*

Returning to God's word in the middle of the day sets the noonday meal in the spiritual context of God's sustaining grace. Prayer at the height of the day reminds us that we do not live by bread alone and that the food we are about to enjoy is also a form of God's word to us. This is also the hour when physical or spiritual fatigue may overtake us. Listening and responding to God's revivifying voice can restore vitality to a wilting spirit. We may choose to follow our pattern for Morning Prayer or to select another order of worship from a different prayer resource.

12:00—**Noonday Meal**

There is no need to hurry through this meal. Indeed, it can be a continuation of our prayer. As we savor the flavor of each bite, delight in the color of each food item, and note the texture of each portion, we are tasting and seeing that the Lord is good (Psalm 34:8). Here before us is a visible sign of God's love for us. Our meal truly can be for us a sacramental event through which God draws near, responding to the hunger of our heart by meeting the hunger of our body.

1:00—**Spiritual Reading** *(lectio)*

- *Finding hints, signs, and wonders of God in literature, music, art*

This time in the day affords us the opportunity to cast our nets on the other side of the boat (John 21:6), trusting that God has a word for us in the deep waters of culture. Novels, poetry, music from diverse times and places, art both ancient and contemporary—all can open fresh vistas onto God's astonishing creativity in wooing us to greater intimacy.

2:00—Journaling, Walking Mediation *(meditatio)*

In this afternoon period for meditation we can begin to gather up the riches of the preceding hours in a process of reflection and integration. What have we heard God saying to us? What questions do we have for God? What hopes for this day have been fulfilled or remain unfulfilled? Walking meditation on the grounds or in the neighborhood of our retreat location may restore needed physical energy at this point in the day.

2:30—Rest *(contemplatio)*

An extended period of rest and refreshment in God's company allows integration and evaluation of the day's insights, questions, and concerns to continue outside the limitations of conscious reflection. A second nap may be in order. Perhaps a craft project or art piece needs further work. There might be a book chapter calling for completion or a personal psalm pressing toward expression. Play is both delightfully open-ended and profoundly edifying. We may learn more about God and our relationship with God in one hour of true play than in eight hours of diligent theological study.

4:00—Evening Prayer *(lectio* and *oratio)*

Our day apart is coming to a close. Psalms, scripture passages, and prayers for this time emphasize gratitude for God's sustaining love throughout the day and trust that God will bring us safely through the night: "Living in the Most High's shelter, camping in the Almighty's shade, I say to the Lord, 'You are my refuge, my stronghold! You are my God—the one I trust!'" (Ps. 91:1-2).

4:30—Examen of Consciousness

• *Finding hints, signs, and wonders of God in this day of retreat*

The quiet day concludes with a prayerful review of the hours we have spent with God. Several questions provide guidance for our examen: When or how was I particularly aware of God's presence? What did I learn about myself that brings joy to God and me? What did I learn about myself that grieves God and me? What next steps in my journey will allow me to respond to the great invitation: "'Friend, move up higher'" (Luke 14:10, NRSV)?

5:00—Depart in Peace

We gather our belongings and straighten up our space without rush, grateful for the hospitality our surroundings have provided for our day apart. Before departing, we might say a prayer for the next retreatant who will occupy our room or for the family or friends with whom we share our abode.

What can we expect to come from the practice of taking quiet days for personal retreat? The words Jesus spoke to those who believed in him are given as promise to us as well:

If you make my word your home you will indeed be my disciples;

You will come to know the truth, and the truth will set you free (John 8:31-32, JB).

Index of Authors

Numbers after author names indicate weeks in which their writings appear.

Bibliography of Works Cited

Abbreviations

CIC—Companions in Christ
GDC—Great Devotional Classics
URSC 1—Upper Room Spiritual Classics, Series 1
URSC 2—Upper Room Spiritual Classics, Series 2
URSC 3—Upper Room Spiritual Classics, Series 3
Weavings—Weavings: A Journal of the Christian Spiritual Life (published by The Upper Room, Nashville, TN)

Bibliography

Ainsworth, Percy C. "Fear and Joy." *Weavings* (March/April 1999).

———. "The Pilgrim Church." *Weavings* (July/August 2005).

———. "The Waste of the Ointment." *Weavings* (May/June 2008).

Antal, Jim. "Peacemaking in the Congregation." *Weavings* (March/April 1988).

Augustine. *Hungering for God: Selected Writings of Augustine.* Edited by Keith Beasley-Topliffe. URSC 1. Nashville, TN: Upper Room Books, 1997.

Beasley-Topliffe, Keith. "And the Rock Was Christ: Seeking the Deeper Meaning of Scripture for Prayer and Preaching Today." *Weavings* (July/August 1996).

———. "The Beginning of Wisdom." *Weavings* (March/April 1999).

Benedict, Daniel T., Jr. *Patterned by Grace: How Liturgy Shapes Us.* Nashville, TN: Upper Room Books, 2007.

Bernard of Clairvaux. *Selections from the Writings of Bernard of Clairvaux.* Edited by Douglas V. Steere. GDC. Nashville, TN: Upper Room Books, 1961.

Blomquist, Jean M. "Barefoot Basics: Yearning and Learning to Stand on Holy Ground." *Weavings* (September/October 1992).

———. "Fried Dirt and Frayed Faith: Learning to Trust Our Own Wisdom." *Weavings* (July/August 1997).

Bondi, Roberta L. "Becoming Bearers of Reconciliation." *Weavings* (January/February 1990).

———. "Practicing: A Second Flute." *Weavings* (May/June 1996).

Bonhoeffer, Dietrich. *Selections from the Writings of Dietrich Bonhoeffer*. Edited by Orlo Strunk, Jr. GDC. Nashville, TN: Upper Room Books, 1967.

Broyles, Anne. "One More Door into God's Presence." *Weavings* (May/June 1987).

Buchanan, Missy. *Talking with God in Old Age: Meditations and Psalms*. Nashville, TN: Upper Room Books, 2010.

Bunyan, John. *Selections from the Writings of John Bunyan*. Edited by Thomas S. Kepler. GDC. Nashville, TN: Upper Room Books, 1951.

Burrows, Mark S. "A Passion That We Feel." *Weavings* (August/September/October 2011).

———. "The Hardest Love We Carry." *Weavings* (November/December 2008).

Bushnell, Horace. "Living to God in Small Things." *Weavings* (May/June 1987); article condensed from Bushnell's *Sermons for New Life*. Rev. ed. New York: Charles Scribner's Sons, 1901.

Calvin, John. *Selections from the Writings of John Calvin*. Edited by Norman Victor Hope. GDC. Nashville, TN: Upper Room Books, 1958.

Canham, Elizabeth J. "Listen with the Ear of Your Heart." *Weavings* (September/October 1995).

———. "Solo Journey." *Weavings* (March/April 2005).

———. "Strangers and Pilgrims." *Weavings* (September/October 2003).

———. "Where Shall Wisdom Be Found?" *Weavings* (May/June/July 2011).

———. "Wonder, Love, and Praise." *Weavings* (Sept/October 2008).

Catherine of Siena. *A Life of Total Prayer: Selected Writings of Catherine of Siena*. URSC 3. Nashville, TN: Upper Room Books, 2000.

Chilcote, Paul Wesley. *Changed from Glory into Glory: Wesleyan Prayer for Transformation*. Nashville, TN: Upper Room Books, 2005.

———. *A Life-Shaping Prayer: 52 Meditations in the Wesleyan Spirit*. Nashville, TN: Upper Room Books, 2008.

Cunningham, Fred B. "Excerpts from a Pastor's Journal." *Weavings* (September/October 1986).

Dawson, Gerrit Scott. "Gathering Praise." *Weavings* (March/April 2008).

———. "Responding to Our Call," *Companions in Christ: A Small-Group Experience in Spiritual Formation*, Participant's Book. Nashville, TN: Upper Room Books, 2006.

DelBene, Eleanor McKenzie. "As Clay in the Potter's Hands." *Weavings* (November/December 1986).

DelBene, Ron. "A Simple Way to Pray." *Weavings* (September/October 1986).

Donigian, George Hovaness. "All That Glitters May Not Be Gold," *The Upper Room Disciplines 1999*. Nashville, TN: Upper Room Books, 1998.

Donnelly, Doris. "Ambassadors of Reconciliation." *Weavings* (January/February 1990).

———. "Good Tidings of Great Joy." *Weavings* (November/December 1993).

———. "Is the Spiritual Life for Everyone?" *Weavings* (September/October 1986).

Doughty, Stephen V. "Simple Places." *Weavings* (May/June 2003).

———. "Why Are They, Well, So . . . ?!" *Weavings* (May/June 1999).

Doughty, Stephen V. and Marjorie J. Thompson. *The Way of Discernment*, Participant's Book. CIC. Nashville, TN: Upper Room Books, 2008.

Douglas, Deborah Smith. "Enclosed in Darkness (But Not Alone)." *Weavings* (November/December 2010).

———. "Pilgrims, Strangers, and the Hope of the Poor," *Weavings* (May/June 2008).

———. "Unfailing Treasure." *Weavings* (November/December 2005).

Downey, Michael. "Gift's Constant Coming." *Weavings* (November/December 1999).

———. "On Learning How to Look." *Weavings* (August/September/October 2011).

Drew, Anne Marie. "Brave Emptiness: The Geography of Demons." *Weavings* (May/June 2001).

Dreyer, Elizabeth Ann. "Asceticism Reconsidered." *Weavings* (November/December 1988).

Edwards, Tilden H., Jr. "Living the Day from the Heart." *Weavings* (July/August 1992).

Epperly, Bruce G. *Holy Adventure: 41 Days of Audacious Living*. Nashville, TN: Upper Room Books, 2008.

Escamilla, Paul Lynd. "Something Bigger than All of Us: Koinonia, Fruitfulness, and Joy in the Worship of God." *Weavings* (July/August 1995).

Fenelon, Francois. *Selections from the Writings of Francois Fenelon*. Edited by Thomas S. Kepler. GDC. Nashville, TN: Upper Room Books, 1962.

Ford, Stephanie. "A Dance with Gentleness." *Weavings* (July/August 2004).

———. *Kindred Souls: Connecting through Spiritual Friendship*. Nashville, TN: Upper Room Books, 2006.

Francis of Assisi. *Riches of Simplicity: Selected Writings of Francis and Clare*. Edited by Keith Beasley-Topliffe. URSC 2. Nashville, TN: Upper Room Books, 1998.

———. *Selections from the Writings of St. Francis of Assisi*. Edited by J. Minton Batten. GDC. Nashville, TN: Upper Room Books, 1952.

Fraser, Mary L. "Grace: The Return from Exile." *Weavings* (January/February 2008).

Guyon, Jeanne (Madame). *Short and Easy Method of Prayer*. Available at http://www.ccel.org/ccel/guyon/prayer.txt.

Hawkins, Pamela C. *The Awkward Season: Prayers for Lent*. Nashville, TN: Upper Room Books, 2009.

———. *Behold! Cultivating Attentiveness in the Season of Advent*. Nashville, TN: Upper Room Books, 2011.

———. *Simply Wait: Cultivating Stillness in the Season of Advent*. Nashville, TN: Upper Room Books, 2007.

Hinson, E. Glenn. "Having the Mind of Christ." *Weavings* (March/April 1997).

———. "Horizonal Persons." *Weavings* (March/April 1995).

———. *Spiritual Preparation for Christian Leadership*. Nashville, TN: Upper Room Books, 1999.

Hudson, Trevor. *Hope Beyond Your Tears: Experiencing Christ's Healing Love*. CIC. Nashville, TN: Upper Room Books, 2012.

Hudson, Trevor and Stephen D. Bryant. *The Way of Transforming Discipleship*, Participant's Book. Nashville, TN: Upper Room Books, 2005.

Indermark, John. *Do Not Live Afraid: Faith in a Fearful World*. Nashville, TN: Upper Room Books, 2009.

———. *The Way of Grace*, Participant's Book. CIC. Nashville, TN: Upper Room Books, 2004.

Ingram, Kristen Johnson. "The Sacrament of Time." *Weavings* (January/February 1999).

James, Ronald S. "Communion and the Coming Kingdom." *Weavings* (January/February 1987).

Jenkins, J. Marshall. *A Wakeful Faith: Spiritual Practice in the Real World*. Nashville, TN: Upper Room Books, 2000.

Job, Rueben P. *A Guide to Spiritual Discernment*. Nashville, TN: Upper Room Books, 1996.

———. *Spiritual Life in the Congregation: A Guide for Retreats*. Nashville, TN: Upper Room Books, 1997.

Job, Rueben P. and Marjorie J. Thompson. "Embracing the Journey," *Companions in Christ: A Small-Group*

Experience in Spiritual Formation, Participant's Book. Nashville, TN: Upper Room Books, 2006.

John of the Cross. *Loving God through the Darkness: Selected Writings of John of the Cross.* Edited by Keith Beasley-Topliffe. URSC 3. Nashville, TN: Upper Room Books, 2000.

Johnson, Jan. "Weeping with God as a Spiritual Discipline." *Weavings* (May/June 2004).

Jones, W. Paul. *The Art of Spiritual Direction: Giving and Receiving Spiritual Guidance.* Nashville, TN: Upper Room Books, 2002.

———. "Joy and Religious Motivation." *Weavings* (November/December 1993).

Jowett, John Henry. *The Friend on the Road and Other Studies in the Gospels.* New York: The New York Public Library, 2011.Also available at http://www.ccel.org/ccel/jowett/friendonroad.txt.

Julian of Norwich. *Encounter with God's Love: Selected Readings from Julian of Norwich.* Edited by Keith Beasley-Topliffe. URSC 2. Nashville, TN: Upper Room Books, 1998.

Kagawa, Toyohiko. *Living Out Christ's Love: Selected Writings of Toyohiko Kagawa.* Edited by Keith Beasley-Topliffe. URSC 2. Nashville, TN: Upper Room Books, 1998.

Kelly, Thomas. *The Sanctuary of the Soul: Selected Writings of Thomas Kelly.* Edited by Keith Beasley-Topliffe. URSC 1. Nashville, TN: Upper Room Books, 1997.

———. *A Testament of Devotion.* Edited by Douglas V. Steere. GDC. Nashville, TN: Upper Room Books, 1955.

Kempis, Thomas à. *The Imitation of Christ.* Edited by Douglas V. Steere. GDC. Nashville, TN: Upper Room Books, 1950.

———. *A Pattern for Life: Selected Writings of Thomas à Kempis.* Edited by Keith Beasley-Topliffe. URSC 2. Nashville, TN: Upper Room Books, 1998.

Kena, Kwasi. *The Africana Worship Book, Year A*. Edited by Valerie Bridgeman Davis and Safiyah Fosua. Nashville, TN: Discipleship Resources, 2006.

Kidd, Sue Monk. "Birthing Compassion." *Weavings* (November/December 1990).

Kincannon, Karla M. *Creativity and Divine Surprise: Finding the Place of Your Resurrection*. Nashville, TN: Upper Room Books, 2005.

Law, William. *A Serious Call to a Devout and Holy Life*. Edited by Thomas S. Kepler. GDC. Nashville, TN: Upper Room Books, 1952.

———. *Total Devotion to God: Selected Writings of William Law*. Edited by Keith Beasley-Topliffe. URSC 3. Nashville, TN: Upper Room Books, 2000.

Luther, Martin. *Table-Talk*. Edited by William R. Cannon. GDC. Nashville, TN: Upper Room Books, 1950.

Martyn, Henry. *Selections from the Journal and Letters of Henry Martyn*. Edited by Elmer H. Douglas. GDC. Nashville, TN: Upper Room Books, 1959.

McEntyre, Marilyn Chandler. "A Gentle Word." *Weavings* (July/August 2004).

———. "What You Get for the Price." *Weavings* (May/June 2011).

McGinnis, James. "Go Out into the Deep." *Weavings* (March/April 1999).

———. "Living the Vulnerability of Jesus." *Weavings* (July/August 1993).

———. "Mercy in Hard Times and Places." *Weavings* (September/October 2000).

———. "Ordinary Caring Makes Extraordinary Perseverance Possible." *Weavings* (September/October 2005).

Mequi, Bonifacio B., Jr. "Faith in the Balance," *The Upper Room Disciplines 1999*. Nashville, TN: Upper Room Books, 1998.

Mogabgab, John S. "Editor's Introduction." *Weavings*, 1986–2011.

Morris, Robert Corin. "An Altar of Earth: The Bible as Earth-Book." *Weavings* (September/October 2008).

―――. "Disillusionment, Deliverance, and Delight: Stages on the Path Toward Wisdom." *Weavings* (May/June/July 2011).

―――. "Fear or Fascination?: God's Call in a Multicultural World." *Weavings* (September/October 2003).

―――. "Holy Fear and the Wildness of God." *Weavings* (March/April 1999).

―――. "Meek as Moses: Humility, Self-Esteem, and the Service of God." *Weavings* (May/June/July 2000).

―――. "This Far and No Farther: The Life-Giving Power of Limitation." *Weavings* (November/December 2010/January 2011).

Mulholland, M. Robert, Jr. and Marjorie J. Thompson. *The Way of Scripture: A Small-Group Experience in Spiritual Formation*, Participant's Book. CIC. Nashville, TN: Upper Room Books, 2010.

Norberg, Tilda. *The Chocolate-Covered Umbrella: Discovering Your Dreamcode.* Nashville, TN: Upper Room Books, 2008.

Norris, Gunilla. "The Heart of Response-Ability." *Weavings* (July/August 2008).

Nouwen, Henri J. M. "All Is Grace." *Weavings* (November/December 1992).

―――. "Forgiveness: The Name of Love in a Wounded World." *Weavings* (March/April 1992).

―――. *A Spirituality of Fundraising.* Nashville, TN: Upper Room Books, 2010.

―――. "A Spirituality of Waiting: Being Alert to God's Presence in Our Lives." *Weavings* (January/February 1987).

Oden, Marilyn Brown. *Abundance: Joyful Living in Christ.* Nashville, TN: Upper Room Books, 2002.

Palmer, Parker J., "Borne Again: The Monastic Way to Church Renewal." *Weavings* (September/October 1986).

―――. "On Minding Your Call—When No One Is Calling." *Weavings* (May/June 1996).

Parsons, Sarah. *A Clearing Season: Reflections for Lent*. Nashville, TN: Upper Room Books, 2005.

Paulsell, William O. "Ways of Prayer: Designing a Personal Rule." *Weavings* (September/October 1987).

Peacock, Larry James. *Openings: A Daybook of Saints, Psalms, and Prayer*. Nashville, TN: Upper Room Books, 2003.

Pennington, M. Basil. "Bernard's Challenge." *Weavings* (May/June 2000).

Prevallet, Elaine M. "Dancing around the Kingdom: Notes from an Occasional Journal." *Weavings* (January/February 1995).

———. "Grounded in the Holy." *Weavings* (September/October 1992).

———. "Living in the Mercy." *Weavings* (September/October 2000).

———. "Minding the Call." *Weavings* (May/June 1996).

———. "Where Is Your God?" *Weavings* (July/August 2008).

Ptomey, K. C. "This Ferocious Moment." *Weavings* (March/April 1996).

———. "The Waters of Discontinuity." *Weavings* (May/June 2009).

Redding, Mary Lou. *While We Wait: Living the Questions of Advent*. Nashville, TN: Upper Room Books, 2002.

Rensberger, David. "Adoring the Creator." *Weavings* (March/April 2008).

———. "Not Conformed, But Transformed." *Weavings* (March/April 2010).

———. "Thirsty for God." *Weavings* (July/August 2000).

Richardson, Beth A. *Child of the Light: Walking through Advent and Christmas*. Nashville, TN: Upper Room Books, 2005.

———. *The Uncluttered Heart: Making Room for God During Advent and Christmas*. Nashville, TN: Upper Room Books, 2009.

Richardson, Jan L. *In the Sanctuary of Women: A Companion for Reflection and Prayer*. Nashville, TN: Upper Room Books, 2010.

Ross, Maggie. "Practical Adoration." *Weavings* (March/April 2008).

Rouse, Ciona D. *The Africana Worship Book, Year A*. Edited by Valerie Bridgeman Davis and Safiyah Fosua. Nashville, TN: Discipleship Resources, 2006.

Russell, Joseph P. "Baptized for Ministry," *The Upper Room Disciplines 1999*. Nashville, TN: Upper Room Books, 1998.

Shawchuck, Norman. Selections from "Personal Journal."

Shawchuck, Norman and Rueben P. Job. *A Guide to Prayer for All Who Seek God*. Nashville, TN: Upper Room Books, 2003.

Shawchuck, Norman, Rueben P. Job, and Robert G. Doherty. *How to Conduct a Spiritual Life Retreat*. Nashville, TN: Upper Room Books, 1986.

Simsic, Wayne E. "For Darkness Is as Light." *Weavings* (November/December 2010).

Smith, Judith E. "The One Thing Necessary." *Weavings* (May/June 1988).

Smith, Luther E. "The Work of Hope." *Weavings* (February/March/April 2012).

Stathakis, Costa. "God's Purpose for Our Lives," *The Upper Room Disciplines 1999*. Nashville, TN: Upper Room Books, 1998.

Steere, Douglas V. *Dimensions of Prayer: Cultivating a Relationship with God*. Rev. ed. Nashville, TN: Upper Room Books, 1997.

Storey, Peter. *Listening at Golgotha*. Nashville, TN: Upper Room Books, 2004.

Taylor, Jeremy. *Selections from the Writings of Jeremy Taylor*. Edited by James H. Overton. GDC. Nashville, TN: Upper Room Books, 1961.

Temple, William. *Selections from the Writings of William Temple*. Edited by Sulon G. Ferree. GDC. Nashville, TN: Upper Room Books, 1968.

Teresa of Avila. *The Soul's Passion for God: Selected Writings of Teresa of Avila*. Edited by Keith Beasley-Topliffe. URSC 1. Nashville, TN: Upper Room Books, 1997.

Theologia Germanica: *Selections from Theologia Germanica*. Edited by Thomas S. Kepler. GDC. Nashville, TN: Upper Room Books, 1962.

Thibault, Jane Marie. *A Deepening Love Affair: The Gift of God in Later Life*. Nashville, TN: Upper Room Books, 1993.

Thompson, Marjorie J. *Family the Forming Center: A Vision of the Role of Family in Spiritual Formation*. Rev. ed. Nashville, TN: Upper Room Books, 1998.

———. "Moving Toward Forgiveness." *Weavings* (March/April 1992).

———. "Obedience: The Deepest Passion of Love." *Weavings* (May/June 1988).

———. "To Do Justice." *Weavings* (November/ December 1986).

———. *The Way of Forgiveness: A Small-Group Experience in Spiritual Formation*, Participant's Book. CIC. Nashville, TN: Upper Room Books, 2002.

Tracy, Theodore, SJ. "The Body: Pivot-Point of Salvation." *Weavings* (November/December 1987).

Underhill, Evelyn. *Selections from the Writings of Evelyn Underhill*. Edited by Douglas V. Steere. GDC. Nashville, TN: Upper Room Books, 1961.

———. *The Soul's Delight: Selected Writings of Evelyn Underhill*. Edited by Keith Beasley-Topliffe. URSC 2. Nashville, TN: Upper Room Books, 1998.

Vannorsdall, John W. "Behold the Beauty of the Lord." *Weavings* (May/June 2003).

Vestal, Daniel. *Being the Presence of Christ: A Vision for Transformation*. Nashville, TN: Upper Room Books, 2008.

Vogel, Linda J. "Called to Live and Teach God's Commands," *The Upper Room Disciplines 1999*. Nashville, TN: Upper Room Books, 1998.

Wesley, John. *A Longing for Holiness: Selected Writings of John Wesley*. Edited by Keith Beasley-Topliffe. URSC 1. Nashville, TN: Upper Room Books, 1997.

———. "Primitive Physic: Or, An Easy and Natural Method of Curing Most Diseases." *Weavings* (November/December 1987).

———. *Selections from the Journal of John Wesley*. Edited by Paul Lambourne Higgins. GDC. Nashville, TN: Upper Room Books, 1967.

Williams, Michael E. "Gentle and Humble of Heart: Humility as a Response to Imperial Christianity." *Weavings* (May/June 2000).

———. "Saying Grace: Living a Life of Gratitude." *Weavings* (November/December 1992).

Wolf, Janet. "Chosen For . . . ," *The Upper Room Disciplines 1999*. Nashville, TN: Upper Room Books, 1998.

———. Excerpt from Rueben Job's *A Guide to Spiritual Discernment*. Nashville, TN: Upper Room Books, 1996.

Wolpert, Daniel. *Creating a Life with God: The Call of Ancient Prayer Practices*. Nashville, TN: Upper Room Books, 2003.

Woolman, John. *Selections from the Journal of John Woolman*. Edited by J. Manning Potts. GDC. Nashville, TN: Upper Room Books, 1957.

———. *Walking Humbly with God: Selected Writings of John Woolman*. Edited by Keith Beasley-Topliffe. URSC 3. Nashville, TN: Upper Room Books, 2000.

Wright, Wendy M. "Contemplation in Time of War." *Weavings* (July/August 1992).

———. "The Freedom of the Children of God: Notes on Spiritual Poverty." *Weavings* (November/December 2003).

———. "Hints, Signs, and Showings: The Compassion of God." *Weavings* (November/December 1990).

———. "In the Circle of a Mother's Arms." *Weavings* (January/February 1988).

———. "Little Things: A Meditation in Three Parts." *Weavings* (January/February 2003).

———. "Musings on Wisdom and Becoming Wise." *Weavings* (May/June 2011).

———. "Passing Angels: The Arts of Spiritual Discernment." *Weavings* (November/December 1995).

———. "Resting Reaping Times." *Weavings* (January/February 1999).

———. "Tears of a Greening Heart." *Weavings* (March/April 2000).

———. "Thoughts on Solitude." *Weavings* (November/December 2008).

———. *The Vigil: Keeping Watch in the Season of Christ's Coming*. Nashville, TN: Upper Room Books: 1992.

Wuellner, Flora Slosson. *Enter by the Gate: Jesus' 7 Guidelines When Making Hard Choices*. Nashville, TN: Upper Room Books, 2004.

———. *Miracle: When Christ Touches Our Deepest Need*. Nashville, TN: Upper Room Books, 2008.

———. *Prayer and Our Bodies*. Nashville, TN: Upper Room Books, 1987.

Resources for a Life of Prayer

Prayerbooks

Barth, Karl. *Fifty Prayers*. Translated by David Carl Stassen. Louisville, KY: Westminster John Knox Press, 2005.

The Book of Common Prayer. New York: Oxford University Press, 2008.

Brueggemann, Walter. *Prayers for a Privileged People*. Nashville, TN: Abingdon Press, 2008.

Claiborne, Shane, Jonathan Wilson-Hartgrove, and Enuma Okoro. *Common Prayer: A Liturgy for Ordinary Radicals*. Grand Rapids, MI: Zondervan, 2010.

Harper, Steve. *A Pocket Guide to Prayer*. Nashville, TN: Upper Room Books, 2010.

Hauerwas, Stanley. *Prayers Plainly Spoken*. Eugene, OR: Wipf and Stock Publishers, 2003.

Holy Women, Holy Men: Celebrating the Saints. New York: Church Publishing, Inc., 2010.

The Paraclete Psalter: A Four-Week Cycle for Daily Prayer. Brewster, MA: Paraclete Press, 2010.

Redding, Mary Lou. *Prayers for Life's Ordinary and Extraordinary Moments*. Nashville, TN: Upper Room Books, 2012.

Spiritual Classics about Prayer

Baillie, John. *A Diary of Private Prayer*. New York: Charles Scribner's Sons, 1949.

Bonhoeffer, Dietrich. *Psalms: The Prayer Book of the Bible*. Translated by James H. Burtness. Minneapolis, MN: Augsburg Fortress Publishers, 1974.

Brother Lawrence. *The Practice of the Presence of God*. Translated by Robert J. Edmonson. Paraclete Essentials. Brewster, MA: Paraclete Press, 2010.

The Cloud of Unknowing: A New Translation. Translated by Carmen Acevedo Butcher. Boston: Shambhala Publications, Inc., 2009.

Foster, Richard. *Celebration of Discipline: The Path to Spiritual Growth.* San Francisco: HarperSanFrancisco, 1988.

Herman, Brigid E. *Creative Prayer: A Devotional Classic.* Edited by Hal M. Helms. Brewster, MA: Paraclete Press, 1998.

Kelly, Thomas. *A Testament of Devotion.* New York: Harper & Row, 1941.

Merton, Thomas. *Contemplative Prayer.* New York: Doubleday/Image Books, 1971.

Nouwen, Henri J. M. *The Way of the Heart: Desert Spirituality and Contemporary Ministry.* New York: Seabury Press, 1981.

Thompson, Marjorie J. *Soul Feast: An Invitation to the Christian Spiritual Life.* Louisville, KY: Westminster John Knox Press, 2005.

von Balthasar, Hans Urs. *Prayer.* San Francisco: Ignatius Press, 1986.

The Way of a Pilgrim and *The Pilgrim Continues His Way.* Translated by R. M. French. New York: Seabury, 1965.

Introductions to Prayer

Barth, Karl. *Prayer.* Translated by Sara F. Terrien. 50th anniv. ed. Louisville, KY: Westminster John Knox Press, 2002.

Bloom, Anthony. *Beginning to Pray.* Mahwah, NJ: Paulist Press, 1970.

Bondi, Roberta C. *To Pray and to Love: Conversations on Prayer with the Early Church.* Minneapolis, MN: Augsburg Fortress Press, 1991.

DelBene, Ron. *The Breath of Life: A Simple Way to Pray.* Nashville, TN: Upper Room Books, 1992.

Foster, Richard. *Prayer: Finding the Heart's True Home.* San Francisco: HarperSanFrancisco, 1992.

Griffin, Emilie. *Clinging: The Experience of Prayer.* Wichita, KS: Eighth Day Press, 2003.

Guenther, Margaret. *The Practice of Prayer.* Cambridge, MA: Cowley Publications, 1998.

Hauerwas, Stanley and William H. Willimon. *Lord Teach Us: The Lord's Prayer & the Christian Life*. Nashville, TN: Abingdon Press, 1996.

Jones, Timothy. *The Art of Prayer: A Simple Guide to Conversation with God*. Colorado Springs, CO: WaterBrook Press, 2005.

Killinger, John. *Beginning Prayer*. Nashville, TN: Upper Room Books, 2012.

Leech, Kenneth. *True Prayer: An Invitation to Christian Spirituality*. Harrisburg, PA: Morehouse, 1995.

Sangster, W. E. *Teach Me to Pray*. Updated ed. Nashville, TN: Upper Room Books, 2000.

Steere, Douglas V. *Dimensions of Prayer: Cultivating a Relationship with God*. Nashville, TN: Upper Room Books, 2002.

Underhill, Evelyn. *Practical Mysticism: A Little Book for Normal People*. New York: Cosimo, 2006.

———. *The Spiritual Life*. Harrisburg, PA: Morehouse Publishing, 1997.

Yancey, Philip. *Prayer: Does It Make Any Difference?* Grand Rapids, MI: Zondervan, 2010.

Getting Deeper into Prayer

Bourgeault, Cynthia. *Centering Prayer and Inner Awakening*. Cambridge, MA: Cowley Publications, 2004.

Brooke, Avery. *Healing in the Landscape of Prayer*. Cambridge, MA: Cowley Publications, 1996.

Brueggemann, Walter. *Praying the Psalms: Engaging Scripture and the Life of the Spirit*. 2nd ed. Eugene, OR: Cascade Books, 2007.

Carter, Kenneth H., Jr. *"Pray for Me": The Power in Praying for Others*. Nashville, TN: Upper Room Books, 2012.

Casey, Michael. *Sacred Reading: The Ancient Art of Lectio Divina*. Ligouri, MO: Ligouri/Triumph, 1997.

Chilcote, Paul W. *A Life-Shaping Prayer: 52 Meditations in the Wesleyan Spirit*. Nashville, TN: Upper Room Books, 2008.

————. *Praying in the Wesleyan Spirit: 52 Prayers for Today*. Nashville, TN: Upper Room Books, 2001.

Danaher, James P. *Contemplative Prayer: A Theology for the Twenty-First Century*. Eugene, OR: Wipf and Stock Publishers, 2011.

DeLeon, Roy. *Praying with the Body: Bringing the Psalms to Life*. Brewster, MA: Paraclete Press, 2009.

Douty, Linda. *Praying in the Messiness of Life: 7 Ways to Renew Your Relationship with God*. Nashville, TN: Upper Room Books, 2011.

Dunnam, Maxie. *The Workbook of Living Prayer*. Rev. ed. Nashville, TN: Upper Room Books, 1998.

Foster, Richard J. *Sanctuary of the Soul: Journey into Meditative Prayer*. Downers Grove, IL: InterVarsity Press, 2011.

Finley, Mitch. *The Rosary Handbook: A Guide for Newcomers, Old-Timers, and Those in Between*. Frederick, MD: Word Among Us Press, 2007.

Gonzalez, Adele J. "Deepening Our Prayer," *Companions in Christ: A Small-Group Experience in Spiritual Formation*, Participant's Book. Nashville, TN: Upper Room Books, 2006.

Harper, Steve. *Talking in the Dark: Praying When Life Doesn't Make Sense*. Nashville, TN: Upper Room Books, 2007.

Hudson, Trevor. *The Serenity Prayer: A Simple Prayer to Enrich Your Life*. Nashville, TN: Upper Room Books, 2012.

Indermark, John. *Traveling the Prayer Paths of Jesus*. Nashville, TN: Upper Room Books, 2003.

Keating, Thomas. *Open Mind, Open Heart: The Contemplative Dimension of the Gospel*. New York: Continuum, 2006.

Laird, Martin S. *Into the Silent Land: A Guide to the Christian Practice of Contemplation*. New York: Oxford University Press, 2006.

————. *A Sunlit Absence: Silence, Awareness, and Contemplation*. New York: Oxford University Press, 2011.

Magrassi, Mariano. *Praying the Bible: An Introduction to Lectio Divina*. Translated by Edward Hagman. Collegeville, MN: Liturgical Press, 1998.

McQuiston, John, II. *Always We Begin Again: The Benedictine Way of Living*. 15th anniv. ed. Harrisburg, PA: Morehouse Publishing, 2011.

Nouwen, Henri J. M. *Behold the Beauty of the Lord: Praying with Icons*. Notre Dame, IN: Ave Maria Press, 1987.

Peacock, Larry James. *Openings: A Daybook of Saints, Psalms, and Prayer*. Nashville, TN: Upper Room Books, 2003.

Redding, Mary Lou. *The Lord's Prayer: Jesus Teaches Us How to Pray*. Nashville, TN: Upper Room Books, 2011.

Vennard, Jane E. *Intercessory Prayer: Praying for Friends and Enemies*. Minneapolis, MN: Augsburg Fortress Press, 2001.

———. *Praying with Body and Soul: A Way to Intimacy with God*. Minneapolis, MN: Augsburg Press, 1998.

———. *The Way of Prayer*, Participant's Book. Companions in Christ series. Nashville, TN: Upper Room Books, 2007.

Vest, Norvene. *Gathered in the Word: Praying the Scripture in Small Groups*. Nashville, TN: Upper Room Books, 1996.

Wolpert, Daniel. *Creating a Life with God: The Call of Ancient Prayer Practices*. Nashville, TN: Upper Room Books, 2003.

Wuellner, Flora Slosson. *Prayer and Our Bodies*. Nashville, TN: Upper Room Books, 1998.

———. *Prayer, Stress, and Our Inner Wounds*. Nashville, TN: Upper Room Books, 1998.

Youngman, Jenny. *Prayer: Heart of the Pilgrimage*. The Way of Pilgrimage. Vol. 3. Nashville TN: Upper Room Books, 2007.

Zaleski, Irma. *Living the Jesus Prayer*. 2nd ed. Toronto: Novalis, 2011.

*Index of
Weekday
Scripture
References*

Asterisks indicate a paraphrase or allusion rather than a direct quote.

Scripture	Weekly Theme	Affirmation	Psalm	Daily Scripture Readings	Offering of Self	Blessing
Old Testament						
Genesis 1:1-5	25. Creativity			✓		
Genesis 1:9-12	54. Stewards of Creation			✓		
Genesis 1:24-31	7. You Stand on Holy Ground			✓		
Genesis 3:1-13	35. Suffering			✓		
Genesis 2:15-24	31. Many Gifts			✓		
Genesis 6:13-22	56. End Times			✓		
Genesis 9:8-17	52. Compassion			✓.		
Genesis 17:1-8	2. Hope in God			✓		
Genesis 18:1-15	22. Mystery			✓		
Genesis 18:22-33	37. Loneliness			✓		
Genesis 19:1-13	4. Welcome the Stranger			✓		
Genesis 21:1-7	9. The Extraordinary in the Ordinary			✓		
Genesis 22:1-18	48. Gentleness			✓		
Genesis 28:16, 17	7. You Stand on Holy Ground	✓				

Scripture	Weekly Theme	Affirmation	Psalm	Daily Scripture Readings	Offering of Self	Blessing
Genesis 32:22-32	16. We Shall All Be Changed			✓		
Genesis 43:16-34	19. The Gift of Tears			✓		
Genesis 45:1-15	39. Forgiveness			✓		
Exodus 2:1-10	52. Compassion			✓		
Exodus 3:1-6	7. You Stand on Holy Ground			✓		
Exodus 3:7-12	44. Mind Your Call			✓		
Exodus 4:10-17	31. Many Gifts			✓		
Exodus 6:1-13	55. Justice			✓		
Exodus 10:12-20	39. Forgiveness			✓		
Exodus 14:1-19	21. Impasse			✓		
Exodus 14:21-31	24. In the World but Not of It			✓		
Exodus 15:1-18	12. Wonder			✓		
Exodus 16:1-15	27. For the Life of the World			✓		
Exodus 16:22-30	14. Grace Abounding			✓		
Exodus 17:1-7	34. Time of Trial			✓		
Exodus 19:1-11	3. Prepare the Way of the Lord			✓		

Scripture	Weekly Theme	Affirmation	Psalm	Daily Scripture Readings	Offering of Self	Blessing
Exodus 23:1-9	4. Welcome the Stranger			✓		
Exodus 32:1-8	6. The Poverty of God			✓		
Exodus 33:7-23	45. Practicing the Presence of God			✓		
Exodus 33:19	52. Compassion	✓				
Exodus 34:1-9	50. Trust			✓		
Exodus 34:27-35	16. We Shall All Be Changed			✓		
Leviticus 25:8-22	32. Ambassadors of Reconciliation			✓		
Leviticus 26:9-13	24. In the World but Not of It			✓		
Numbers 6:24-26	34. Time of Trial					✓
Numbers 11:10-17	31. Many Gifts			✓		
Deuteronomy 5:1-22	27. For the Life of the World			✓		
Deuteronomy 8	11. Be Still			✓		
Deuteronomy 10:12-22	26. Singleness of Heart			✓		
Deuteronomy 24:10-22	33. Turning the World Upside Down			✓		

Scripture	Weekly Theme	Affirmation	Psalm	Daily Scripture Readings	Offering of Self	Blessing
Deuteronomy 30:11-14	8. The Kingdom of God Is among You					
Deuteronomy 30:15-20	28. Things That Make for Peace			✓		
Deuteronomy 32:1-14	48. Gentleness			✓		
Joshua 4	49. Simplicity			✓		
Joshua 24:13-18	24. In the World but Not of It			✓		
Joshua 24:15	24. In the World but Not of It				✓	
Judges						
Ruth 1:1-18	18. Vulnerability			✓		
1 Samuel 2:1-10	12. Wonder			✓		
1 Samuel 3:1-10	7. You Stand on Holy Ground			✓		
1 Samuel 3:11-21	44. Mind Your Call			✓		
1 Samuel 24:8-22	19. The Gift of Tears			✓		
2 Samuel 12:1-15	18. Vulnerability			✓		
2 Samuel 22:1-20	35. Suffering			✓		

Scripture	Weekly Theme	Affirmation	Psalm	Daily Scripture Readings	Offering of Self	Blessing
1 Kings 3:10-14	42. Discernment			✓		
1 Kings 19:1-18	37. Loneliness			✓		
2 Kings 2:1-22	29. Power from On High			✓		
2 Kings 6:8-23	38. Fear Not			✓		
1 Chronicles 16:8-36	13. Adoration			✓		
1 Chronicles 16:14	55. Justice	✓				
1 Chronicles 28:1-10	26. Singleness of Heart			✓		
2 Chronicles 1:7-13	43. Wisdom			✓		
2 Chronicles 7:11-21	15. The Time is Ripe			✓		
2 Chronicles 20:1-20	50. Trust			✓		
Ezra						
Nehemiah 1:1-11	40. Pray for One Another			✓		
Nehemiah 8:1-12	23. Count It All Joy			✓		
Esther 8	34. Time of Trial			✓		
Job 3:1-10	35. Suffering			✓		
Job 26:5-14	25. Creativity			✓		

Scripture	Weekly Theme	Affirmation	Psalm	Daily Scripture Readings	Offering of Self	Blessing
Job 28:12-28	43. Wisdom			✓		
Psalm 1	53. Responsibility		✓			
Psalm 2:11	56. End Times	✓				
Psalm 3	38. Fear Not		✓			
Psalm 4	11. Be Still			✓		
Psalm 8	25. Creativity		✓			
Psalm 9:1-2	14. Grace Abounding				✓	
Psalm 9:10	50. Trust	✓				
Psalm 10	33. Turning the World Upside Down			✓		
Psalm 11	56. End Times		✓			
Psalm 14	6. The Poverty of God		✓			
Psalm 16:5, 7	42. Discernment				✓	
Psalm 16:7-8	43. Wisdom				✓	
Psalm 16:11	45. Practicing the Presence of God				✓	
Psalm 18	34. Time of Trial			✓		
Psalm 19	49. Simplicity			✓		

Scripture	Weekly Theme	Affirmation	Psalm	Daily Scripture Readings	Offering of Self	Blessing
Psalm 19:1, 14	9. The Extraordinary in the Ordinary	✓				
Psalm 20	50. Trust		✓			
Psalm 23	31. Many Gifts		✓			
Psalm 24	8. The Kingdom of God Is among You		✓			
Psalm 25	41. Contemplative Life		✓			
Psalm 26	26. Singleness of Heart		✓			
Psalm 26:1-12	47. Gratitude			✓		
Psalm 27:4	10. Behold the Beauty of the Lord	✓				
Psalm 27:13	27. For the Life of the World	✓				
Psalm 27:14	2. Hope in God	✓				
Psalm 27:7-14	37. Loneliness			✓		
Psalm 27	1. Active Waiting		✓			
Psalm 29	44. Mind Your Call		✓			
Psalm 29:11	28. The Things That Make for Peace					✓
Psalm 30	16. We Shall All Be Changed		✓			
Psalm 31	17. Put a New & Right Spirit within Me		✓			

Scripture	Weekly Theme	Affirmation	Psalm	Daily Scripture Readings	Offering of Self	Blessing
Psalm 32	30. The Freedom of the Christian			✓		
Psalm 33	2. Hope in God		✓			
Psalm 33:20-22	41. Contemplative Life					✓
Psalm 34:1-10	14. Grace Abounding			✓		
Psalm 34:8	46. Attentiveness	✓				
Psalm 34:11-13	28. The Things That Make for Peace			✓		
Psalm 34:18	37. Loneliness	✓				
Psalm 36:5-10	16. We Shall All Be Changed			✓		
Psalm 37	34. Time of Trial		✓			
Psalm 38	19. The Gift of Tears		✓			
Psalm 39:1-5	56. End Times			✓		
Psalm 40	30. The Freedom of the Christian		✓			
Psalm 40:17	17. Put a New & Right Spirit within Me	✓				
Psalm 41	32. Ambassadors of Reconciliation		✓			
Psalm 42:2	1. Active Waiting	✓				
Psalm 46	11. Be Still		✓			

Scripture	Weekly Theme	Affirmation	Psalm	Daily Scripture Readings	Offering of Self	Blessing
Psalm 47	23. Count It All Joy		✓			
Psalm 49	33. Turning the World Upside Down		✓			
Psalm 51	17. Put a New & Right Spirit within Me			✓		
Psalm 53	21. Impasse			✓		
Psalm 55	20. Letting Go		✓			
Psalm 56	38. Fear Not			✓		
Psalm 61:1	40. Pray for One Another	✓				
Psalm 62:1-2, 5-8	41. Contemplative Life			✓		
Psalm 63	23. Count It All Joy			✓		
Psalm 64	22. Mystery			✓		
Psalm 66	46. Attentiveness		✓			
Psalm 67	5. The Word Became Flesh		✓			
Psalm 68:28-35	29. Power from On High			✓		
Psalm 71	36. Perseverance		✓			
Psalm 72	55. Justice		✓			
Psalm 74:1-10	6. The Poverty of God			✓		

Scripture	Weekly Theme	Affirmation	Psalm	Daily Scripture Readings	Offering of Self	Blessing
Psalm 77:11-20	7. You Stand on Holy Ground			✓		
Psalm 80	22. Mystery		✓			
Psalm 81	4. Welcome the Stranger		✓			
Psalm 84	50. Trust			✓		
Psalm 85	28. The Things That Make for Peace		✓			
Psalm 86:11-12	44. Mind Your Call				✓	
Psalm 89:1-14	55. Justice			✓		
Psalm 91	29. Power from On High		✓			
Psalm 92:1	47. Gratitude	✓				
Psalm 93	10. Behold the Beauty of the Lord			✓		
Psalm 94	32. Ambassadors of Reconciliation			✓		
Psalm 95:1-7	15. The Time Is Ripe			✓		
Psalm 96	3. Prepare the Way of the Lord		✓			
Psalm 97	10. Behold the Beauty of the Lord		✓			
Psalm 98	3. Prepare the Way of the Lord			✓		
Psalm 99	13. Adoration			✓		

Scripture	Weekly Theme	Affirmation	Psalm	Daily Scripture Readings	Offering of Self	Blessing
Psalm 100	13. Adoration		✓			
Psalm 102	37. Loneliness		✓			
Psalm 103	52. Compassion		✓			
Psalm 104	9. The Extraordinary in the Ordinary		✓			
Psalm 104:1	10. Behold the Beauty of the Lord				✓	
Psalm 104:24	14. Grace Abounding	✓				
Psalm 104:24, 31	54. Stewards of Creation				✓	
Psalm 105	14. Grace Abounding		✓			
Psalm 111	43. Wisdom		✓			
Psalm 113	12. Wonder		✓			
Psalm 114	7. You Stand on Holy Ground		✓			
Psalm 115:12-13	20. Letting Go					✓
Psalm 116	49. Simplicity		✓			
Psalm 118:6	34. Time of Trial	✓				
Psalm 119:65-72	51. Humility			✓		
Psalm 119:73-80	48. Gentleness		✓			

Scripture	Weekly Theme	Affirmation	Psalm	Daily Scripture Readings	Offering of Self	Blessing
Psalm 119:159-170	2. Hope in God			✓		
Psalm 120	24. In the World but Not of It		✓			
Psalm 121	4. Welcome the Stranger			✓		
Psalm 125	18. Vulnerability		✓			
Psalm 126	15. The Time Is Ripe		✓			
Psalm 130	1. Active Waiting			✓		
Psalm 131	51. Humility		✓			
Psalm 132	45. Practicing the Presence of God		✓			
Psalm 136	47. Gratitude		✓			
Psalm 138	35. Suffering		✓			
Psalm 139	42. Discernment		✓			
Psalm 143:1	18. Vulnerability	✓				
Psalm 143	40. Pray for One Another		✓			
Psalm 144:3	5. The Word Became Flesh	✓				
Psalm 145	8. The Kingdom of God Is among You			✓		
Psalm 145:13	8. The Kingdom of God Is among You	✓				

Scripture	Weekly Theme	Affirmation	Psalm	Daily Scripture Readings	Offering of Self	Blessing
Psalm 146	27. For the Life of the World		✓			
Proverbs 2:1-15, 20-22	43. Wisdom			✓		
Proverbs 3:3-8	20. Letting Go			✓		
Proverbs 3:13-14	43. Wisdom	✓				
Proverbs 3:19-23	9. The Extraordinary in the Ordinary					✓
Proverbs 7:1-3	36. Perseverance			✓		
Proverbs 15:23-33	51. Humility			✓		
Proverbs 18:15	42. Discernment	✓				
Proverbs 28	53. Responsibility			✓		
Ecclesiastes 2:1-11	49. Simplicity			✓		
Ecclesiastes 3:1, 4	19. The Gift of Tears	✓				
Ecclesiastes 3:1-8	15. The Time Is Ripe			✓		
Ecclesiastes 9:11-18	11. Be Still			✓		
Song of Songs						
Isaiah 3:1-5	6. The Poverty of God			✓		
Isaiah 6:1-7	22. Mystery			✓		

Scripture	Weekly Theme	Affirmation	Psalm	Daily Scripture Readings	Offering of Self	Blessing
Isaiah 11:1-9	48. Gentleness			✓		
Isaiah 12:1-6	38. Fear Not			✓		
Isaiah 25:1	20. Letting Go	✓				
Isaiah 26:7-10	1. Active Waiting			✓		
Isaiah 29:13-24	33. Turning the World Upside Down			✓		
Isaiah 30:15	41. Contemplative Life				✓	
Isaiah 40:10-31	10. Behold the Beauty of the Lord			✓		
Isaiah 41:10-13	20. Letting Go			✓		
Isaiah 42:1-9	31. Many Gifts			✓		
Isaiah 43:18-25	16. We Shall All Be Changed			✓		
Isaiah 45:16-19	25. Creativity			✓		
Isaiah 48:12-19	46. Attentiveness			✓		
Isaiah 49:13	35. Suffering	✓				
Isaiah 51:1-16	9. The Extraordinary in the Ordinary			✓		
Isaiah 53	18. Vulnerability			✓		
Isaiah 53:3, 5	4. Welcome the Stranger	✓				

Scripture	Weekly Theme	Affirmation	Psalm	Daily Scripture Readings	Offering of Self	Blessing
Isaiah 57:15	29. Power from On High	✓				
Isaiah 58:1-12	35. Suffering			✓		
Isaiah 61:1-4	15. The Time Is Ripe			✓		
Isaiah 63:7-14	45. Practicing the Presence of God			✓		
Isaiah 64:8	25. Creativity	✓				
Isaiah 65:17-25	23. Count It All Joy			✓		
Jeremiah 6:16-19	46. Attentiveness			✓		
Jeremiah 7:1-7	4. Welcome the Stranger			✓		
Jeremiah 13:15-19	51. Humility			✓		
Jeremiah 17:7-8	50. Trust			✓		
Jeremiah 29:8-14	26. Singleness of Heart			✓		
Jeremiah 29:11	44. Mind Your Call	✓				
Jeremiah 31:1-13	27. For the Life of the World			✓		
Jeremiah 33:10-17	47. Gratitude			✓		
Lamentations 3:19-26	1. Active Waiting			✓		
Lamentations 3:25-26	41. Contemplative Life	✓				

Scripture	Weekly Theme	Affirmation	Psalm	Daily Scripture Readings	Offering of Self	Blessing
Lamentations 4	21. Impasse			✓		
Ezekiel 11:17-20	46. Attentiveness			✓		
Ezekiel 34:1-16	55. Justice			✓		
Ezekiel 36:22-36	36. Perseverance			✓		
Ezekiel 37:1-14	17. Put a New & Right Spirit within Me			✓		
Daniel 1	34. Time of Trial			✓		
Daniel 2:17-23	42. Discernment			✓		
Daniel 2:24-45	22. Mystery			✓		
Daniel 3:8-18	30. The Freedom of the Christian			✓		
Daniel 4:1-3	13. Adoration			✓		
Hosea 2:14-23	32. Ambassadors of Reconciliation			✓		
Hosea 11:1-9	14. Grace Abounding			✓		
Joel 2:12-13	17. Put a New & Right Spirit within Me			✓		
Joel 2:18-27	45. Practicing the Presence of God					
Amos 4:13	54. Stewards of Creation	✓				
Obadiah						

Scripture	Weekly Theme	Affirmation	Psalm	Daily Scripture Readings	Offering of Self	Blessing
Jonah 1:1-3; 3	44. Mind Your Call			✓		
Micah 3	29. Power from On High			✓		
Micah 6:1-8	28. The Things That Make for Peace			✓		
Nahum						
Habakkuk						
Zephaniah 2:1-3	51. Humility			✓		
Haggai 2:1-9	21. Impasse			✓		
Zechariah 2:10b-11, 13	45. Practicing the Presence of God	✓				
Zechariah 9:9-12	2. Hope in God			✓		
Malachi 3:1	3. Prepare the Way of the Lord	✓				
New Testament						
Matthew 1:18-25	45. Practicing the Presence of God			✓		
Matthew 2:1-12	7. You Stand on Holy Ground			✓		
Matthew 4:1-11	18. Vulnerability			✓		
Matthew 4:18-22	44. Mind Your Call			✓		
Matthew 5:1-12	8. The Kingdom of God Is among You			✓		

Scripture	Weekly Theme	Affirmation	Psalm	Daily Scripture Readings	Offering of Self	Blessing
Matthew 5:5	51. Humility	✓				
Matthew 5:13-16	14. Grace Abounding			✓		
Matthew 5:38-42	28. The Things That Make for Peace			✓		
Matthew 5:43-48	40. Pray for One Another			✓		
Matthew 6:5-15	40. Pray for One Another			✓		
Matthew 6:25-34	20. Letting Go			✓		
Matthew 7:1-6	53. Responsibility			✓		
Matthew 7:7-8	53. Responsibility	✓				
Matthew 10:16-31	5. The Word Became Flesh			✓		
Matthew 11:28-30	48. Gentleness	✓				
Matthew 12:1-23	2. Hope in God			✓		
Matthew 14:22-33	38. Fear Not			✓		
Matthew 15:32-39	47. Gratitude			✓		
Matthew 17:1-13	9. The Extraordinary in the Ordinary			✓		
Matthew 18:1-5	43. Wisdom			✓		
Matthew 18:10-14	54. Stewards of Creation			✓		

Scripture	Weekly Theme	Affirmation	Psalm	Daily Scripture Readings	Offering of Self	Blessing
Matthew 18:21-35	39. Forgiveness			✓		
Matthew 19:14	49. Simplicity	✓				
Matthew 19:16-22	33. Turning the World Upside Down			✓		
Matthew 20:29-34	52. Compassion			✓		
Matthew 24:1-21	56. End Times			✓		
Matthew 24:22-42	56. End Times			✓		
Matthew 25:1-13	1. Active Waiting			✓		
Matthew 25:31-46	4. Welcome the Stranger			✓		
Matthew 26:36-44	41. Contemplative Life			✓		
Matthew 27:27-31	10. Behold the Beauty of the Lord			✓		
Matthew 28:1-10	25. Creativity			✓		
Mark 1:1-11	31. Many Gifts			✓		
Mark 1:15	8. The Kingdom of God Is among You					✓
Mark 1:35-39	27. For the Life of the World			✓		
Mark 4:21-25	46. Attentiveness			✓		
Mark 6:1-6	6. The Poverty of God			✓		

Scripture	Weekly Theme	Affirmation	Psalm	Daily Scripture Readings	Offering of Self	Blessing
Mark 6:31-44	5. The Word Became Flesh			✓		
Mark 7:1-13	13. Adoration			✓		
Mark 9:2-13	11. Be Still			✓		
Mark 10:17-22	42. Discernment			✓		
Mark 10:23-31	33. Turning the World Upside Down			✓		
Mark 12:41-44	8. The Kingdom of God Is among You			✓		
Mark 13:3-13	34. Time of Trial			✓		
Mark 13:28-37	3. Prepare the Way of the Lord			✓		
Mark 14:32-50	37. Loneliness			✓		
Mark 15:1-37	35. Suffering			✓		
Luke 1:26-38	25. Creativity			✓		
Luke 1:51-53	33. Turning the World Upside Down	✓				
Luke 1:67-79	15. The Time Is Ripe			✓		
Luke 1:78-79	28. The Things That Make for Peace	✓				
Luke 2:1-7	6. The Poverty of God			✓		
Luke 2:25-32	1. Active Waiting			✓		

Scripture	Weekly Theme	Affirmation	Psalm	Daily Scripture Readings	Offering of Self	Blessing
Luke 4:18-19	32. Ambassadors of Reconciliation				✓	
Luke 4:35-41	11. Be Still			✓		
Luke 5:12-26	12. Wonder			✓		
Luke 6:39-49	24. In the World but Not of It			✓		
Luke 8:4-15	44. Mind Your Call			✓		
Luke 9:51-58	4. Welcome the Stranger			✓		
Luke 10:27	26. Singleness of Heart	✓				
Luke 11:5-13	40. Pray for One Another			✓		
Luke 11:37-44	55. Justice			✓		
Luke 12:13-21	49. Simplicity			✓		
Luke 12:22-32	11. Be Still			✓		
Luke 12:35-40	3. Prepare the Way of the Lord			✓		
Luke 13:31-35	5. The Word Became Flesh			✓		
Luke 14:25-33	53. Responsibility			✓		
Luke 15:11-32	17. Put a New & Right Spirit within Me			✓		
Luke 17:20-21	8. The Kingdom of God Is among You			✓		

Scripture	Weekly Theme	Affirmation	Psalm	Daily Scripture Readings	Offering of Self	Blessing
Luke 18:9-14	51. Humility			✓		
Luke 18:18-30	26. Singleness of Heart			✓		
Luke 19:1-10	16. We Shall All Be Changed			✓		
Luke 19:29-44	19. The Gift of Tears			✓		
Luke 21:5-19	36. Perseverance			✓		
Luke 22:31-34	40. Pray for One Another			✓		
Luke 22:47-62	19. The Gift of Tears			✓		
Luke 22:63-71	18. Vulnerability			✓		
Luke 24:13-35	45. Practicing the Presence of God			✓		
Luke 24:36-53	29. Power from On High			✓		
John 1:1-18	14. Grace Abounding			✓		
John 1:29-39	48. Gentleness			✓		
John 3:1-3, 7-12	5. The Word Became Flesh			✓		
John 4:7-26	52. Compassion			✓		
John 5:19-29	12. Wonder			✓		
John 6:48-51	27. For the Life of the World			✓		

Scripture	Weekly Theme	Affirmation	Psalm	Daily Scripture Readings	Offering of Self	Blessing
John 8:1-11	39. Forgiveness			✓		
John 8:12-20	42. Discernment			✓		
John 10:1-18	30. The Freedom of the Christian			✓		
John 10:22-33	21. Impasse			✓		
John 11:17-44	19. The Gift of Tears			✓		
John 14:1-14	50. Trust			✓		
John 14:21-27	28. The Things That Make for Peace			✓		
John 15:1-11	23. Count It All Joy			✓		
John 15:12-17	26. Singleness of Heart			✓		
John 16:12-15	17. Put a New & Right Spirit within Me			✓		
John 17:10-23	24. In the World but Not of It			✓		
John 18:1-14	18. Vulnerability			✓		
John 18:15-18, 25-27	32. Ambassadors of Reconciliation			✓		
John 20:1-18	22. Mystery			✓		
John 21:15-19	32. Ambassadors of Reconciliation			✓		
Acts 2:22-36	37. Loneliness			✓		

Scripture	Weekly Theme	Affirmation	Psalm	Daily Scripture Readings	Offering of Self	Blessing
Acts 2:42-47	49. Simplicity			✓		
Acts 3:1-10	12. Wonder			✓		
Acts 4:32-35	49. Simplicity			✓		
Acts 5:12-42	36. Perseverance			✓		
Acts 8:26-40	48. Gentleness			✓		
Acts 10:1-8	44. Mind Your Call			✓		
Acts 10:9-33	41. Contemplative Life			✓		
Acts 14:21-28	50. Trust			✓		
Romans 6:1-14	17. Put a New & Right Spirit within Me			✓		
Romans 8:19-29	2. Hope in God			✓		
Romans 8:31-39	20. Letting Go			✓		
Romans 11:1-6	37. Loneliness			✓		
Romans 12:1-8	13. Adoration			✓		
Romans 13:11-14	3. Prepare the Way of the Lord			✓		
Romans 15:13	2. Hope in God					✓
*Romans 15:33	43. Wisdom					✓

Scripture	Weekly Theme	Affirmation	Psalm	Daily Scripture Readings	Offering of Self	Blessing
1 Corinthians 1:18-31	6. The Poverty of God			✓		
1 Corinthians 2:6-16	43. Wisdom			✓		
1 Corinthians 2:12	31. Many Gifts	✓				
1 Corinthians 4:1-13	51. Humility			✓		
1 Corinthians 10:14-33	30. The Freedom of the Christian			✓		
1 Corinthians 11:17-34a	33. Turning the World Upside Down			✓		
1 Corinthians 12:4-11	31. Many Gifts			✓		
1 Corinthians 15:12-22	2. Hope in God			✓		
1 Corinthians 15:35-58	22. Mystery			✓		
*2 Corinthians 2:10	39. Forgiveness				✓	
2 Corinthians 1:7-14	49. Simplicity			✓		
2 Corinthians 3:17	30. The Freedom of the Christian	✓				
2 Corinthians 3:18	16. We Shall All Be Changed	✓				

Scripture	Weekly Theme	Affirmation	Psalm	Daily Scripture Readings	Offering of Self	Blessing
2 Corinthians 4:1-15	9. The Extraordinary in the Ordinary			✓		
2 Corinthians 5:11-21	32. Ambassadors of Reconciliation			✓		
2 Corinthians 5:17	24. In the World but Not of It	✓				
2 Corinthians 6:1-10	36. Perseverance			✓		
2 Corinthians 6:2	15. The Time Is Ripe	✓				
2 Corinthians 8:1-15	23. Count It All Joy			✓		
2 Corinthians 12:1-5	12. Wonder			✓		
Galatians 5:1-15	30. The Freedom of the Christian			✓		
Galatians 6:1-10	32. Ambassadors of Reconciliation			✓		
Ephesians 1:18-19	44. Mind Your Call					✓
Ephesians 2:1-10	24. In the World but Not of It			✓		
Ephesians 2:11-22	28. The Things That Make for Peace			✓		
Ephesians 3:14-21	29. Power from On High			✓		
Ephesians 4:1-6	53. Responsibility			✓		
Ephesians 4:7-16	42. Discernment			✓		
Ephesians 4:17-24	55. Justice			✓		

Scripture	Weekly Theme	Affirmation	Psalm	Daily Scripture Readings	Offering of Self	Blessing
Ephesians 4:25–5:2	52. Compassion			✓		
Ephesians 5:8-15	15. The Time Is Ripe			✓		
Ephesians 5:15-21	47. Gratitude			✓		
Philippians 1:3-11	42. Discernment			✓		
*Philippians 1:9	43. Wisdom					✓
Philippians 2:7	6. The Poverty of God	✓				
Philippians 3:1-12	36. Perseverance			✓		
Philippians 2:12-15	5. The Word Became Flesh			✓		
Philippians 3:12-21	19. The Gift of Tears			✓		
*Philippians 4:4-6	40. Pray for One Another				✓	
*Philippians 4:7	40. Pray for One Another					✓
Philippians 4:10-13	20. Letting Go			✓		
Colossians 1:3-14	40. Pray for One Another			✓		
Colossians 1:15-23	7. You Stand on Holy Ground			✓		
Colossians 2:1-6	9. The Extraordinary in the Ordinary			✓		
Colossians 2:3	42. Discernment					✓

Scripture	Weekly Theme	Affirmation	Psalm	Daily Scripture Readings	Offering of Self	Blessing
Colossians 3:1-11	16. We Shall All Be Changed			✓		
*Colossians 3:15	52. Compassion					✓
Colossians 3:12-17	39. Forgiveness			✓		
1 Thessalonians 5:12-24	47. Gratitude			✓		✓
*2 Thessalonians 3:16	18. Vulnerability					✓
1 Timothy 1:12-17	39. Forgiveness			✓		
1 Timothy 4:7b-16	53. Responsibility			✓		
2 Timothy 4:1-8	26. Singleness of Heart			✓		
Titus 2:11-15	14. Grace Abounding			✓		
Philemon						
Hebrews 1:1-9	10. Behold the Beauty of the Lord			✓		
Hebrews 4:14-16	9. The Extraordinary in the Ordinary			✓		
Hebrews 5:7-10	5. The Word Became Flesh			✓		
Hebrews 10:23-25	46. Attentiveness			✓		
Hebrews 12:1	36. Perseverance	✓				
Hebrews 12:1-2	20. Letting Go			✓		

Scripture	Weekly Theme	Affirmation	Psalm	Daily Scripture Readings	Offering of Self	Blessing
Hebrews 12:18-29	8. The Kingdom of God Is among You			✓		
Hebrews 13:1-6	38. Fear Not			✓		
James 1:2-18	23. Count It All Joy			✓		
James 1:19-27	43. Wisdom			✓		
James 3:13-18	55. Justice			✓		
James 4:1-10	21. Impasse			✓		
James 5:13-20	40. Pray for One Another			✓		
1 Peter 1:3-12	52. Compassion			✓		
1 Peter 1:13-16	3. Prepare the Way of the Lord			✓		
1 Peter 1:17-25	48. Gentleness			✓		
1 Peter 2:2-9	25. Creativity			✓		
1 Peter 2:9-25	30. The Freedom of the Christian			✓		
1 Peter 4:7-11	56. End Times			✓		
1 Peter 5:1-11	35. Suffering			✓		
2 Peter 1:2	45. Practicing the Presence of God					✓
2 Peter 1:1-8	53. Responsibility			✓		

Scripture	Weekly Theme	Affirmation	Psalm	Daily Scripture Readings	Offering of Self	Blessing
2 Peter 1:10-19	46. Attentiveness			✓		
2 Peter 3:8-13	1. Active Waiting			✓		
1 John 4:9-12	27. For the Life of the World			✓		
1 John 4:13-21	38. Fear Not			✓		
2 John						
3 John						
Jude						
Revelation 4:1-11	13. Adoration			✓		
Revelation 5	48. Gentleness			✓		
Revelation 7:9-17	56. End Times			✓		
Revelation 12:10	56. End Times					✓
Revelation 21:1-7	45. Practicing the Presence of God			✓		